TEACHING PROBLEM-SOLVING STRATEGIES

Daniel T. Dolan
James Williamson

Addison-Wesley Publishing Company
Menlo Park, California • Reading, Massachusetts
London • Amsterdam • Don Mills, Ontario • Sydney

This book is published by the ADDISON-WESLEY INNOVATIVE DIVISION.

Design and cover: Betsy Bruneau

Illustrations: Jane McCreary

ISBN-0-201-10231-5

16 17 18 19 20 - ML - 95

ACKNOWLEDGEMENTS

We would like to acknowledge the contributions that several people have made to the development of this book. Alex Hilsendeger, Superintendent of Schools in Columbus, Montana, and Al Kober, junior high school principal, have encouraged our efforts to develop new materials and allowed us the freedom to try them. Without this support, the book would not have been possible.

Eight junior high school teachers in Montana—Stan Hassman, Lance Johnson, Keith Thompson, Glenda Tinsley, Larry Moye, Doug Ferkin, Rich Dengel, and Ray Meyers worked with us for three years on a Title IV-C junior high school mathematics project. This book is an outgrowth of that project and the contribution of these teachers to the success of the project and the book is greatly appreciated. In addition, some of them field tested these materials with their students and evaluated the results for us. We thank their students and our own for being willing participants.

Thanks to Glenn Allinger, Montana State University, and Richard Billstein, University of Montana, for their review of the first drafts of the text and the many suggestions they made to improve it.

Special thanks to Coleen Ekle and Sandi Walter who typed, retyped, corrected, and recorrected the many drafts. They were always willing to do whatever was requested to improve the final copy.

CONTENTS

INTRODUCTION

The purpose of this book is to provide junior high school mathematics teachers with a carefully developed, systematic approach to teaching six problem-solving strategies. The book is a result of our frustration with students' inability to solve problems and apply previously learned concepts. It contains lessons and activities that we have used successfully during the past six years in our classrooms and that have resulted in significant gains in our students' ability to solve problems.

The materials in the book are intended to complement the subject matter normally taught in a junior high mathematics course. However, most of the materials have been used successfully with classes in grades six through ten. They have proved especially valuable when used in general math and pre-algebra type courses.

WHY PROBLEM-SOLVING?

In the spring of 1977, the National Council of Supervisors of Mathematics published its now famous *Position Paper on Basic Mathematical Skills.* In it, they defined skills in ten vital areas which would provide students with the basic mathematical ability needed by adults. The first area listed is *problem solving*, and the NCSM points out that "learning to solve problems is the principal reason for studying mathematics."

In April 1980, following two years of extensive research regarding the beliefs that many segments of society hold with respect to the objectives and priorities of mathematics education, the National Council of Teachers of Mathematics published *Recommendations for School Mathematics of the 1980's.*

Recommendation 1 states that problem solving must be the focus of school mathematics in the 1980's. The recommendation goes on to state that "the definition and language of problem solving in mathematics should be developed and expanded to include a broad range of strategies." Further, "appropriate curricular materials to teach problem solving should be developed for all grade levels. Most current materials strongly emphasize an algo-rithmic approach to the learning of mathematics, and as such they are inadequate to support or implement fully a problem-solving approach."

WHAT IS PROBLEM-SOLVING AND HOW DO WE TEACH IT?

A significant problem that one encounters when attempting to implement the above recommendations is the decision as to what constitutes problem solving. The renowned master teacher of problem solving, George Polyà, states, "To have a problem means to search consciously for some action appropriate to attain some clearly conceived but not immediately attainable aim. To solve a problem means to find such an action." "What is know-how in mathematics? The ability to solve problems—not merely routine problems but problems requiring some degree of independence, judgment, originality, creativity. Therefore the first and foremost duty of the high school in teaching mathematics is to emphasize methodical work in problem solving."

One must be extremely careful not to fall into the trap of defining problem solving as another basic skill which can be treated as an algorithm. The National Assessment of Educational Progress findings on mathematics achievement made in 1979, reported that "evidence shows that students proceed mechanically and thoughtlessly through problems—if they forget the rule, then they are unable to do the problem on their own." This analysis of results of achievement in problem solving is consistent with the usual methodology of teaching it. Problem solving in mathematics has become a set of words which are wrapped around some computational exercises.

We believe that to successfully teach problem solving, we must do more than simply assign problems to students. We must teach *strategies*.

Webster defines a strategy as a careful plan—the art of devising a plan toward a goal. The latter definition is consistent with Polyà's concept of problem solving: to search for some action to attain a goal. It seems to us that a problem really means selecting an appropriate strategy, not simply deriving an answer.

To teach problem solving, we must approach it as we do addition or multiplication. The strategy to be taught must be susceptible to analysis and must be broken down into constituent parts. These parts must then be taught individually in a sequence that eventually results in the development of the complete strategy.

HOW DO WE SELECT STRATEGIES?

It is impossible to include all of the strategies that can be used in problem solving in one book. Our primary concern in selecting strategies to include was that they be ones that could be taught effectively at the junior high level. While the criterion is simple to state, it is very difficult to actually apply.

In addition to teachability, the strategies we selected had to be versatile ones that could be applied to a wide variety of problems and also be useful in advanced courses in mathematics. Whenever possible, we also wanted strategies whose use could be extended to areas other than mathematics. The six we chose were: Guess and Check, Make a Table, Patterns, Make a Model, Elimination, Simplify.

Mathematics textbooks typically contain only one type of problem solving material: story problems. Each set of problems is usually located immediately after the materials that develop the operations required to solve the problems. This sequencing eliminates the need for the students to determine the operations necessary to solve a problem, and, in some instances, even eliminates the need to read the problem. Limiting the content of the problem-solving strand to story problems also ignores the fact that problem solving is used in a variety of everyday situations, and that problem solving techniques also provide valuable tools that can be used to discover and develop new concepts.

These weaknesses are further compounded by the fact that most texts teach only the translation method of problem solving: read the problem, write an equation, check the result. Because of its power and versatility, every student should eventually develop a proficiency in using this method. However, it is a fallacy to assume that this is the only strategy that need be taught.

Teaching just one problem-solving strategy gives students the false impression that all problems can be solved using it. This poses a particular difficulty since students are too often conditioned to equate learning mathematics with memorizing specific procedures to apply in particular situations. These students expect to memorize an algorithm for problem solving that they can apply to every problem. Teaching just one problem-solving strategy establishes a mind set in these students: "If I can't solve the problem by writing an equation, then the problem can't be solved."

There are many problems that cannot be solved by the *translation* method, but even more important, what happens to the students who are able to read and comprehend a problem that can be solved by the translation method but then are still unable to write the equation? Without alternate strategies to apply, there is no way for these students to analyze the problem and find a solution. All students need to know a variety of problem-solving strategies, and teachers need materials that will teach the strategies.

HOW DO WE COMMUNICATE WITH STUDENTS?

Our final observation on the problem-solving strand in textbooks concerns communication. When students are unable to solve a problem, it often seems that the only way to help them is to actually solve the problem for them. This is due to the fact that most textbooks do not develop a language that can be used to suggest approaches to a problem or to provide hints on how to carry out the solution.

Throughout the Instructional Strategies section in the Introductory Lessons, we have consistently encouraged the teacher to discuss the procedures used in solving problems. By doing so, the students can talk about the solution process rather than just the answer. When a student asks for help after the problem-solving strategies have been introduced, one may be able to simply suggest, "try a table, or look for a pattern," rather than offering a *solution* to the problem.

A note concerning pedagogy seems appropriate at this point. Junior high mathematics classes are often very monotonous, not only for the student, but also for the teacher. This fact was very much on our minds as we prepared materials for this text. If the materials are to be successful, the role of the student must change from one of passive recipient of knowledge to one of active involvement in learning. To this end, we have varied the instructional techniques using not only traditional lecture-discussion approach, but also activity, game, and discovery formats.

In summary, we wrote *Teaching Problem-Solving Strategies* to accomplish four things.

1. Teach students a variety of problem-solving strategies.

2. Present students with a variety of problem-solving experiences.

3. Develop a language to communicate with students about the problem-solving process.

4. Provide alternatives to the usual lecture-textbook teaching process.

WHAT DOES *Teaching Problem-Solving Strategies* CONTAIN?

The book is divided into four sections. Section I, Introductory Lessons, contains six units. Each unit includes detailed lesson plans for a systematic development of one of the six problem-solving strategies. At each stage in the development, materials for practice are provided. On the next page is a suggested time schedule for these introductory activities.

Section II, Activities, contains nineteen student activities, each of which involves one or more of the strategies. Each one is keyed to a strand in the junior high mathematics curriculum (see the Skills Chart on page 111). These activities can be utilized to: (1) develop new concepts, (2) reinforce concepts already introduced, (3) maintain skills previously taught.

Section III, Practice Problems, contains additional problems keyed to the six strategies. The strategies involved are indicated by which wizards appear on the page. These problems can

be used during the year to reinforce each strategy after the units in Section I have been completed.

Section IV, Student Pages, contains all the student worksheets, without answers, to be used as black-line masters for reproduction.

HOW IS *Teaching Problem-Solving Strategies* USED?

Section I Introductory Lessons

These six units are the nucleus of this text. Through carefully structured use of these units, a teacher may help students to develop the most important skill in mathematics—the ability to solve problems.

The units may be taught in various ways. All six may be presented during a three- to five-week period, or they may be taught as individual units interspersed with regular textbook material. As a result of field testing these materials, we have determined that the greatest student achievement and retention resulted when the strategies were taught during the first two months of the course and then reinforced throughout the year. The reinforcement can be accomplished through use of activities which utilize the strategies and problems from the Practice Problem section. We have included a suggested time schedule on page xiii. It is based on our experience using these materials with students and indicates approximate times necessary to teach these units.

The lessons that teach the use of each strategy should be completed in order, since each one carefully develops some aspect of the strategy that is essential to the next lesson.

Careful notice should be made of the carriers, or wizard, which is used on the student pages. The function of this carrier is twofold:

1. It acts as an "assistant" teacher, defining terms, offering suggestions, and explaining step-by-step procedures in the development of the strategies.

2. It offers hints to the student at specific points in order to bridge gaps in the process of solving a problem.

Page xiv shows the way the six strategies are identified by varying the *hat* on the wizard. You may want to introduce this figure to your students by using an overhead projector.

A teacher unaccostomed to the use of class activities or games may be reluctant to use some of the lessons, e.g., "The Listing Game" in Unit II. Be assured that every activity, game, and problem presented in this book has been classroom tested and proved to be successful with students in grades six through ten.

The games and class activities used in the Introductory Lessons are written specifically to teach the objective of that lesson. Be willing to try them and don't be alarmed if small problems arise at first.

Several of the objectives for the lessons contain the words *to teach*. We do not intend to imply that students will have completely mastered the objective after completing the lesson. In using the words *to teach*, we intend that the lesson will instruct the students by means of appropriate examples and provide them with meaningful experiences related to the understanding and learning of that strategy.

Once a unit has been completed, the strategy should be reinforced throughout the year by using the activities and the Practice Problems.

Section II Activities

The materials in this section are designed to physically involve students in activities that utilize one or more of the problem-solving strategies in the process of: (1) developing mathematical concepts, (2) reinforcing concepts and basic skills previously taught.

The activities may also reinforce one or more of the strategies in the context of regular course material.

Since the activities are correlated to the six strategies and to content areas, they may be utilized to extend either. As an example, "Square Fractions" is keyed to the Model strategy and the Fraction area. This activity could be used after the Model unit has been presented to provide an application of the strategy, or it might instead be used to reinforce the concept of a fraction and introduce

multiplication and addition of fractions through concrete experiences.

The activities that are designed to develop concepts can replace the usual teacher lecture and explanation of the concepts. By actively involving the students in the learning of concepts, we may greatly increase the probability of making a lasting impression on our students.

An oft repeated Chinese proverb says:

"I hear and I forget
I see and I remember
I do and I understand."

Because students are doing rather than listening, they may better understand and remember those concepts developed through activities.

The Skills Chart on page 111 shows the relationship between a particular activity, the problem-solving strategies, and the strand area to which the activity is related.

Section III Practice Problems

This section is designed to:

1. Provide problems that can be used in addition to those in the introductory lessons while the strategies are first being presented.

2. Provide additional problems for use after the introductory lessons have been presented to reinforce the use of the strategies.

3. Provide enrichment problems for use throughout the year as supplementary work for students.

4. Provide problems for the purpose of evaluating student progress and achievement.

Suggested Time Schedule for Introductory Lessons

(1 period = 45 to 60 minutes)

Strategy	Lesson	Number of Class Periods	
		Minimum	Maximum
Guess	1	1.0	1.0
and	2	0.5	0.5
Check	3	0.5	1.0
	4	1.0	1.0
	Total	3.0	3.5
Make	1	0.5	1.0
a	2	0.5	1.0
Table	3	0.5	1.0
	4	1.5	2.0
	Total	3.0	5.0
Patterns	1	0.5	0.5
	2	0.5	0.5
	3	0.5	1.0
	4	1.5	2.0
	5	1.0	1.0
	Total	4.0	5.0
Make	1	1.0	1.5
a	2	0.5	1.0
Model	3	1.0	1.5
	4	0.5	1.0
	Total	3.0	5.0
Elimination	1	1.0	1.5
	2	1.0	1.5
	Total	2.0	3.0
Simplify	1	1.5	2.0
	2	1.5	2.0
	Total	3.0	4.0

THE WISE SAGES OF PROBLEM SOLVING

GUESS AND CHECK

MAKE A TABLE

PATTERNS

USE A MODEL

SIMPLIFY

ELIMINATE

SECTION I

INTRODUCTORY LESSONS

UNIT I

GUESS AND CHECK

This unit is designed to introduce students to the Guess and Check problem-solving strategy. This is probably the simplest and most natural of all problem-solving strategies. Unfortunately, beginning with the student's earliest experiences in a mathematics classroom, solving problems through the application of the guess and check strategy instead of the direct application of a particular algorithm is often discouraged. As a result, many students are very reluctant to guess at the solution to a problem. Thus, to teach this strategy, it is first necessary to encourage students to make guesses. Only after they are comfortable with making them, can they be taught the essential features of the guess and check strategy:

1. Make an "educated" guess at the solution.
2. Check the guess against the conditions of the problem.
3. Use the information obtained in checking to make a better guess.
4. Continue this procedure until the correct answer is obtained.

"Certainly, let us learn proving, but also *let us learn guessing.*"

George Pólya

LESSON 1

OBJECTIVE:

This lesson introduces the Guess and Check strategy and encourages students to make guesses.

MATERIALS:

A copy of Worksheet 1 for each student.

INSTRUCTIONAL STRATEGY:

The Guess and Check strategy is easily introduced by playing the game "What's My Number?" and its variations. The games are very simple and accomplish the following:

1. Encourage students to guess.
2. Instill the idea of developing a system for improving successive guesses and eliminating possibilities.
3. Provide an opportunity for emphasizing the use of correct terminology, and reviewing some fundamental number theory concepts.

Step 1: Begin the period by playing the "Bigger or Smaller?" game. Draw a chart similar to the following on the chalkboard, or on an overhead transparency.

The Number Is	
Bigger Than	Smaller Than

Explain to the students that you are thinking of a number between 1 and 100, and that you want them to guess the number. Call on a student to make a guess. Tell whether your number is bigger or smaller than the guess, and record the guess in the appropriate column on the chart. Continue this process until the correct number is obtained. To motivate the game, you may want to allow the student who guessed the number to select a new number and conduct the next round.

Step 2: After half the period, switch to "What's My Number?" Divide the class into teams of three or four, and have each team select a captain who will ask the questions for the team. Explain that you are thinking of a number less than 100 (you may want to change this to 1000 after one or two rounds), and they are to guess it by asking questions to which you can answer either yes or no. To encourage questions such as Is it even?, Is it a multiple of *n* ?, Is it prime?, Is the number in the tens place odd?, and so forth, place the limit on number of questions you will answer that involve "greater than," "less than," and "between." Draw lots to determine the order in which the teams will ask questions. A team may continue asking questions until they receive a "No" answer. Record each question and your answer on the overhead or chalkboard. Any team may break in and guess the number regardless of whether it is their turn to ask questions or not. However, if their guess is wrong, they are eliminated from the competition. To motivate the game, you may wish to give each member of the team that guesses the number two or three extra credit points.

Step 3: Assign Worksheet 1.

WORSHEET 1—*Guess the Answer*

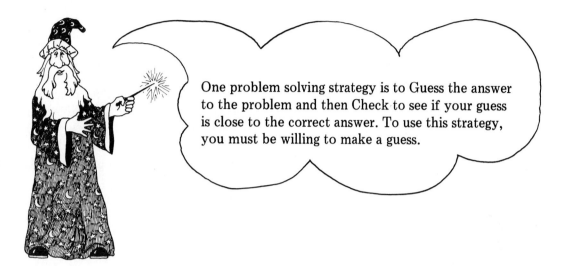

One problem solving strategy is to Guess the answer
to the problem and then Check to see if your guess
is close to the correct answer. To use this strategy,
you must be willing to make a guess.

Write your guess for the answer to each question in the blank.

0.5kg–1kg

1. What is the weight of your math book?

**2,400,000
or 2.3 to 2.5 million**

2. How many people will visit Yellowstone National Park in an average year? (based on average numbers for 1979-1982.)

1260m

3. How long is the Golden Gate Bridge? (length of longest span)

6060 km

4. How far is it from New York to Paris?

144

5. How many shirts are in a gross?

100 mph.

6. What is the greatest speed ever recorded for a fastball thrown by a major league pitcher? (record 100.9mph set by Nolan Ryan in 1974.)

1600–2300kg

7. How much does a pickup truck weigh?

228 cm

8. What is the greatest height ever recorded for a woman?

498 kg

9. What is the heaviest weight ever recorded for a human being?

30min. 40 sec.

10. How fast can a man run 1500 meters? (1980 world record 3min. 31.36 sec.)

6632 km

11. How long is the longest river in the world?

LESSON 2

OBJECTIVE:

This lesson introduces the concept of an "educated guess" and teaches the student how to make one.

MATERIALS:

A copy of Worksheet 2 for each student.

INSTRUCTIONAL STRATEGY:

Step 1: Discuss the students' guesses on Worksheet 1. Emphasize that since all they had to do was make a guess, any answer they have is correct. However, some guesses are better than others. If their answer falls in the range given for each question, they made a good guess.

Step 2: Continue playing "What's My Number?"

Step 3: Assign Worksheet 2.

LESSON 3

OBJECTIVE:

This lesson teaches the student to check a guess for accuracy and reinforces the procedures used in making "educated" guesses.

MATERIALS:

A copy of Worksheet 3 for each student.

INSTRUCTIONAL STRATEGY:

Step 1: Discuss the answers to Worksheet 2. The most important questions are 7–12. In discussing them, the emphasis should be on the questions students had to answer before making their decision as to whether the statement was "Likely" or "Unlikely."

Step 2: Give each student a copy of Worksheet 3. Explain to them that the important thing is to make a good guess so they should think about each question before answering.

Step 3: After the students have recorded their guesses on Worksheet 3, discuss each question with the class by having individual students tell their guess and explain the reasoning they used to make it. Then use the individual guesses to determine a class estimate, and, finally, discuss what methods could be used to check individual guesses and the class estimate.

For example, to determine how many times your heart beats in one hour, take your pulse rate for one minute and multiply it by 60.

Step 4: Assign two or three students to check the answer to each question using the procedures developed in the discussion.

WORKSHEET 2—Likely or Unlikely

Tell whether the following statements are likely or unlikely:

_____U_____   1. The center on the high school basketball team is three meters tall.

_____L_____   2. A ladybug is 5 millimeters long.

_____L_____   3. A recipe for a casserole that serves four people calls for 500 grams of hamburger.

_____U_____   4. Your math teacher weighs 150 kilograms.

_____U_____   5. He drank 350 milliliters of lemonade in one swallow.

_____U_____   6. It is 100° C outside.

_____L_____   7. A tour group consisting of six young married couples is visiting the Washington Monument. The elevator to the top has a load limit of 1000 kg. It is safe for all six couples to ride the elevator at once.

Did you have trouble with number 7? The following might help you make a good guess.

What is the weight of an adult female? __50kg__

What is the weight of an adult male? __80kg__

What is the weight of the 6 couples? __780kg__

_____U_____   8. A stack of notebook paper 50 centimeters tall contains 7000 sheets of paper.

_____L_____   9. Bob and Steve are planning a 400-mile trip to Collegeville in Bob's car. $20.00 will pay for the gas for the trip.

_____U_____   10. The 16 members of the Drama Club are planning
                   to go to the pizza parlor for pizza and soft
                   drinks after the school play. Sixty-five dollars
                   will be enough to pay the bill.

Having trouble? Think;

One large pizza will feed ____2-4____ people.

To feed everyone, they will need ____4-8____ large pizzas.

One large pizza costs ____$8.00-$10.00____.

They will need ____16____ large soft drinks.

Each soft drink will cost ____$0.60-0.90____.

_____L_____   11. If you were to count continuously for eight
                   hours a day, five days a week, it would take more
                   than two weeks to count to one million.

_____U_____   12. A restaurant chain claims that it sells one billion
                   hamburgers each year. If you could stack up all
                   the hamburgers they sell in one year, the stack
                   would reach from the earth to the moon.

WORSHEET 3—An Educated Guess

Use your knowledge of the real world and the methods you learned in Worksheet 2 to try to make a good guess.

Estimate the answer to each of the following questions.

_____	1.	What is the length of this room?
_____	2.	How high is the ceiling in this room?
4200	3.	How many times does your heart beat in an hour?
25000	4.	How many breaths do you take in a day?
600 g	5.	How heavy is a basketball?
175 cm	6.	What is the length of a 10-speed bike?
10-15 min.	7.	How long would it take an average junior high student to walk one kilometer?
18500	8.	How many drops of water from a medicine dropper will it take to fill a one liter jar?
_____	9.	How many egg cartons can you stack in your classroom? (A standard egg carton (1 doz.) is approximately 2000 cm³.)
_____	10.	How far is it from your school to the state capitol building?
100 m	11.	What is the height of a stack containing 1,000,000 one-dollar bills? (A stack of 100 new $1 bills is approximately 1 cm tall.)

LESSON 4

OBJECTIVE:

This lesson teaches the student to refine each successive guess and continue the Guess and Check procedure until a solution is found.

MATERIALS:

A copy of Worksheet 4 for each student.

INSTRUCTION STRATEGY:

Step 1: Discuss the answers that students obtained for the questions on Worksheet 3, and have them compare the answers to their guesses.

Step 2: To introduce the new idea, play 3 or 4 rounds of "What Are My Numbers?." Divide the class into teams. Explain that you are thinking of two whole numbers whose product (or quotient, sum or difference) is _____ . The procedure is the same as in "What's My Number?." After each game, explain how a list of the possibilities could have been made, and how questions such as "Is one of the factors prime?," "Are both factors even?," "Is one factor less than 10?," and so forth could be asked which would eliminate various possibilities.

> *Sample Games:*
>
> Product is 180.
> Choices: 1 × 180, 2 × 90, 3 × 60, 4 × 45, 5 × 36, 6 × 30, 9 × 20, 10 × 18, 12 × 15.
>
> Sum is 12.
> Choices: 0 + 12, 1 + 11, 2 + 10, 3 + 9, 4 + 8, 5 + 7, 6 + 6.

Step 3: Assign Worksheet 4. Allow some time for the students to start it in class. If they need help, ask questions that will get them to make a guess and check it, but don't do the problems for them. This worksheet should be carefully

discussed after the students are finished. Emphasize how to use the process of making a guess, checking it, using the information obtained to make another guess, and continuing until all the solutions are obtained. The continuation process is very important in problems 5 and 6 where there is more than one solution. Since tables are very helpful in organizing the Guess and Check procedure, the material in this section will be reviewed after the Table Strategy has been introduced.

For additional problems to reinforce the Guess and Check strategy, see the Practice Problems section of this book

WORKSHEET 4—Check Your Guess

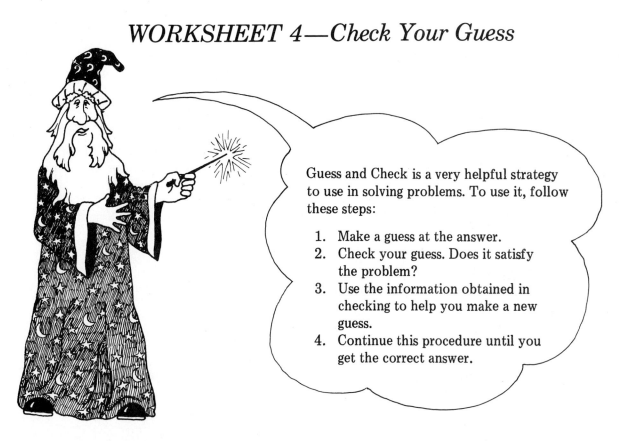

Guess and Check is a very helpful strategy to use in solving problems. To use it, follow these steps:

1. Make a guess at the answer.
2. Check your guess. Does it satisfy the problem?
3. Use the information obtained in checking to help you make a new guess.
4. Continue this procedure until you get the correct answer.

Use Guess and Check to solve the following problems.

1. "I am thinking of two whole numbers," Jose said. "When I add them the answer is 118, and when I subtract the smaller number from the larger one the result is 36. What are my numbers?"

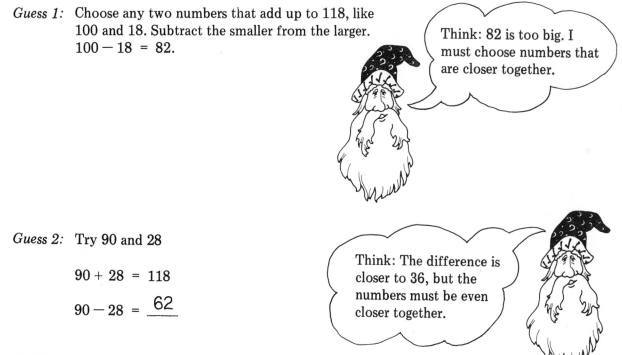

Guess 1: Choose any two numbers that add up to 118, like 100 and 18. Subtract the smaller from the larger. $100 - 18 = 82$.

Think: 82 is too big. I must choose numbers that are closer together.

Guess 2: Try 90 and 28

$$90 + 28 = 118$$

$$90 - 28 = \underline{62}$$

Think: The difference is closer to 36, but the numbers must be even closer together.

Guess 3: Try 82 and ___36___

82 − ___36___ = ___46___

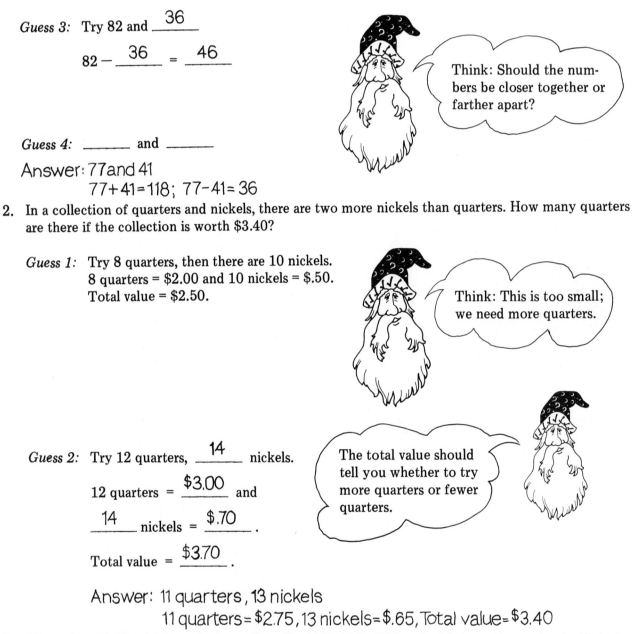

Think: Should the numbers be closer together or farther apart?

Guess 4: _____ and _____

Answer: 77 and 41
77 + 41 = 118; 77 − 41 = 36

2. In a collection of quarters and nickels, there are two more nickels than quarters. How many quarters are there if the collection is worth $3.40?

Guess 1: Try 8 quarters, then there are 10 nickels.
8 quarters = $2.00 and 10 nickels = $.50.
Total value = $2.50.

Think: This is too small; we need more quarters.

Guess 2: Try 12 quarters, ___14___ nickels.

12 quarters = ___$3.00___ and

___14___ nickels = ___$.70___ .

Total value = ___$3.70___ .

The total value should tell you whether to try more quarters or fewer quarters.

Answer: 11 quarters, 13 nickels
11 quarters = $2.75, 13 nickels = $.65, Total value = $3.40

3. "I am also thinking of two whole numbers," said Matilda. "When I add them, the answer is 45, but when I multiply them the answer is 486. What are my numbers?"

27 and 18

4. Carmen bought some sweaters for $16 each and some blouses for $10 each. She spent $98. How many did she buy?

No. of blouses	1	2	3	4	5	6	7	8	9
Cost of blouses	10	20	30	40	50	60	70	80	90
Amount remaining	88	78	68	58	48	38	28	18	8
No. of sweaters	—	—	—	—	3	—	—	—	—

5. The sum of two numbers is 47, their difference is less than 10. What are *all* the possible pairs of numbers?

23 and 24
22 and 25
21 and 26
20 and 27
19 and 28

6. Dan's father makes furniture for a hobby. Last Christmas he made 4-legged tables and 3-legged stools as gifts for relatives. When he finished, he had used 37 legs. What are all of the possible combinations for the number of tables and stools that he made?

No. of tables	1	2	3	4	5	6	7	8	9
No. of legs	4	8	12	16	20	24	28	32	36
No. remaining	33	29	25	21	17	13	9	5	1
No. of stools	11	—	—	7	—	—	3	—	—

7. In order to encourage Sandy to do her science problems, Sandy's father promised to pay her $.25 for every problem she got right, but he would take away $.15 for every problem she missed. After working 20 problems, Sandy was paid $.20 by her father. How many of Sandy's answers were correct?

8

UNIT II

MAKE A TABLE

This unit is designed to introduce the Make a Table problem-solving strategy.

Many students have considerable difficulty solving word problems. Their confusion often lies in the fact that they are unable to write number sentences for the problems, which is the method of solution typically taught. If they cannot use that approach, they are lost and often give up. A majority of these same students do have an understanding of the basic problem. If they are taught an alternate strategy that will give them a less sophisticated approach to solving the problem, they may be able to arrive at a solution. The table strategy quite often provides such an approach.

Unit II is divided into two sections, Make a List and Make a Table. In the first section, Make a List, a procedure for constructing an organized list containing all the possibilities for a given situation is developed, and the fundamental concepts of permutations and combinations are introduced. The listing procedure becomes especially important when using the process of elimination, for one must first determine all the possibilities before specific cases can be excluded. This application will be explored in a later unit.

The Make a Table section develops methods for setting up a table for a problem and for using entries in a table to solve word problems. It also shows how tables can be used as an organizer when using the Guess and Check strategy.

LESSON 1

OBJECTIVE:

This lesson introduces the Make a List strategy.

MATERIALS:

Sheets of paper or large cards with the letters A–F printed on them.

INSTRUCTIONAL STRATEGY:

The Make a List strategy can be introduced easily by playing "The Listing Game." It is simple to manage and does the following:

  a. Reinforces the idea of multiple solutions to a problem.

  b. Develops the concepts of permutations and combinations.

  c. Assists in developing a procedure for exhaustive listing.

Step 1: Play "The Listing Game" as follows:

  a. Divide the class into two equal groups. Have groups sit on opposite sides of the room.

  b. Each group then chooses a team of three to represent it.

  c. Each team of three stands in a row in front of the opposing group as shown. Each student standing should be identified with a letter printed on a card.

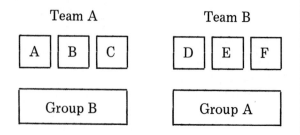

  d. At the command of the teacher, each team must step forward to form a different order. On a second command, each team steps back, but must be in an order different from the previous ones used.

Example:

Team A	A B C	*Team B*	D E F
Move Frwd	C A B		F D E
Move Back	B A C		E F D

  e. The procedure continues until one team repeats an order previously used. The students sitting should record the orders of the opposing team and serve as judges.

  f. When a team repeats an order, both teams must sit down and new teams are chosen to represent the groups.

  g. A team receives one point for each new order derived. The initial one is not counted.

  h. When new teams begin, they both start over. That is, they may repeat "orders" used by the first teams.

If this procedure is too easy with teams of three, or if students quickly find the six orders, try teams of four or five.

Step 2: After all students have participated as team members, the following variation may be used to develop the concept of *combinations.* Put four members on each team; all rules will be the same except rule d. It will now be:

  At the command of the teacher, two of the four team members must step forward to form a combination. However in this game, any combination of two letters such as AB or BA is considered as being the same. On the second command, the two step back into the team of four and two of the four must step forward to form a new combination.

Once students find the six combinations of four people taken two at a time, change the rule so that they use combinations of three. The number of team members and number used for the combination can be changed to make the game more challenging.

Motivation for the games can be provided by awarding some extra credit points to the winning team members.

LESSON 2

OBJECTIVE:

This lesson develops a method for making an exhaustive list of all possibilities.

MATERIALS:

One copy of Worksheet 1 and Worksheet 2 for each student.

INSTRUCTIONAL STRATEGY:

Step 1: During the previous activity, "The Listing Game," students probably listed arrangements randomly. It is important to stress the point that in order to be sure that all possibilities are obtained, we need to develop a method of ORGANIZING our list. Worksheet 1 should be handed out with little or no explanation except that students read carefully and follow the hints given. Students should work independently. However, those who finish early can be encouraged to check answers with a neighbor to see if all possible answers have been derived.

Step 2: When everyone has completed the assignment, the results should be thoroughly discussed. The answer columns for the first problem should have led students toward the idea of an exhaustive list. We anticipate that students will derive the following answers for number 1. They should be listed on the overhead or chalkboard and carefully analyzed.

Problem 1: Worksheet 1

$$\underline{4} \quad \underline{5} \quad \underline{6} \qquad \underline{5} \quad \underline{4} \quad \underline{6} \qquad \underline{6} \quad \underline{4} \quad \underline{5}$$
$$\underline{4} \quad \underline{6} \quad \underline{5} \qquad \underline{5} \quad \underline{6} \quad \underline{4} \qquad \underline{6} \quad \underline{5} \quad \underline{4}$$

The main idea is the process of listing one number in the first position (for example, 4) and altering the others in order, so as to develop all possibilities using that number in the first position.

A second number (for example, 5) should then be used in the first position and all remaining numbers altered in order as shown above.

The answer columns for the second problem contain fewer answers. However, students should understand that there are 10 different answers. They must also understand the listing procedure that is being developed.

Problem 2: Worksheet 1

A	R	St		A	Se	W
A	R	Se		R	St	Se
A	R	W		R	St	W
A	St	Se		R	Se	W
A	St	W		St	Se	W

Again, the main idea is the process of listing one item in the first position (for example, Air) and then altering the others in order. However, in this case, A R St (Air, Radio, Stripes) is the same option package as A St R (Air, Stripes, Radio), since two cars having these packages have exactly the same options. Consequently, one item is listed *first* (A), one second (R), and all others are used in the third position. Then (R) is dropped, (A) is still used first, a new item is put in the second place (St), and the remaining items placed third. This process continues until all arrangements have been derived with (A) in the first place. (A) is then dropped entirely from the list, and a new item (R) is used in the first place. The order of the remaining items is then altered as shown.

Step 3: Following the discussion of Worksheet 1, ask the students how many ways they could

have coins which total 13¢. This problem involves the listing procedure developed above; however, it is important that students first determine which coins are possible and then make an organized list.

P	13	8	3	3
N	0	1	2	0
D	0	0	0	1

Step 4: Completion of Worksheet 1 and the discussion following will probably take up the entire period. Assign Worksheet 2. Each problem on Worksheet 2 should be thoroughly discussed, emphasizing again the procedure for ORGANIZING a list.

WORKSHEET 1—Complete the List

Solve the following problems by completing the list which is started for you.

To be a good problem solver, you must learn to organize your work.

1. How many three digit numbers can you make with the digits 4, 5, and 6.

| 4 | 5 | 6 | | 5 | 4 | 6 | | 6 | 4 | 5 |
| 4 | 6 | 5 | | 5 | 6 | 4 | | 6 | 5 | 4 |

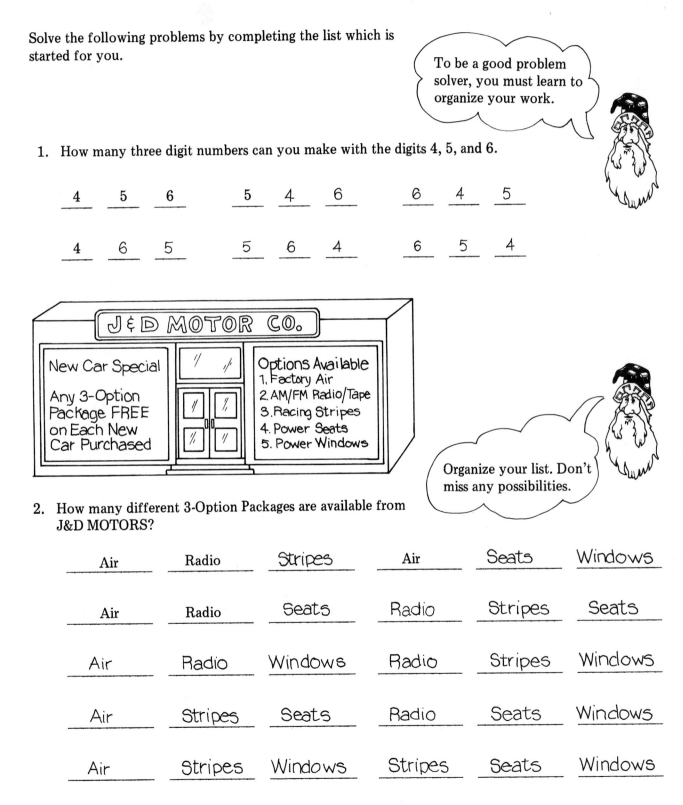

Organize your list. Don't miss any possibilities.

2. How many different 3-Option Packages are available from J&D MOTORS?

Air	Radio	Stripes		Air	Seats	Windows
Air	Radio	Seats		Radio	Stripes	Seats
Air	Radio	Windows		Radio	Stripes	Windows
Air	Stripes	Seats		Radio	Seats	Windows
Air	Stripes	Windows		Stripes	Seats	Windows

WORKSHEET 2—Make the List

1. The Busy Bee Cafe offers these choices on its dinner menu. If you choose one item from each category, how many days can you eat meals at the Busy Bee before you eat the same dinner a second time?*

2. After a football game, a group of students go to the Super Burger for a snack. Hamburgers cost 80¢, soft drinks are 40¢. They have $10 to spend.

   If they must buy at least 5 hamburgers and 5 drinks, how many of each can they buy? They must spend exactly $10.

3. The five tags below are put in a box and drawn out three at a time. If a score is the *sum of the numbers* on the tags drawn, how many different scores are possible?

   What are they?

4. How many ways can you have coins that total exactly 37¢?

*Answers next page.

ANSWERS FOR WORKSHEET 2—*Make the List*

1. Since $3 \times 2 \times 2 \times 2 = 24$, you can eat 24 meals before you eat the same dinner twice.

2.

Hamburgers	5	6	7	8	9	10
Soft drinks	15	13	11	9	7	5

3. There are 9 different scores, 13 appears twice.

Tag 1	4	4	4	4	4	4	7	7	7	0
Tag 2	7	7	7	0	0	6	0	0	6	6
Tag 3	0	6	2	6	2	2	6	2	2	2
Score	11	17	13	10	6	12	13	9	15	8

4. There are 24 ways.

25¢	1	1	1	1																				
10¢	1				3	3	2	2	2	2	1	1	1	1	1	1								
5¢		2	1		1		3	2	1		5	4	3	2	1		7	6	5	4	3	2	1	
1¢	2	2	7	12	2	7	2	7	12	17	2	7	12	17	22	27	2	7	12	17	22	27	32	37

LESSON 3

OBJECTIVE:

This lesson teaches the student to (1) make a table by identifying the unknowns in the problem, labeling the table correctly and making entries for the unknowns; (2) write a number sentence for the table.

MATERIALS:

A copy of Worksheet 3 and Worksheet 4 for each student.

INSTRUCTIONAL STRATEGY:

Step 1: Pass out Worksheet 3 and instruct students to complete it. Assistance should be minimal. Simply explain that words may be used for the unknowns in the rule, but operations should be indicated by symbols as in the first problem. If the use of variables has been introduced previously, their use should be encouraged. However, any rule using words or symbols, should be accepted if it correctly describes the situation. Point out that any numbers can be used in the table as long as they fit the situation.

Step 2: Students will complete this worksheet quickly. Follow-up discussion is important and should focus on some important points:

    a. Proper identification of the unknowns in the table is essential.

    b. Students should check each pair of entries to see if they satisfy the given situation.

    c. The rule for each problem can be derived by answering one of the following questions:

    • Can you multiply the entries in one row of the table by a constant to obtain the corresponding entry in the other row? (number 1)

    • Do the pairs of entries have a constant sum? (number 2)

    • Do the pairs of entries have a constant difference? (number 4)

    • Do the pairs of entries have a constant product? (number 3)

    • Do the pairs of entries have a constant ratio? (number 5)

Step 3: Following a thorough discussion of Worksheet 3, assign Worksheet 4.

NOTE: As we have stated previously, many students have difficulty with word problems because they are unable to write a number sentence that fits the problem. These students need a problem-solving strategy that will bridge the gap between a problem and the number sentence.

    The situations on Worksheet 3 do not ask questions which demand that students analyze a general statement (for example, wages = $15.50/hour) and then relate a specific question to it (for example, how much is earned in 5 hours?). Students are generally capable of completing the table with little difficulty. By observing the numbers in the table and asking the key questions noted in Step 2, they may then be able to write a rule which describes how the pairs of entries are related. To complete the blanks in the table on Worksheet 4, the student is required to answer a specific question related to the general statement. However, the question is not asked in a verbal manner. Thus students do not have to become involved in the translation from words to mathematical symbolism. Once again, students will probably complete these tables with little difficulty.

    Once the page has been completed, the results can be used to have students develop word problems that are indicated by the blanks in the tables.

For example:

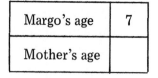

Margo's age	7
Mother's age	

Margo's mother is 27 years older then Margo. How old is her mother if Margo is 7?

If students will build a table and make the entries that are indicated by the general state-ment, they may then be able to solve the specific problem by:

a. adding entries to the table and com-bining entries in the table to answer the question, or

b. generating some additional entries, writing a number sentence that describes the related entries, and then solving the equation.

WORKSHEET 3—Make the Table

For each situation below, make a table that shows at least six entries. Explain how you filled in the table by stating a rule for each situation:

1. A mechanic is paid $15.50 per hour.

Hours Worked	1	2				
Wages	15.50	31.00				

   Rule: Wages = $15.50 × hours worked.

2. Two ropes are tied together to form a rope 35m long.

Rope 1	15	25	30			
Rope 2	20	10	5			

   Rule: Rope 1 + Rope 2 = 35.

3. The 80 chairs in the auditorium are arranged in rows with the same number of chairs in each row.

Rows	8	4	5			
Chairs	10	20	16			

   Rule: Rows x Chairs = 80

4. Sam is seven years older than Maria.

Sam's Age	8	9	17			
Maria's Age	1	2	10			

   Rule: Sam = Maria + 7

5. The small wheel on a pulley goes around 3 times when the large wheel goes around 2 times.

Small wheel	3	6	9			
Large wheel	2	4	6			

   Rule: Small wheel / large wheel = 3/2.

WORKSHEET 4—Table the Situation

Complete the table and state a rule for each situation.

1. Margo's mother is 27 years older than Margo.

Margo's Age	2	7	14	12	18	30	31
Margo's Mother's Age	29	34	41	39	45	57	58

Rule: Mother = Margo + 27.

2. Each year of a dog's life is approximately equal to seven years of a human's life.

Human's Age	7	28	70	105	21	35	63
Dog's Age	1	4	10	15	3	5	9

Rule: Human's age = 7 x Dog's age.

3. The seventh and eighth grade classes sold a total of 127 tickets to the school play.

Tickets sold by 8th	70	85	96	62	80	106	33
Tickets sold by 7th	57	42	31	65	47	21	94

Rule: 7th grade + 8th grade = 127.

4. The directions on Sun Pak Orange Drink mix are: "Mix 16 g of Sun Pak Orange mix with one liter of cold water, stir, and chill."

Orange Drink Mix	16 g	8 g	64 g	48 g	4 g	1.6 g	160 g
Water	1 L	500mL	4 L	3L	250 mL	100 mL	10 L

Rule: Grams = 16 x Liters.

5. Amy saves 30¢ from each $1.00 she earns babysitting.

Amount earned	1.00	3.00	.50	5.00	8.00	8.50	12.00
Amount saved	.30	.90	.15	1.50	2.40	2.55	3.60

Rule: Amount saved = .3 x Amount earned.

LESSON 4

OBJECTIVE:

This lesson teaches the student to use some entries in a table to generate other information not given.

MATERIALS:

A copy of Worksheets 5 and 6 for each student.

INSTRUCTIONAL STRATEGY:

Step 1: Distribute Worksheet 5 and have students complete it. Some hints are given in problem 1 to assist them. If questions arise, instruct students to combine the numbers given in the table to obtain the desired number. In problems 3–6, some entries are made, but others must be filled in. Advise students that they may need to add more entries to the table in order to answer all questions.

Step 2: Once the class has completed the assignment, review the procedures for deriving the answers. Be sure to emphasize that several options are available when combining given entries to generate others. Bring out as many as possible in the discussion.

It is imperative that students understand the relation between the pairs of hints (1a, b, and 2a, b) given in problem 1. If in deriving 10 bags, you add 6 bags and 4 bags, then the cost of 10 bags will be the cost of 6 bags plus the cost of 4 bags. If an operation is performed on one entry or a pair of entries then it must be performed on the related entries.

Let individual students explain their method of solution to these problems. It is especially worthwhile to have different methods described.

NOTE: Students that have difficulty solving problems can often read the problem and understand what is given. Usually their inability to complete the solution is a result of the fact that they cannot translate the words into mathe-matical symbols in order to make a number sentence. If students will construct a table and make the first entry, it is generally possible for them to generate additional entries. In doing so, they may arrive at the desired answer immediately. If not, it is important that they realize that some entries can be combined to derive others.

Example: Problem 5, Worksheet 5

	1	2	3	4	5	6
Cars	35	70	140	280	350	385
Minutes	1	2	4	8	10	11
Cost	.77	1.54	3.08	6.16	7.70	8.47

a. The entries in the first column can be made by simply reading the problem.

b. The second column can be derived by doubling all entries in the first column. The doubling process is usually well understood by students.

c. The entries in column 3 and 4 are also a result of doubling entries in the preceding column.

d. Doubling the entries in column 4 would result in 560 cars which is greater than the desired answer. The question we now ask is: can we combine some numbers in the table to get close to 385? Yes, $280 + 70 = 350$, so column 5 is derived by adding the corresponding numbers in columns 2 and 4.

e. Since $350 + 35 = 385$, the numbers for column 6 are obtained by adding the entries in columns 1 and 5.

Some students will immediately see that $385 \div 35 = 11$, therefore $11 \times 0.77 = \$8.47$ is the correct solution. This should not be discouraged. However, those students should also realize that this process is being developed so that when they are faced with a problem where the solution is not immediately recognized, they will have some method to use.

Step 3: Assign Worksheet 6 which reviews the use of a Table to organize the Guess and Check strategy.

For additional problems to reinforce the Table strategy, see the Practice Problems section of this book.

WORSHEET 5—Using Tables

Use the information given in the following tables to solve the problems:

59¢/BAG

CINNAMON BALLS

1.

Bags	1	2	3	4	5	6	7	8
Cost	$.59	$1.18	$1.77	$2.36	$2.95	$3.54	$4.13	$4.72

10 bags
cost = $5.90

13 bags
cost = $7.67

cost = $17.70
30 bags

24 bags
cost = $14.16

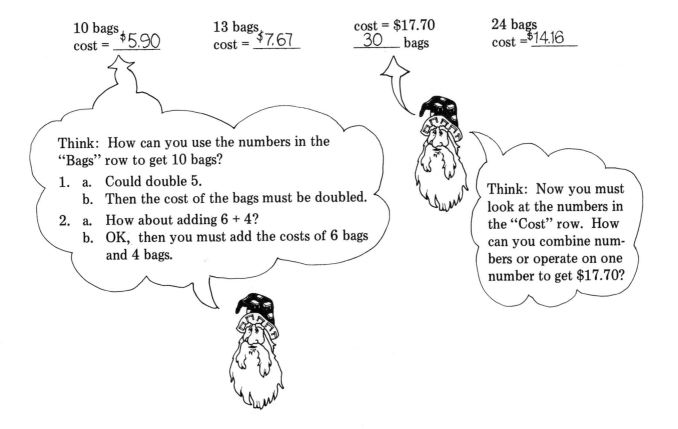

Think: How can you use the numbers in the "Bags" row to get 10 bags?

1. a.   Could double 5.
    b.   Then the cost of the bags must be doubled.

2. a.   How about adding 6 + 4?
    b.   OK, then you must add the costs of 6 bags and 4 bags.

Think: Now you must look at the numbers in the "Cost" row. How can you combine numbers or operate on one number to get $17.70?

2. Beginning salary $4.50 per hour.

Hours worked	1	2	3	4	5	6	7
Salary	4.50	9.00	13.50	18.00	22.50	27.00	31.50

TIME CARD	TIME CARD	TIME CARD	TIME CARD	TIME CARD
Name: Joan	Name: Eric	Name: Kevin	Name: Linda	Name: Tanya
Hours: 10	Hours: 20	Hours: 8	Hours: 18	Hours: 42
Salary:	Salary:	Salary:	Salary:	Salary:
$ 45.00	$ 90.00	$ 36.00	$ 81.00	$ 189.00

3. During last year's softball season Andrea got a hit 3 out of every 5 times at bat.

Hits	3	6	9	12	15	36
Times at Bat	5	10	15	20	25	60

Times at Bat 20; Hits ___12___ .

Hits 36; Times at Bat ___60___ .

Times at Bat 45; Hits ___27___ .

Hits 75; Times at Bat ___125___ .

4. Peppermint Sticks cost 15¢ apiece, 2 for 25¢.

P. Sticks	1	2	3	4	5	6
Cost	15	25	40	50	65	75

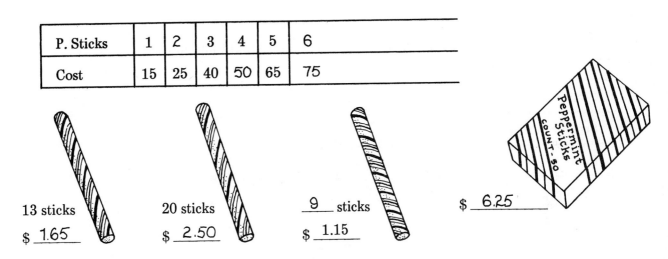

13 sticks

$ 1.65

20 sticks

$ 2.50

9 sticks

$ 1.15

$ 6.25

Be sure you found the *least* cost.

5. A stamping machine in a toy factory can produce 35 toy cars each minute at a cost of 77¢.
    What does it cost to produce 385 toy cars? How long does it take?

Cars	35	70	140	280	385
Minutes	1	2	4	8	11
Cost	.77	1.54	3.08	6.16	8.47

Combine some of the numbers in your table to obtain the 385 cars you need to solve the problem.

6. Ms. Smith's third period math class has 32 students.

Boys	5	9	20	19	16	8
Girls	27	23	12	13	16	24

1. If there are the same number of boys and girls, how many girls are there? _____ 16

2. If there are six more girls than boys, how many girls are there? _____ 19

3. If there are three times as many girls as boys, how many boys are there? _____ 8

4. If the ratio of boys to girls is 5 to 3, how many boys are there? _____ 20

WORKSHEET 6—Table Problems

Make a Table to solve the following. Use the Guess and Check strategy. The table should help you to organize the guessing procedure.

1. Tracy said, "When I add two whole numbers, the result is 46. If I multiply them the answer is 493. What are the two numbers?"

First Number	40	35	32	30	29	
Second Number	6	11	14	16	17	
Sum	46	46	46	46	46	
Product	240	385	448	480	493	

The numbers are 29 and 17

Think: Need two numbers whose sum is 46. Product is TOO SMALL. Second number should be larger.

Think: Getting closer, second number still needs to be larger. Try 14 and __32__ .

2. The sum of two whole numbers is 41. If you subtract the smaller from the larger, the result is 5. What are the two numbers?

Larger Number	40	30	25	23	
Smaller Number	1	11	16	18	
Sum	41	41	41	41	
Difference	39	19	9	5	

The numbers are 23 and 18.

Sample entries

3. Gwen said, "If I multiply two numbers the result is 360. When I divide the larger by the smaller the result is 40." What are the two numbers?

1ˢᵗ Number	360	180	120	
2ⁿᵈ Number	1	2	3	
Product	360	360	360	
Quotient	360	90	40	

The numbers are 120 and 3.

Sample entries

4. The product of two whole numbers is 36. When the first number is added to three times the second, the answer is 31. What are the numbers?

1ˢᵗ Number	1	2	3	4
2ⁿᵈ Number	36	18	12	9
3 x 2 Number	108	54	36	27
1ˢᵗ + 3 x 2ⁿᵈ	109	56	39	31

The numbers are 9 and 4.

Sample entries

5. On a TV game show called "The Big 24", a contestant is paid $7 for each correct answer, but must pay back $5 for each wrong answer. After answering 24 questions on the show, Sam broke even (he did not win or loose money). How many questions did he answer correctly?

Number Right	20	15	12	10
Number Wrong	4	9	12	14
Amount Won	140	105	84	70
Amount Paid back	20	45	60	70
Net Winnings	⁺120	⁺60	⁺24	0

Sam answered 10 questions correctly.

Sample entries

6. When asked about the ages of her brothers, Carmen said, "Al is twice as old as Doug; Lance is 3 years older than Doug, and their ages add up to 35." How old is each brother?

Doug	3	6	10	8
Al (2 x Doug)	6	12	20	16
Lance (Doug+3)	6	9	13	11
Sum	15	27	43	35

Doug is 8, Al is 16, Lance is 11.

Sample entries

UNIT III

PATTERNS

This unit is designed to introduce students to the Pattern strategy for problem solving.

Patterns pervade most of mathematics. Students are introduced to them at the most elementary level in counting processes, and continue to utilize them in addition tables, multiplication tables, and so forth. While students are exposed to a variety of pattern situations in the early grades, generally there is no application of them as a strategy for problem solving.

This unit is divided into two sections. In the first four lessons, students will progress from simple identification of a pattern and completion of next terms to a final stage in which they will find the term of a sequence given any term number and in the case of a linear sequence, determine a rule to describe it.

In the final lesson Tables are used once again as an organizer for the Pattern strategy.

We are cognizant of the possibility that the procedures developed in this unit may lead students to make generalizations on the basis of insufficient information, and leave them with the feeling that the methods used to obtain the generalizations constitute a proof of their validity. Because patterns play an integral role in the discovery and application of mathematical concepts, at some point in their mathematics education, students must be taught

1. To analyze patterns and make generalizations based on their observations,
2. To check the generalization against known information, and finally

3. To construct a formal proof to verify the generalization.

The techniques, such as proof by induction, which are required to accomplish the final goal are too sophisticated for the students to whom this book is addressed. However, these stude_ts have reached a level of maturity at which they should be introduced to the first two goals. The objective of this unit is to provide such an introduction.

Stated briefly: we believe that students must have the tools necessary to make generalizations before learning the formal methods of proving the generalizations becomes meaningful or relevant.

"A mathematician, like a painter or a poet, is a maker of patterns. If his patterns are more permanent than theirs, it is because they are made with ideas."

G. H. Hardy

"The mathematician's patterns, like the painter's or the poet's, must be beautiful; the ideas, like the colours or the words, must fit together in a harmonious way. Beauty is the first test: there is no permanent place in the world for ugly mathematics."

G. H. Hardy

LESSON 1

OBJECTIVE:

This lesson introduces the student to the concept of numerical and pictorial sequences which involve a specific pattern.

MATERIALS:

One copy of worksheet 1 for each student.

INSTRUCTIONAL STRATEGY:

Step 1: This worksheet contains both numerical and geometric sequences. It should be completed by the students with a minimum of instruction. Students should simply be advised to study the terms given and then fill in the blanks so that they continue the given pattern.

Step 2: When the assignment is completed, the sequences should be discussed with the class. Allow students to describe the patterns and the methods they used to complete the sequences.

CAUTION: It is important to note that knowing only the initial terms in a sequence is not sufficient to determine a unique rule for the sequence. To illustrate this point, consider the sequence whose first three terms are 1, 2, 4. By using the method of analysis to be developed in this unit, a student might conclude that the sequence is:

    a. 1, 2, 4, 7, 11, 16 $\cdots$

$$\frac{n^2 - n + 2}{2}$$

    b. 1, 2, 4, 8, 16, 32 $\cdots$

$$2^{n-1}$$

    c. 1, 2, 4, 8, 15, 26 $\cdots$

$$\frac{n^3 - 3n^2 + 8n}{6}$$

Even knowing five terms, 1, 2, 4, 8, 16, one may conclude that the sequence is:

    a. 1, 2, 4, 8, 16, 32

$$2^{n-1}$$

    b. 1, 2, 4, 8, 16, 31

$$\frac{n^4 - 6n^3 + 23n^2 - 18n + 24}{24}$$

In general, similar situations can occur regardless of the number of initial terms that are known. Thus, even though a rule generates the known initial terms, a formal proof that it works in all cases is still required. However, this is a topic for more advanced courses.

To help alleviate these problems and at the same time still include meaningful materials, as far as possible, the problems presented throughout the unit will involve sequences with unique rules and sufficient information will be given to determine them.

Explanation of these considerations should be given if students discover the problem of deriving a general term. Otherwise the explanation should wait until the entire unit is completed and students are comfortable with the procedures developed in it.

WORKSHEET 1—What's Missing?

Look at the sequences below and fill in the blanks so that your answers complete the Pattern.

1. 1, 4, 7, 10, ___13___ , ___16___ , ___19___ , ___22___ , 25

2. 0, 5, 10, 15, ___20___ , ___25___ , ___30___ , ___35___ , 40

3. 61, 57, 53, ___49___ , ___45___ , ___41___ , ___37___ , 33

4. 1 × 2, 2 × 3, 3 × 4, ___4 × 5___ , ___5 × 6___ , ___6 × 7___ , ___7 × 8___ , 8 × 9

5. 3, 6, 12, ___24___ , ___48___ , ___96___ , ___192___ , 384

6. 1, 3, 6, 10, ___15___ , ___21___ , ___28___ , ___36___ , 45

7. 101, 99, 96, ___92___ , ___87___ , ___81___ , ___74___ , 66

8. 2, 4, 8, ___16___ , ___32___ , ___64___ , ___128___ , 256

9. 720, 360, 120, ___30___ , ___6___ , ___1___ , 1/7

10. 1, 4, 3, 6, 5, ___8___ , ___7___ , ___10___ , 9, 12

Use the last term to check your Pattern.

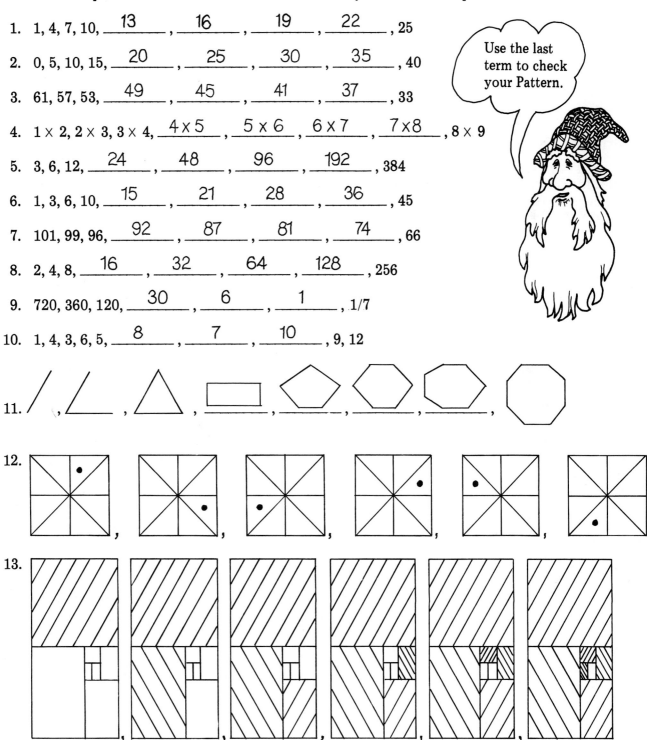

LESSON 2

OBJECTIVE:

This lesson develops a procedure that the student can apply to identify a pattern and determine the missing terms in a sequence.

MATERIALS:

One copy of worksheet 2 for each student.

INSTRUCTIONAL STRATEGY:

Step 1: Pass out the worksheet and instruct students to complete it. Directions should be minimal since they are included on the worksheet.

Step 2: The worksheet is fairly simple and should be completed quickly. Discussion with the class should focus on the four steps outlined on the worksheet. These steps should be emphasized since they constitute the framework for generating a given term in a sequence. A special point should be made concerning sequences that are NOT LINEAR. Students should look for the pattern in the sequence of DIFFERENCES. They must then continue THAT pattern to determine the missing terms.

WORKSHEET 2—What Comes Next?

Given the sequence 15, 21, 27, 33, · · ·

Term Number	1	2	3	4	5	6	7
Term	15	21	27	33			

First: Number the terms in the space above the sequence.

Term Number	1	2	3	4	5	6	7
Term	15	21	27	33			

21 − 15 = 6   27 − 21 = _6_

What is the difference between successive terms? __6__

Second: Find the difference between the 1st and 2nd terms, 2nd and 3rd terms, and so forth.

Term Number	1	2	3	4	5	6	7
Term	15	21	27	33	39	45	51

+6   +6   +6   + _6_   + _6_   + _6_

What do you add to each term to get the next term? __6__

Third: If the difference each time is the SAME, add that difference to the last given term to get the next one.

Fourth: If the difference each time is DIFFERENT, find the pattern of change and continue that pattern to get the next terms.

Term Number	1	2	3	4	5	6	7	8	9
Term	3	4	6	9	13	18	24	31	39

+1   +2   +3   +4   +5   + _6_   + _7_   + _8_

What is the pattern in the difference? __The difference increases by 1.__

USE these Four Steps and find WHAT COMES NEXT.

1.

Term Number	1	2	3	4	5	6	7
Term	2	6	10	14	18	22	26

+4 +4 +4 +4

2.

Term Number	1	2	3	4	5	6	7
Term	74	67	60	53	46	39	32

+$^-$7 +$^-$7 +$^-$7 +$^-$7

3.

Term Number	1	2	3	4	5	6	7
Term	1	4	9	16	25	36	49

+3 +5 +7 +9

LESSON 3

OBJECTIVE:

This lesson introduces the idea that many sequences can be constructed by utilizing a rule which relates each term of the sequence to its term number.

MATERIALS:

One copy of worksheet 3 for each student.

INSTRUCTIONAL STRATEGY:

Step 1: Pass out the worksheet and go through the example with the class. Make sure that they understand the terminology before starting. Emphasize the difference between the TERM NUMBER and the TERM itself. Students should understand that the TERM NUMBERS are simply the COUNTING NUMBERS. Each TERM of the sequence is determined by following the given rule.

Step 2: Once the students have completed the worksheet, the results should be reviewed quickly with the class. Three points should be stressed in the discussion:

    a. If the rule involves a constant multiplier, it is the difference between successive terms.

Example: Problem 4, Worksheet 3

$$9, \qquad\qquad 16, \qquad\qquad 23$$

$$16 - 9 = 7 \qquad 23 - 16 = 7$$
$$\text{Constant Multiplier} = 7$$

    b. If the constant multiplier is negative, as in 3 and 5, the sequence is DECREASING.

NOTE: If students have not been exposed to negative numbers prior to this time, a short explanation will be necessary. It has been the experience of many teachers who have successfully used these materials that students will pick up the needed concepts very quickly. Complete coverage of all negative number concepts is not a prerequisite to successful use of these sheets.

    c. In sequences such as 6 and 7, the difference is not constant. Students should notice that there is no constant multiplier, hence no constant difference.

Step 3: As an assignment have students make up their own rules for generating a sequence. Suggest that they use constant factors to develop increasing and decreasing sequences, and others in which the difference between successive terms is NOT constant.

When the assignment is completed, it would be most valuable to have several students explain their rules and have other students construct the sequences. This will help students to understand the distinction between the *term* and the *term number*.

WORSHEET 3—Make a Sequence

Compute the first seven terms in each sequence.

EXAMPLE: Use the term number, multiply it by 5.

1st Term	2nd Term	3rd Term	4th Term	5th Term
1×5	2×5	3×5	4×5	$\underline{5} \times \underline{5}$
5	10	15	20	25

1. Term number times 2.

Term Number	1st	2nd	3rd	4th	5th	6th	7th
Term	2	4	6	8	10	12	14

2. Term number times 3, minus 1.

Term number	1st	2nd	3rd	4th	5th	6th	7th
Term	2	5	8	11	14	17	20

3. Term number times (−5), plus 55.

Term number	1st	2nd	3rd	4th	5th	6th	7th
Term	50	45	40	35	30	25	20

4. Term number times 7, plus 2.

Term Number	1st	2nd	3rd	4th	5th	6th	7th
Term	9	16	23	30	37	44	51

5. Term number times (−4), plus 91.

Term Number	1st	2nd	3rd	4th	5th	6th	7th
Term	87	83	79	75	71	67	63

6. Square the term number.

Term Number	1st	2nd	3rd	4th	5th	6th	7th
Term	1	4	9	16	25	36	49

7. Term number times the next term number.

Term Number	1st	2nd	3rd	4th	5th	6th	7th
Term	2	6	12	20	30	42	56

LESSON 4

OBJECTIVE:

This lesson develops a procedure that the student can apply to determine the rule which describes a linear sequence.

MATERIALS:

One copy of Worksheet 4 and Worksheet 5 for each student.

INSTRUCTIONAL STRATEGY:

Step 1: Pass out Worksheet 4. This worksheet will be completed as a class exercise and students should be advised to retain it for future reference.

The following important points should be carefully explained during the class discussion:

a. Remind students of the four hints given in Lesson 2. Direct students to complete these steps for the first sequence.

b. Question the students concerning the value of continuing to add the *constant difference* in order to obtain the 50th, 100th, or 1000th term. Be sure the students understand that this is a way to find a particular term in the sequence, however if the term number is large, it is too time consuming and allows too much chance for error.

c. Review the major point of the previous worksheet, that many sequences are constructed by utilizing a rule which relates each term of the sequence to its term number. In particular, those sequences that contained a constant difference as in number 4 had a rule which involved a constant multiplier. Review several such examples including both increasing and decreases sequences.

d. The key to determining the rule for a linear sequence involves building a TABLE as shown. Term numbers should be listed through 4 or 5, although this can be shortened after students are comfortable with the procedure. Each term number is then multiplied by the constant difference. The products are not the terms of the desired sequence, but they are directly related to them.

e. The next step is the most important. The column is headed WHAT TO DO? since the question we now ask is, WHAT DO YOU DO to the numbers in the previous column to obtain the TERMS? What do you do to 3 to obtain 5? to 6 to obtain 8?, and so forth. Once students see that the answer is always the same, it is easy to find any term, the 50th, 100th, or 1000th.

Step 2: At this point, give students different term numbers, and ask them for the related terms. Following this, put a sequence on the chalkboard or overhead and ask them to follow these steps to find the 100th term such as 7, 12, 17, 22, · · ·

Step 3: The second sequence is decreasing and involves some special consideration. The steps as previously outlined can be followed exactly, however students must realize that since the constant difference is negative, the constant multiplier will be negative. Problems 3 and 5 from the previous worksheet can be reviewed at this time.

Step 4: Following the explanation, repeat the suggestions in step 2. Sample sequence: 51, 49, 47, 45, · · ·

Step 5: While these steps are simple and can be applied successfully by students, they must be cautioned that this method will work only on sequences that are linear, that is, those sequences in which the difference between successive terms is constant.

This procedure *WILL NOT* produce a rule when quadratic or higher degree expressions are used to generate sequences.

Step 6: Assign Worksheet 5. Instruct students to build a table as shown in the previous steps to solve each problem.

WORKSHEET 4—The Constant Difference

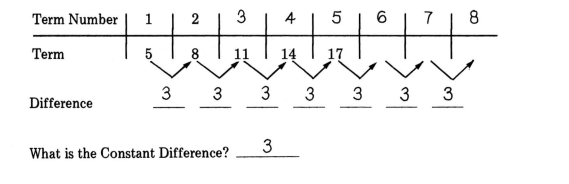

Term Number	1	2	3	4	5	6	7	8
Term	5	8	11	14	17			
Difference		3	3	3	3	3	3	3

What is the Constant Difference? ____3____

Term Number		Constant Difference			What To Do?				
1	×	3	=	3	→	3	+ 2	= 5	1st Term
2	×	3	=	6	→	6	+ 2	= 8	2nd Term
3	×	3	=	9	→	9	+ 2	= 11	3rd Term
4	×	3	=	12	→	12	+ 2	= 14	4th Term
.									
.									
.									
10	×	3	=	30	→	30	+ 2	= 32	10th Term
.									
.									
50	×	3	=	150	→	150	+ 2	= 152	50th Term

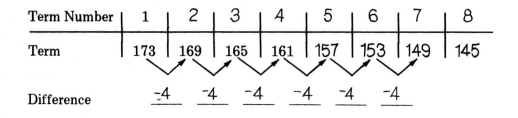

Term Number	1	2	3	4	5	6	7	8
Term	173	169	165	161	157	153	149	145

Difference $^-4$ $^-4$ $^-4$ $^-4$ $^-4$ $^-4$

What is the Constant Difference? ___$^-4$___

Term Number		Constant Difference			What To Do?					
1	×	$^-4$	=	$^-4$	$\longrightarrow$	$^-4$	+	177	=	173	1st Term
2	×	$^-4$	=	$^-8$	$\longrightarrow$	$^-8$	+	177	=	169	2nd Term
3	×	$^-4$	=	$^-12$	$\longrightarrow$	$^-12$	+	177	=	165	3rd Term
4	×	$^-4$	=	$^-16$	$\longrightarrow$	$^-16$	+	177	=	163	4th Term
⋮										
10	×	$^-4$	=	$^-40$	$\longrightarrow$	$^-40$	+	177	=	137	10th Term
⋮										
30	×	$^-4$	=	$^-120$	$\longrightarrow$	$^-120$	+	177	=	57	30th Term

WORKSHEET 5—Guess My Rule

Build a table for each sequence as shown on the previous worksheet. Answer each question for each sequence.

a. What are the missing numbers?
b. What is the 20th term?
c. What is the 50th term?
d. What is the rule you used to determine the 50th term?

	20th term	50th term	Rule
1. 8, 13, 18, 23, _28_ , _33_ , _38_ , ...	103	253	$5 \times t + 3$
2. 4, 5, 6, 7, _8_ , _9_ , _10_ , ...	23	53	$t + 3$
3. 4, 9, 14, 19, _24_ , _29_ , _34_ , ...	99	249	$5 \times t - 1$
4. 5, 8, 11, 14, _17_ , _20_ , _23_ , ...	62	152	$3 \times t + 2$
5. 23, 30, 37, 44, _51_ , _58_ , _65_ , ...	156	366	$7 \times t + 16$
6. 200, 197, 194, _191_ , _188_ , _185_ , ...	143	53	$-3 \times t + 203$
7. 8, 22, 36, 50, _64_ , _78_ , _92_ , ...	274	694	$14 \times t - 6$
8. 6, 10, 14, 18, _22_ , _26_ , _30_ , ...	82	202	$4 \times t + 2$
9. 383, 379, 375, 371, _367_ , _363_ , _359_ , ...	307	187	$-4 \times t + 387$
10. 1, 4, 7, 10, _13_ , _16_ , _19_ , ...	58	148	$3 \times t - 2$

LESSON 5

OBJECTIVE:

This lesson teaches the student how to use a table as an organizer when applying the patterns strategy.

MATERIALS:

One copy of worksheet 6 for each student.

INSTRUCTIONAL STRATEGY:

Step 1: The worksheet should be distributed with no special instructions except that students show their solutions for each problem. Some hints leading to a solution are given in problems 1 and 2.

Step 2: Upon completion of the worksheet, the problems should be thoroughly discussed with the class. Allow students to explain their method of solution and be alert to different or unusual solutions. Be sure to emphasize the difference between the two patterns in problem 2. The sequence for "the number of passengers that get on the train" is linear. The methods learned in the previous lessons can be used to find the general term. However, the sequence for "the total number of passengers" is not linear. The methods previously used for finding the rule for the general term will not work and students must carry out the table to the fifteenth stop. This is also true in problem 3, Worksheet 6, since the sequence involves the powers of two.

NOTE: As mentioned previously, it is impossible to determine a unique rule for a sequence given a few initial terms. Thus, you need to be aware of the fact that there are possible solutions other than those presented in the Answer Key. If a student derives an answer different from that given, allow him or her the opportunity to explain the solution and how it was determined.

For additional problems to reinforce the Patterns strategy, see the Practice Problem section of this book.

WORKSHEET 6—Solve with Patterns

Use your knowledge of Patterns to solve the following:

1. An empty commuter train is picking up passengers at the following rate. One passenger jumped on at the first stop, three jumped on at the second stop, five at the third stop, seven at the fourth, and so on. How many passengers got on the train at the 15th stop?

Stops	1	2	3	4	5	6
Number of Passengers that get on the Train	1	3	5	7	9	11

Do you see a pattern in the problem? Let's set up a table to help solve it.

What is the constant difference in the number of passengers? _____2_____
Rather than carry the table to 15 stops, use the method you learned in the last lesson to find the correct answer.

$$2 \times 15 - 1 = 29$$

2. Now that you know how many passengers got on at each stop, what was the total number of passengers on the train after 10 stops? After 15 stops?

Be sure you understand the question—Now you want total passengers. How about using a table again—but now add a third row—Total Passengers.

10th stop 100 passengers

15th stop 225 passengers

Stops	1	2	3	4	5	6	
Number of Passengers that get on the Train	1	3	5	7	9	11	
Total Passengers on the Train	1	4	9	16	25	36	

3. Suppose you were offered a job and the employer said she would pay your salary as follows: one penny the first day, 2 pennies the second day, 4 pennies the third day, 8 pennies the fourth day and so on to the end of the month.

How much would you be paid for working on the thirteenth day?

Day	1	2	3	4	5	6	7	13
Salary	1	2	4	8	16	32	64	$2^{12} = \$40.96$

How much money would you have earned altogether for 13 days?

Total Earned	1	3	7	15	31	63	127	$2^{13} - 1 = \$81.91$

4.

1   2   3   4

a. Describe the pattern in the twentieth picture. __20 dots high, 21 dots wide__

b. How many dots are there in the twentieth picture? __420 dots__

5. The Talk-A-Lot Phone Company installs party lines with various numbers of customers. It charges $7 a month per phone. After much research on costs, it discovered that it costs $2 a month to install and service one phone on a line, $4 a month for two phones, $7 a month for three phones, and so forth. If this pattern continues, how many phones can be put on a party line before the company would lose money?

Phones	1	2	3	4	5	6	7	8	9	10	11	12	13
Income	7	14	21	28	35	42	49	56	63	70	77	84	91
Cost	2	4	7	11	16	22	29	37	46	56	67	79	92
Net Profit	+5	+10	+14	+17	+19	+20	+20	19	+17	+14	+10	+5	−1

6. Harry Heartburn had the largest garden in the neighborhood. Instead of growing beets, carrots, corn, and beans (vegetables that everyone enjoys), he had a garden of exotic foods.

Ten days after he planted, the first shoots began to appear. The kohlrabi came up first at the rate of one plant a day. The collards started a day after the first kohlrabi at a rate of two a day. The first rutabagas came up two days after the first collards at a rate of three plants a day.

Thirty days after the first kohlrabi came up, how many total plants could be seen growing in Harry's garden?

Rule for Pattern

Days	1	2	3	4	5	6
Kohlrobi	1	2	3	4	5	6
Collards	0	2	4	6	8	10
Rutabagas	0	0	0	3	6	9

Days	30
1 x Day	30
2 x Day – 2	58
3 x Day – 9	81

Total plants = 169

UNIT IV

Make a Model

The proverb, one picture is worth more than 10,000 words, expresses a truth that is very important in mathematics education. A perceivable model is often the most effective tool for discovering and explaining mathematical concepts as well as for solving problems. In this unit, students are introduced to the Make a Model problem-solving strategy.

It is important to note that we are referring to a simple model, an object or a drawing, that serves as an aid to the intuition or to understanding rather than a mathematical model of an abstract system. Educators often assume that students have an innate ability to construct such models, but experience in the classroom suggests that this is a fallacy. Students need to be taught how to construct and use models, and they must be provided with experiences in which they can develop this skill.

The Make a Model strategy uses physical objects or drawings to help solve problems. There are two essential steps in applying the strategy:

1. Decide on a model that is appropriate for the problem.

There is usually more than one appropriate model for a given problem. The selection of one of these models generally depends on the ability to perceive what is important in the problem, the materials that are available, and, to a large extent, on previously acquired knowledge. It should also be noted that since there isn't a unique algorithm for constructing a useful model, the ability to do so is best developed by providing students with experiences with a wide variety of different types of models that are useful in problem solving.

2.   Use the model selected to aid in solving the problem.

In some instances, the model is itself the solution. In others, it represents only one of the possible solutions, and the other solutions can be obtained by suitable alteration of the model. Finally, many models serve only as an aid to organizing the information in the problem or as an aid to understanding the problem. In this case, the information or understanding gained from the model should suggest another procedure which can then be applied to solve the problem.

LESSON 1

OBJECTIVE:

This lesson introduces two basic types of models, the physical type and the paper–pencil type.

MATERIALS:

Weights (large metal washers work well), string, graph paper, rulers, a clock with a second hand, and masking tape.

INSTRUCTIONAL STRATEGY:

Step 1: To start the lesson, tie a weight to one end of a string and demonstrate that it will swing back and forth readily, thus forming a pendulum. Ask the students what they think determines the *period* of a pendulum, the time required to make one complete swing over and back.

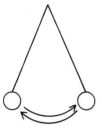

Several answers may be suggested: the amount of weight used, the length of the string, how far to the side you hold the weight before releasing it. Ask how they would determine which of these actually affect the period.

Step 2: Divide the class into small groups. Give each group 50 cm of string and some weights. Allow the groups some time to experiment to answer the question, but first emphasize these things.

    a. It is difficult to measure the period accurately, so they should time ten swings and use the average.

    b. If the pendulum is held by hand, the motion of the hand will affect the motion of the pendulum. Thus, the pendulum should be tied to a pencil, and the pencil taped to a desk in such a way that the pendulum can swing freely.

    c. To determine the length of the pendulum, measure the distance from the pencil to the center of the weight.

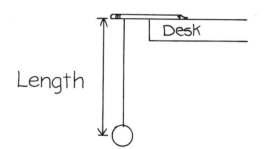

Step 3: When the students have finished experimenting, discuss the methods used by the various groups and their results. They should have discovered that:

    a. If the length is fixed, the amount of weight does not affect the period.

    b. The amount of deflection does affect the period when large deflections are used, but it is not a factor for small amounts of 5 cm or less.

    c. The length of the pendulum always affects the period.

Step 4: Write the following problem on the board.

What is the length of a pendulum that makes one complete swing in *one* second?

(The correct answer is approximately 25 cm. It will be less for large deflections.

Suggest that in doing the problem each group make a table similar to the one below to record their results.

TIME

LENGTH

After the students have determined the correct length, point out that they have used a *physical model* to solve a problem, and that the experimenting in step 2 was necessary to insure that the model was *appropriate*.

Step 5: Write the following problem on the board, or give each group a copy.

Every weekday, Mrs. Jones leaves her home and drives 4 km west, 2 km north, 6 km east, 3 km south, and 4 km east to get to her law office.

Her husband leaves their home at the same time and drives 5 km east, 3 km south, 8 km west, 4 km north, and 2 km west to get to the factory where he works.

The factory in which Mr. Jones works is

_____ km (east, west) and _____ km (north, south) of the office in which his wife works.

(The answer is: 11 km west, 2 km north. It can be obtained by using a model similar to this:

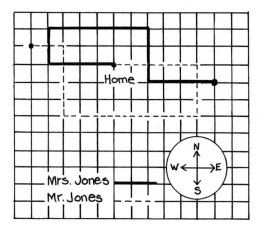

Have each group solve the problem. Allow them to use graph paper or any other special materials that might help to solve the problem, but only if requested.

Step 5: Upon completion, have some groups explain the model they used and discuss the appropriateness of it. Stress that in this case, they have used a paper-pencil model to solve a problem, and that their choice of an appropriate model was strongly influenced by their general knowledge of such things as map and compass bearings.

LESSON 2

OBJECTIVE:

This lesson teaches the student to select a model that is appropriate for a problem.

MATERIALS:

One copy of worksheet 1 for each student.

INSTRUCTIONAL STRATEGY:

Step 1: Hand out worksheet 1. Instruct the students to follow the directions on the worksheet and complete it.

Step 2: When the students have completed the worksheet, discuss it thoroughly, restricting your comments to the appropriateness of the model. With the exception of problems 2, 3, and 7, avoid giving the correct answers to the problems as they will be covered later.

Problem 1: The key point is that postage stamps have a distinct top and a distinct front. The model must have these same properties. One possibility is a set of three rectangles with an arrow pointing up drawn on the front of each.

   Some students may suggest using a sheet of graph paper to represent the sheet of stamps. This is a good approach, however, they must also indicate the top and the front of each stamp in some manner. If they don't, when they cut off the arrangements shown below, they wouldn't be able to tell them apart. (See problem 2, Worksheet 2.)

Problem 2: This problem is easily solved using a table instead of a model.

ml Orange Juice	4	16	160
ml Pineapple Juice	6	24	240

The constant quotient is 2/3.

Problem 3: Students who do not use a model to help solve this problem generally fail to recognize what is really important in the problem: the time varies directly as the number of cuts, not the number of pieces. They reason that it takes 4 minutes per piece and consequently 16 minutes to cut 4 pieces. A simple model such as a strip of paper to represent the log and a scissors for making the cuts used in conjunction with a table will yield the correct result.

Cuts	1	2	3
Pieces	2	3	4
Time	6	12	18

Problem 4: A drawing of a rectangle is the only model needed. It is used to organize the information in the problem rather than to solve it.

Problem 5: A good model is a set of marbles or cubes that can be stacked to form a pyramid. An alternate model would be a drawing of each layer of the pyramid.

Problem 6: A set of 3×5 rectangles and one 10×20 rectangle in which to place them is an appropriate model.

Problem 7: Some students will probably tell you that the situation described is impossible so the question is meaningless. Clearly, they are thinking of a map drawn on a plane as the model. If a globe is used however, it is easily seen that the only place this situation can occur is at the north pole. Thus the bear is a polar bear and is white.

Problem 8: Simple drawings are the only models necessary.

WORKSHEET 1—Selecting a Model

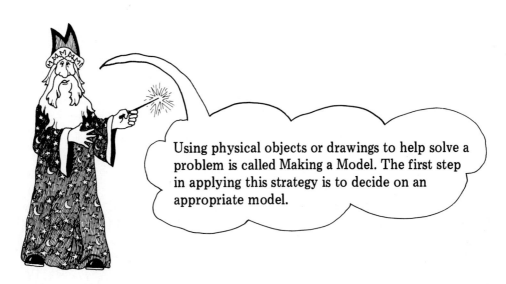

Using physical objects or drawings to help solve a problem is called Making a Model. The first step in applying this strategy is to decide on an appropriate model.

For each of the following problems:

a.   Decide whether or not a model would help you solve the problem.

b.   If you WOULD NOT use a model, give the answer to the problem and explain your solution.

c.   If you think a model would help, describe the model you would use, but DO NOT solve the problem.

1.   How many different ways can three postage stamps be torn from a sheet so that all three stamps are still attached to one another?

   See teacher pages for answer.

2.   A fruit punch dispenser mixes 4 mL of orange juice with 6 mL of pineapple juice. How many milliliters of orange juice does it mix with 240 mL of pineapple juice?

   See teacher pages for answer.

3.   If it takes 12 minutes to cut a log into 3 pieces, how long would it take to cut the log into 4 pieces?

   See teacher pages for answer.

4. The length of a tennis court is six feet more than twice its width. If the court is 36 feet wide, what is its perimeter?

See teacher pages for answer.

5. Cannon balls for an antique cannon are stacked next to it in four layers forming a square pyramid. How many cannon balls are there in the pyramid?

See teacher pages for answer.

6. Find the maximum number of 3 cm × 5 cm rectangles that can be placed inside a 10 cm × 20 cm rectangle, if none of the small rectangles overlap.

See teacher pages for answer.

7. In the spring, a bear left its cave in search of food. It walked 10 km due south, 10 km due west, and 10 km due north and arrived back at its cave. What color was the bear?

See teacher pages for answer.

8.   a.   Is it possible to plant roses, mums, and asters in a single plot so that the roses are next to the asters, but the asters are not next to the mums?

See teacher pages for answer.

b.   Is it possible to plant the flowers so that each type of flower is next to each of the other two types?

LESSON 3

OBJECTIVE:

This lesson teaches the student various ways to use the model chosen to solve a problem.

MATERIALS:

One copy of worksheet 2 for each student, graph paper, squares cut from tagboard, rulers, scissors.

INSTRUCTIONAL STRATEGY:

Step 1: Hand out the worksheet and instruct the students to complete it. All the necessary instructions are on the worksheet.

Step 2: When everyone has finished, discuss the worksheet and explain the solutions where necessary. Problems 1, 3, and 4 explain the three basic ways in which a model can be used to help solve a problem. Be sure to emphasize these techniques in the discussion.

Problem 1: This problem illustrates the idea of altering a model to find all the solutions. There are six arrangements altogether, the two given in the problem and the four shown here.

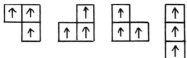

Problem 2: This problem reinforces the technique introduced in problem 1. However its major importance is that it expands on the concept of selecting an appropriate model. Unlike stamps, the squares do not have a definite front or a definite top. The model must also exhibit this property. Thus a good model for the problem would be four squares cut from paper which have no marking to indicate a front or a top. This property is important because then an individual square cannot be distinguished from its image under the geometric transformations of reflection and rotation. The same idea should be carried over into the solution of the

problem. An arrangement of the squares and its image under one or more of the transformations really represent the same arrangement. However, many students have poorly developed spatial perception and will not recognize this fact. Depending on the students perception of the problem, there are two solutions: five arrangements if one does not consider transformations of an arrangement to be distinct, and an infinite number otherwise. The five basic arrangements are:

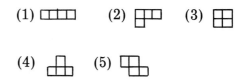

Many students will believe there are others. In these cases, a careful explanation of how a "new" arrangement can be obtained from one of the five basic arrangements by using rotations and reflections should be given.

For example: ⊞ can be obtained from ⊟

as follows:

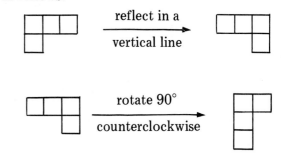

Problems of this type are extremely important because they help to develop students' spatial perception. They also provide an informal introduction to the concept of congruence, the transformations of rotation, translation, and reflection, and the idea of composition of functions.

Problem 3: This problem demonstrates how a model can be used to help discover a quicker method of solution. It also previews the Simplify strategy which is presented in Unit VI.

Layer	Model	Number in Layer	Total
1	•	1	1
2	• • • •	4	5
3	• • • • • • • • •	9	14
4	• • • • • • • • • • • • • • • •	16	30
5		25	55
6		36	91
7		49	140
8		64	204
9		81	285
10		100	385

Problem 4: This problem provides a very simple example of how a model is used to organize the information in a problem.

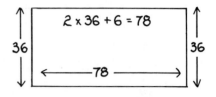

Perimeter = 36 + 78 + 36 + 78 = 228 feet

Problem 5:

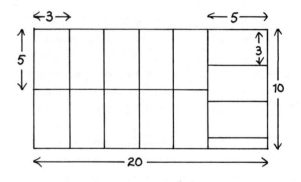

Problem 6:

a. | Asters | Roses | Mums |

b. | Asters |
   | Roses | Mums |

WORKSHEET 2—Using a Model

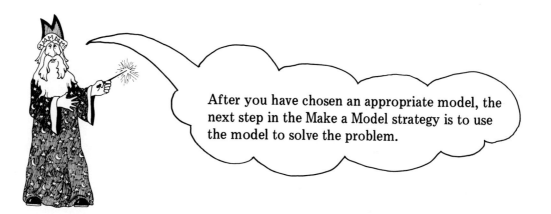

After you have chosen an appropriate model, the next step in the Make a Model strategy is to use the model to solve the problem.

Use the hints provided to solve the following problems.

1. **How many different ways can three postage stamps be torn from a sheet so that all three stamps are still attached to one another?**

Placing the rectangles side by side like this gives one solution.

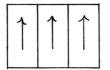

For a model, cut out three rectangles and draw an arrow on one side of each of them.

Here is one new arrangement:

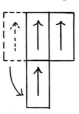

But there are others. To find them, change the model by moving one rectangle around the other two.

Continue moving this rectangle around the other two to find three other arrangements and draw them below.

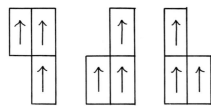

Now see if you can find any new arrangements by moving two of the rectangles in the original arrangement.

2. How many different ways can four squares be arranged in a single shape so that if two squares touch they border along a full side?

What model would you use?   <u>Four squares cut from paper.</u>

Use the procedure in problem 1 to find all the possible arrangements. Be sure to keep a record of each one!

3. Cannon balls for an antique cannon are stacked next to it in four layers to form a square pyramid. How many cannon balls are in the pyramid?

A good model for this problem would be to stack marbles (or cubes) in a square pyramid and count the number of marbles in the top four layers. If you don't have marbles, you can accomplish the same thing by making a drawing of each layer.

Layer	Drawing	Number of Cannon Balls in the Layer	Total Number of Cannon Balls
1		1	1
2		4	5
3		9	14
4		16	30

Suppose that the original problem asked for the number of cannon balls in 10 layers.

Layer	Number of Cannon Balls in the Layer	Total Number of Cannon Balls
5	25	55
6	36	91
7	49	140
8	64	204
9	81	285
10	100	385

Sometimes a model suggests another strategy that could be used to solve a problem more quickly.

Use *patterns* to extend the last two columns in the table and answer the question.

4. The length of a tennis court is six feet more than twice its width. If the court is 36 feet wide, what is its perimeter?

The model here is very simple. Its main purpose is to help us organize the information in the problem.

Draw a rectangle to represent the tennis court, and label the length and width using the information in the problem.

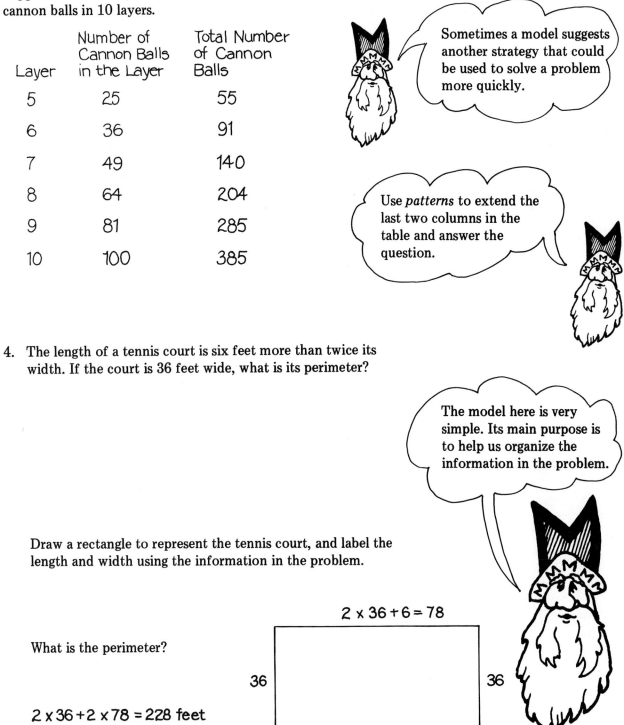

2 x 36 + 6 = 78

What is the perimeter?

36   36

2 x 36 + 2 x 78 = 228 feet

78

5. Find the maximum number of 3 cm × 5 cm rectangles that can be placed inside a 10 cm × 20 cm rectangle, if none of the small rectangles overlap.

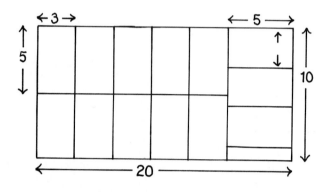

6. a. Is it possible to plant roses, mums, and asters in a single plot so that the roses are next to the asters, but the asters are not next to the mums?

Asters	Roses	Mums

b. Is it possible to plant the flowers so that each type of flower is next to each of the other two types?

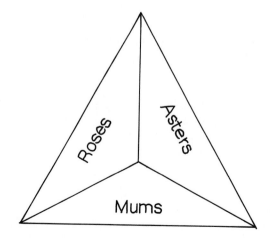

LESSON 4

OBJECTIVE:

This lesson reinforces the concepts of selecting an appropriate model and using it to solve a problem.

MATERIALS:

One copy of worksheet 3 for each student, squares cut from tagboard, graph paper, scissors, cubes.

INSTRUCTIONAL STRATEGY:

Step 1: Hand out the worksheet and instruct the students to complete it. No additional instructions are necessary, but you may want to move about the room and give help to individual students as needed.

Step 2: When all of the students have completed the worksheet, a thorough discussion of individual answers and the models used to obtain them would be helpful.

In problem 1, the students determined the twelve pentimento pieces. The activities section of this book contains additional materials involving pentominoes. You may want to use them at this time.

For additional problems to reinforce the Make-a-Model strategy, see the Practice Problems section of this book.

WORKSHEET 3—Solve Using Models

Use a model to solve each of the following problems.

1. How many different ways can five squares be arranged in a single shape so that if two squares touch, they border along a full side?

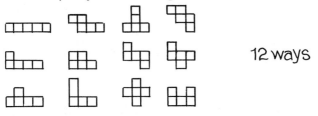

12 ways

2. How many of the arrangements in problem 1 can be folded to form an open topped box?

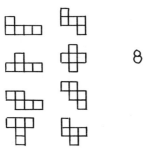

8

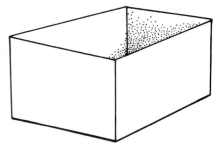

3. If it costs a nickel each time you cut and weld a link, what is the minimum cost to make a length of chain out of five separate links?

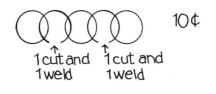

10¢

↑ 1 cut and   ↑ 1 cut and
1 weld   1 weld

4. A little squirrel went up a tree,
   Which was forty feet and three.
   Every day she climbed up eleven;
   Every night she slid down seven.
   Tell me, if she did not drop,
   When did her paws touch the top?

   at the end of the 9th day.

5. Each of the following is a different view of the same cube. What are the two missing numbers?

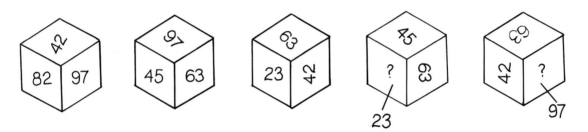

6. Have you ever heard a story about people who are lost in a forest? They often walk for hours thinking they are traveling in a straight line, and suddenly find themselves back where they started. The reason for this is simple. No one's legs are exactly the same length, so the length of a step taken with one leg is longer than the length of a step taken with the other. This difference in the lengths of the steps causes people to walk in circles.

Wierd Willie had a similar problem. While hiking in a forest one day, he became lost. He came upon a marker which indicated he was at the exact center of the forest. Now Willie knew that the forest area was a square 60 km on a side, so he decided to walk out in a straight line. But, the route he actually traveled went like this: 5 km south, then 10 km west, then 15 km north, 20 km east, 25 km south, and so on.

How far did Willie walk before he got out of the forest, and on which side of the forest did he exit?

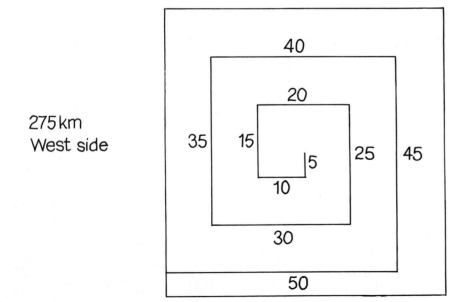

UNIT V

ELIMINATION

This unit is designed to provide students with an informal introduction to deductive logic and the use of *Elimination* as a strategy for problem solving.

As the problem solving strategy most commonly used by people in everyday life, Elimination is probably second only to Guess and Check. While it may not be recognized as a use of formal logic, the decision made by a consumer when choosing a particular brand of appliance may be based on eliminating other models because of price, consumer-report information, dealer service, model repair records, or the advice of other owners.

Logic is the cornerstone upon which mathematics is built. In the high school curriculum most students are first introduced to formal logic in geometry. Throughout higher level mathematics courses, the understanding of the correct use of deductive logic is a virtual necessity.

The materials in this unit are not intended to teach students all of the facets of formal logic. Junior high students are at an age when they are entering the "formal operational stage" as defined by Piaget. As such, they may not be ready for a complete development of logic. This unit will provide a good introduction to the use of logic in a manner consistent with the level of understanding of students in this age group.

The unit is divided into two lessons. In the first, the students will eliminate possible solutions from a given set to determine a correct answer. In the second, the students are introduced to the concept of first developing a set of possible solutions and then using Elimination to determine the correct answer. Construction of a Table is used again to organize the set of possible solutions and to lead students to an orderly use of Elimination.

Within these two lessons, three important aspects of the Elimination process are stressed:

1. The careful selection of the first clue to be used. Consideration must be given to the one that is easiest to use, and/or that will eliminate the most possibilities.

2. The use of direct reasoning in the process of elimination.

3. The use of the indirect method, whereby a possible solution is tested and a contradiction is obtained.

"When you have eliminated the impossible, whatever remains, however improbable, must be the truth."

Sir Arthur Conan Doyle

LESSON 1

OBJECTIVE:

This lesson teaches the student to use information contained in a problem to eliminate all but the correct answer from a given set of possible solutions.

MATERIALS:

One copy of Worksheets 1 and 2 for each student.

INSTRUCTIONAL STRATEGY:

Step 1: Pass out Worksheet 1 and instruct students to complete it. Directions are included on the worksheet. If the students have difficulty solving the problems by themselves, suggest that they discuss the clues with a fellow student.

Step 2: Once the students have completed the worksheet, the results should be discussed with the class. Allow students to analyze each clue in the detective problem and explain how it can be used to eliminate a suspect. By itself, the first clue will not eliminate a suspect since being "registered at the hotel" does not necessarily indicate that he spent the night.

Ask the students which clue they used first to solve the second problem. There may be some discussion of the exact order, however there will probably be agreement on the use of clues b, c, and e, before a and d. The choice of the first clue is important. Students should learn to read all of the statements first and then determine which one is easiest to use, and/or which one will eliminate the most choices.

Throughout the students' early years of learning arithmetic, they are generally instructed to begin working at the beginning of a problem and continue. In many problem-solving situations, and especially when using the Elimination strategy, this may not be the best procedure. It

is important that students realize this, and that it be stressed during these first lessons.

Step 3: Assign Worksheet 2.

Step 4: During the discussion with the class, reemphasize the choice of a *first* clue to be used. A statement is chosen first because it (1) is the easiest one to use, or (2) will eliminate the most possibilities.

The hints given in the first two problems are carefully ordered to introduce students to the use of an indirect argument in the process of Elimination.

In Game A, students should be able to determine that 9 and 12 complete the first and fourth blanks respectively.

Since two numbers remain (19 and 14), either may be used to complete the third blank. If 14 is used, the response must be "smaller." Then 19 would not be a *good guess* for the next blank. Therefore, 19 must precede 14.

In Game B, students can determine that 85 completes the first blank. We know that the correct answer is *bigger than 72* and that the response to the following guess is *smaller*. The only numbers possible for the last two blanks are 74 and 75. If 74 is chosen, the response *smaller* would be incorrect, therefore the correct order is 75 and then 74. Once these are determined, blanks 2-5 can be completed with the remaining numbers in increasing order. All responses are bigger.

Game B, problem 3, involves a similar argument. There are two possible choices for the second blank 45 and 35. If 45 is chosen, the response will be *bigger*. The contradiction will not occur until blank 4, where 35 will not be a *good guess*.

In problem 2, the relation between (a) the choice of a blue marble from the Red–Blue box, and (b) the switching of the lids to the correct boxes is very subtle.

The selection of a blue marble from box C allows two possibilities for the other marble. However, if the marble is red, the lid on box C is correct, which we know is *false*.

If box B contains Red and Blue marbles as suggested in hint #2, then box A must have a Red lid. However, this is *false* as no box has the correct lid.

WORKSHEET 1—Solve by Elimination

1. Ace Detective Shamrock Bones of the City Homicide Squad is investigating a murder at the Old Grand Hotel. Five men are being held as suspects.

    • "Giant Gene" Green. He is 250 cm tall, weighs 140 kg, and loves his dear mother so much that he has never spent a night away from home.

    • "Yoko Red." He is a 200 kg Sumo wrestler.

    • "Hi" Willie Brown. He is a small man only 130 cm tall; he hates high places because of a fear of falling.

    • "Curly" Black. His nickname is a result of his totally bald head.

    • Harvey "The Hook" White. He lost both of his hands in an accident. Answer: Yoko Red

    Use the following clues to help Detective Bones solve this crime.

    a. The killer was registered at the hotel.

    b. Before he died, the victim said the killer had served time in prison with him.

    c. Brown hair from the killer was found in the victim's hand.

    d. The killer escaped by diving from the third floor balcony into the river running by the hotel and then swimming away.

    e. Smudges were found on the glass table top indicating that the killer wore gloves.

2. Find the number described by the clues below. Circle the correct number.

    a. It is divisible by 4.

    b. It is larger than 8641.

    c. It is an even number.

    d. The sum of the digits is 21.

    e. It is less than 9756.

    What does this eliminate? odd numbers

    Which clue(s) should you use first? b, e, c

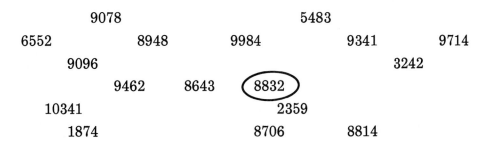

WORKSHEET 2—*Bigger or Smaller Revisited*

1. The object of the Bigger or Smaller game is to determine an unknown number by a series of guesses. The strategy is to eliminate certain guesses based on each response of the teacher.

   In each game below, put the guesses and the responses of the teacher in the correct order. Use the hints to help you solve the problems. *WATCH the order.*

   In these games, each guess is a *good* one. That is, if the guess is 54 and the response is SMALLER, all guesses after that will be LESS THAN 54.

Game A

Guesses   12,   19,   9,   14,   13

Guess	Teacher Response
9	Bigger
19	Smaller
14	Smaller
12	Bigger
13	Right

1. All guesses are good. This FIRST response tells you what guess was made.

3. There are two numbers left. Could 14 be a correct guess here? Explain.

No, because 19 would be incorrect as next guess.

2. You know the number is 13. This response should tell you what guess was made here.

Game B

Guesses 63, 74, 11, 72, 85, 24, 75, 47

Guess	Teacher Response
85	Smaller
11	Bigger
24	Bigger
47	Bigger
63	Bigger
72	Bigger
75	Smaller
74	Right

1. This FIRST response tells you what guess was made.

3. Now you can fill in these guesses and responses.

2. You know the number and response to Guess #1 and the previous guess. Could 74 be the correct guess here? Explain.

No, 74 and 75 are the only numbers bigger than 72. If 74 is used, then 75 could not be the right answer.

2. For the Bigger or Smaller games below, put the guesses and the teacher responses in the correct order. All guesses are *GOOD* guesses.

Game A

Guesses 35, 30, 25, 33, 50, 31

Guess	Teacher Response
50	Smaller
25	Bigger
35	Smaller
30	Bigger
33	Smaller
31	Right

Game B

Guesses 65, 49, 55, 35, 47, 45

Guess	Teacher Response
65	Smaller
35	Bigger
55	Smaller
45	Bigger
49	Smaller
47	Right

3. Study the clues that are given below and explain how you can tell exactly which marbles are in each box.

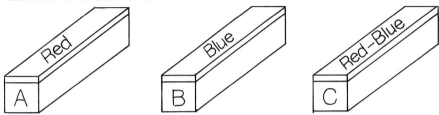

a. One box contains 2 red marbles.

b. One box contains 2 blue marbles.

c. One box contains 1 red and 1 blue marble.

d. None of the lids are on their correct box.

e. Jason reached into the box with the Red–Blue lid and pulled out a blue marble.

(1.) Since a blue marble was picked, can the other marble be red? ___No.___

Explain. A red marble would mean Box C has the correct lid which contradicts clue (d).

What is the correct lid for Box C?

Blue

(2.) Can Box B contain the Red and Blue marbles? ___No.___

Explain. If so, then Box A would have red marbles. This contradicts clue (d).

What are the correct lids for boxes A, B, and C?

Box	Correct Lid
A	Red–Blue
B	Red
C	Blue

4. Three teams in the Ice-Cold Hockey League played each other at home and away. Find the win-loss record for the six games shown in the schedule below if:

   a.   The Ants never defeated the Bats.

   b.   The Cats never lost a home game.

   c.   The Cats lost 2 games.

Winner is circled.

Game	1	2	3	4	5	6
Home Team	(Ants)	(Cats)	(Bats)	Ants	(Bats)	(Cats)
Visitors	Cats	Ants	Ants	(Bats)	Cats	Bats

Team	Ants	Bats	Cats
Won	1	3	2
Lost	3	1	2

5. Study the clues. Eliminate all but the correct number.

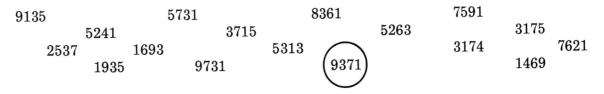

```
9135              5731           8361          7591
      5241            3715          5263        3175
   2537      1693         5313              3174      7621
      1935       9731          (9371)            1469
```

   a.   The sum of the first and last digit is equal to the sum of the two middle digits.

   b.   The four digits in the number are all different.

   c.   The hundreds digit is smaller than the thousands digit and the tens digit.

   d.   All of the digits are odd.

   e.   The units digit is the smallest natural number.

LESSON 2

OBJECTIVE:

This lesson teaches the student to construct a list of possible solutions on the basis of information given in the problem, and then eliminate all but the correct answer.

MATERIALS:

One copy of Worksheets 3 and 4 for each student.

INSTRUCTIONAL STRATEGY:

Step 1: Pass out Worksheet 3. Instruct students to complete it paying careful attention to the hints given. It might be valuable to review the use of an indirect argument with students. It may also be necessary to define *square number* and explain a Guess-and-Check method so that students can determine whether a number is a perfect square.

Step 2: After students have completed the problems, discuss the strategies used. Allow students to explain their reasons for choosing a particular clue with which to begin the elimination process.

In problem 1, students may use the clue concerning divisibility by five to develop a list of possible solutions since the multiples of five are very familiar to them and easy to write. You may wish to point out that the multiples of nine would be a better choice as the list would be shorter. When using the third clue, Elimination can be used to narrow the list of numbers to be squared. Since the list of possible solutions contains only numbers with 5 in the ones place, the whole numbers chosen to be squared must also contain 5 in the ones place.

In problems 2 and 4, a Table is given so that students can fill in the blanks as they read the clues. The construction of a Table as an organizer should be discussed and the labeling of the entries should be emphasized. The hint given in problem 4 is intended to lead the student to use an indirect argument, trying the choice given in the hint and

then finding that this choice leads to a contradiction.

Step 3: Assign worksheet 4.

The game Pico Centro in the Activities section is an excellent follow up to the Elimination strategy.

For additional problems to reinforce the Elimination strategy, see the Practice Problem section of this book.

WORSHEET 3—Elimination Illustrated

1. Clues:

   (a) I am not even.

   (b) I am greater than 200.

   (c) I am not a square number.

   (d) I am divisible by 5.

   (e) I am less than 400.

   (f) I am divisible by 9.

   Who am I?

Which clue(s) might best be used FIRST? (b), (d), (e)

205	275	345
215	285	355
225	295	365
235	305	375
245	(315)	385
255	325	395
265	335	

Would it help to make a list based on these clues? Try it.

List the multiples of 5 between 200 and 400 which are odd. Then check if divisible by 9 and not a square number.

2. Linda received four stamps from England, Spain, France, and Italy for her collection. The stamps are not marked so she does not know which stamp came from each country. A fellow stamp collector gave her the following clues:

   The French stamp is red.

   The English stamp has a picture of a castle.

   The white stamp has a picture of a fountain.

   The flower is on the blue stamp.

   The Spanish stamp is not white.

   The tower is not on the green stamp.

   Use the clues and complete the table below.

Color	Red	White	Blue	Green
Picture	Tower	Fountain	Flower	Castle
Country	France	Italy	Spain	England

3. Old MacDonald was on his way to market when a case of eggs fell off the back of the truck. Looking at the huge omelet on the road, a man asked how many eggs were in the case.

"When I counted by 2s, there was one left over; when I counted by 3s or 4s, there was one left over; but when I counted by 5s, there were no eggs left over," said MacDonald.

If MacDonald had less than 100 eggs in the case, what are the possible numbers of eggs he could have had?

Make a list of multiples of 5 that are odd.

Check division by 3 and 4 for a remainder of 1.

5	45	(85)
15	55	95
(25)	65	
35	75	

4. Juanita, Ester, and Grace left school together. In their rush to leave, they mixed up their caps and gloves. Each one wore someone else's cap and the gloves that belonged to yet another. If Grace wore Ester's cap, determine whose cap and whose gloves each girl wore.

Name	Cap	Gloves
Grace	Ester	Juanita
Juanita	Grace	Ester
Ester	Juanita	Grace

Can Juanita be wearing Grace's gloves?

No   . Explain.

If so, then she would have to wear Ester's cap.

WORKSHEET 4—Constructing Solutions

1. An archeologist digging in a ruin found a set of measuring containers used by an ancient tribe of people. There were five different jars with the names MUG, LUG, PUG, BUG, and HUG printed on them. Study of some writings which were also found indicated that the names were not on the correct jars.

   Use the following clues and place the correct name on each jar shown below.

   a. A LUG is more than a BUG.

   b. A MUG is never the least.

   c. A LUG is not the greatest.

   d. Only one thing is less than a HUG.

   e. A PUG is more than a MUG.

   f. More than one thing is greater than a MUG.

2. Lee has a collection of records. When he puts them in piles of two, he has one left over. He also has one left over when he puts them in piles of 3 or piles of 4. He has none left over when he puts them in piles of 7. What is the least number of records he can have?

   Make a list of multiples of 7 that are odd. Check division by 3 and 4 for remainder of 1.

   7
   21
   35
   (49)

3. The Lopez family, the Stein family, and the Brewster family live in 3 houses on the same side of 54th Street.

   a. The Lopez's live next to the Steins.

   b. There are no children in the middle house.

   c. The family on the right does not have the Shepherd.

   d. Kathy thinks her Poodle is the best dog a person can have.

   e. Ramona Lopez and Kathy Brewster are best friends and go to the same junior high.

   f. The Shepherd and the Poodle are not neighbors.

   From the clues, determine which family lives in each house and who has which dog.

Family	Lopez	Stein	Brewster
Dog	Shepherd		Poodle

4. There was a dog show in which four places were awarded. A poodle, beagle, setter, and terrier all entered. All had collars of different colors. There were no ties. Find which dog won each place and the color of his collar.

   a. The poodle wore the red collar, not the green collar.

   b. The beagle received the place next to the dog with the purple collar.

   c. The dog with the yellow collar received first.

   d. The dog with the purple collar was second.

   e. The colors of the poodle's collar and the terrier's collar mix to form orange.

Place	1	2	3	4
Color	Yellow	Purple	Green	Red
Dog	Terrier	Setter	Beagle	Poodle

UNIT VI

SIMPLIFY

In this unit, students are introduced to the *Simplify* strategy for problem solving. Simplifying a problem involves changing its form so that:

1. The problem becomes more understandable,
2. A method of solution is more easily discovered, or
3. The solution process is facilitated.

Since it is not a method of solving a problem which is complete in itself, it is generally used in conjunction with one or more of the other strategies.

It would be impossible to define and enumerate all of the methods of simplifying. However, there are four techniques which are frequently employed and which can be taught successfully.

1. Reword the problem using different numbers or a more familiar setting to help discover the operation which should be used.

This is probably the most commonly used method of simplifying. The following problem illustrates how it is used:

If the distance from the sun to the earth is 1.55×10^8 km, and the speed of light is 3.1×10^5 km per second, how long does it take for sunlight to reach the earth?

If a student is unable to solve the problem, it is generally for one of the following reasons:

a. The type of numbers involved or their magnitude,
b. The nature of the setting for the problem,
c. Inability to recognize the correct operation, or
d. Inability to determine how to use the numbers in the operation.

To overcome these difficulties, he is often encouraged to reword the problem using a more familiar setting and numbers with which he is more comfortable.

If it is 360 km from Columbus to Dillon, and you drive 90 km per hour, how long will it take you to drive from Columbus to Dillon?

By solving this problem the student discovers the correct operation for solving the original problem and how to use the numbers in the operation.

This approach is used routinely in teaching students to solve word problems, and the material in most textbooks provides ample situations for teaching it to individual students. For these reasons, no additional materials are presented here.

2. Separate the problem into distinct subproblems which can be solved individually or in sequence.

Students are familiar with this technique from the "two-step" problems of arithmetic, but they require additional exposure to it in nonstandard settings. This technique provides a natural prelude to the method of defining subgoals which is an essential part of more advanced courses.

3. Solve the problem by cases.

This procedure involves partitioning the set over which the problem is to be solved into disjoint subsets and finding the solutions in each subset separately. The solution set for the problem is the union of the solution sets for the individual subsets. This technique introduces the method of proof by cases which is employed in deductive logic.

4. Begin with a simpler case of the problem and work through successive cases until a general method of solution is discovered.

This technique is essentially an informal analogy of proof by induction. It assumes that the problem to be solved is a member of a hierarchy of identical problems. By solving the initial problem in the hierarchy, information or insight is gained which enables one to solve the next problem, and so on until a general solution which applies to any member of the hierarchy is discovered.

"Divide each problem that you examine into as many parts as you can and as you need to solve them more easily."

René Déscartes

"This rule of Descartes is of little use as long as the art of dividing . . . remains unexplained. . . . By dividing the problem into unsuitable parts, the inexperienced problem solver may increase his difficulty."

G. W. Leibnitz

LESSON 1

OBJECTIVE:

This lesson teaches the student to solve a complex problem by separating it into simpler problems or cases.

MATERIALS:

One copy of worksheet 1 for each student.

INSTRUCTIONAL STRATEGY:

Step 1: Introduce the lesson by dividing the class into pairs and playing the following version of the ancient game of NIM. Beginning with 0, the two players alternate turns adding 1, 2, or 3 to the previous sum. The first player to reach 21 is the winner.

Example:

Start	0		Sum	11
A	+ 3		B	+ 3
Sum	3		Sum	14
B	+ 2		A	+ 2
Sum	5		Sum	16
A	+ 2		B	+ 3
Sum	7		Sum	19
B	+ 3		A	+ 2
Sum	10		Sum	21
A	+ 1			
Sum	11		A wins	

The game is nicely adapted to play on calculators if they are available. To be certain that the students understand the rules, it is a good idea to select a student as an opponent and play a sample game at the board.

After a few games, some students generally notice that the player who leaves his opponent with a sum of 17 always wins, and they start looking for a method of obtaining 17. They quickly discover that the first player can always win by leaving his opponent with the sums 1, 5, 9, 13, and 17.

(This sequence of key numbers can always be found by repeated subtraction of $n + 1$ where n is the largest number a player can add. The desired sequence is decreasing, begins with the target number, and contains only nonnegative terms. For example, in the game above, the target number is 21 and n is 3. The sequence is found as follows:

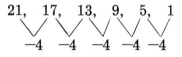

If the target number is 25 and a player can add 1, 2, 3 or 4, the sequence would be:

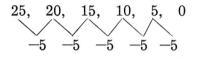

If the sequence ends with 0, the second player can always win, otherwise the first player can always win.)

At this point, you may either go directly to step 2, or you may want to continue playing the game; there are several possible variations:

    a. Change the target number,

    b. Change the numbers that may be added,

    c. Change the operation to subtraction,

    d. Change the rules so that the person who reaches the target number loses, or

    e. Use any combination of the above.

(In all the variations, an analysis similar to the one shown previously will yield a winning strategy.)

Step 2: Have some students who discovered a winning strategy explain their method and the procedure they used to obtain it. Emphasize that the winning strategy can be discovered by considering simpler problems. Explain that this is a valuable problem solving technique which can also be applied in other situations.

Step 3: Hand out Worksheet 1 and have the students complete it. Emphasize the instruction to use the lettered hints to help solve each problem.

Step 4: When the worksheet has been completed, it should be thoroughly discussed. The key point in each of the problems is that the solution involved breaking the problem into simpler problems or considering separate cases.

Additional points to emphasize are:

a. In problem 1, there are too many cases in c to make listing practical. However, by starting an organized list, a Pattern can be discovered that will quickly yield the total number. These same considerations apply in problem 2.

b. In problem 4, it is helpful to have individual students explain how they decided what the two problems are. This is a facet of the Simplify strategy which can only be learned through experience, but the process can be enhanced by sharing insights.

c. In problem 5, once the students have obtained one solution, they should still consider the remaining cases as there may be more than one solution. This is not true in this problem, but it is in many others.

WORKSHEET 1—Divide and Conquer

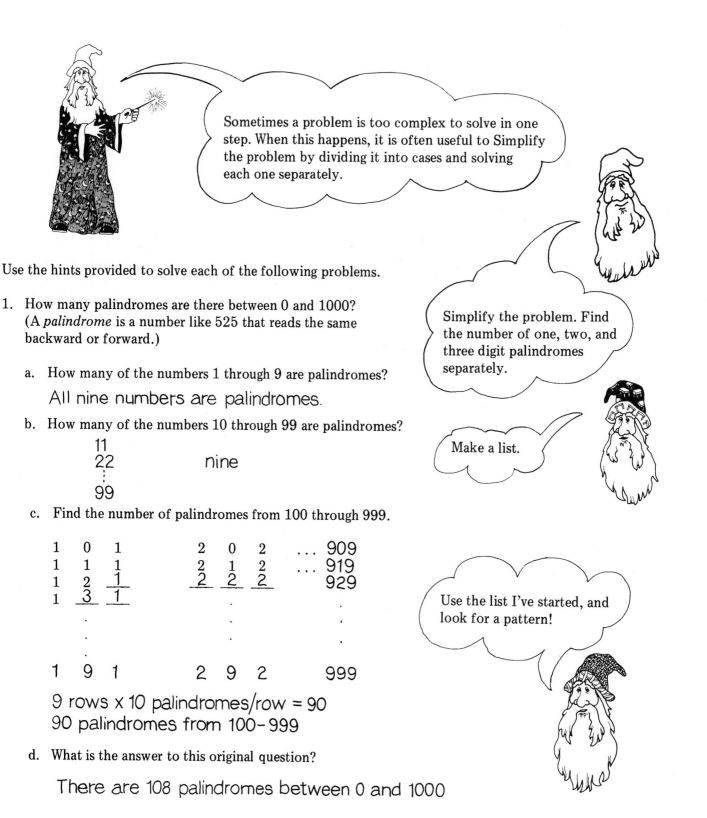

Sometimes a problem is too complex to solve in one step. When this happens, it is often useful to Simplify the problem by dividing it into cases and solving each one separately.

Use the hints provided to solve each of the following problems.

1. How many palindromes are there between 0 and 1000? (A *palindrome* is a number like 525 that reads the same backward or forward.)

    a. How many of the numbers 1 through 9 are palindromes?

    All nine numbers are palindromes.

    Simplify the problem. Find the number of one, two, and three digit palindromes separately.

    b. How many of the numbers 10 through 99 are palindromes?

    11
    22
    ⋮   nine
    99

    Make a list.

    c. Find the number of palindromes from 100 through 999.

1	0	1		2	0	2	...	909
1	1	1		2	1	2	...	919
1	2	1		2	2	2		929
1	3	1						

    1 9 1   2 9 2   999

    9 rows x 10 palindromes/row = 90
    90 palindromes from 100-999

    Use the list I've started, and look for a pattern!

    d. What is the answer to this original question?

    There are 108 palindromes between 0 and 1000

2. If you add the digits in a number, how many numbers between 0 and 1000 have a sum of 10? (One of the numbers is 334 because 3 + 3 + 4 = 10.)

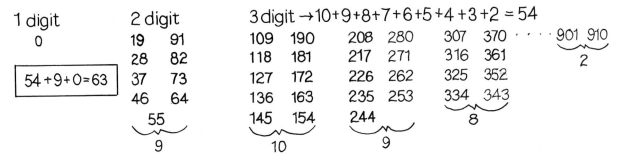

3. During a recent sale, the Sound Palace sold $2070 worth of records and tapes. They received twice as much income from the tapes as from the records. They sold 150 records—classical lps selling for $5 each and country-western lps selling for $4 each. They sold 210 tapes—disco tapes selling for $8 each and rock tapes selling for $6 each. How many classical lps did they sell? Country-western lps? Each variety of tape?

> There are really three separate problems to solve.

a. First, determine how much of the $2070 was from records, and how much was from tapes.

Record Sales	500	690
Tape Sales = 2 × Record Sales	1000	1380
Total Sales	1500	2070

> The tape sales must be two times the record sales. Build a Table and use Guess and Check. Total sales must be $2070.

b. How many classical lps and how many country-western lps did they sell?

Number of classical	100	90	
Number of country-western	50	60	
Total	150	150	
Value of classical lps	500	450	
Value of country-western lps	200	240	
Total Value	700	690	

The number of classical lps plus the number of country-western lps is 150. Classical lps sell for $5 each, country-western lps sell for $4 each. Try a Table and use Guess and Check.

c. How many disco tapes and how many rock tapes did they sell?

Disco tapes	60
Rock tapes	150
Total	210
Disco value	480
Rock value	900
Total value	1380

Build a Table and use Guess and Check.

4. A man's age at death was 1/29th of the year of his birth. He was alive in 1900. How old was he in 1900?

There are really two problems to be solved. What do you need to know to find his age in 1900?

The year he was born.

year of birth	1856	1885
age at death	64	65
year of death	1920	1950
age in 1900	44	15

5. Harry is twice Becky's age now. Four years ago Becky was twice as old as Jill. However, Jill is now 1/3 Harry's age. Which one will be 13 on their next birthday?

One of the people is 12 years old now, but we don't know which one. Try three separate cases and use Elimination.

a. Suppose Harry is 12?

How old is Becky? ___6___

How old is Jill? ___4___

How old was Becky 4 years ago? ___2___

How old was Jill 4 years ago? ___0___

Was Becky twice as old as Jill? ___no___

What does this tell you? Harry isn't 12 now.

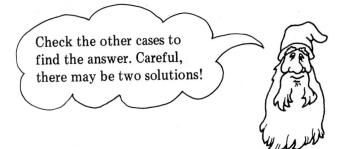

Check the other cases to find the answer. Careful, there may be two solutions!

b. Suppose Jill is 12.
    Harry is 36.
    Becky is 18.

    4 years ago:
      Jill was 8.
      Becky was 14.
    Becky was not twice
    as old as Jill. Thus
    Jill is not 12.

c. Suppose Becky is 12.
    Harry is 24.
    Jill is 8.

    4 years ago:
      Becky was 8.
      Jill was 4.
    Becky was twice as
    old as Jill. Thus
    Becky will be 13
    on her next birthday.

LESSON 2

OBJECTIVE:

This lesson teaches the student to solve a problem by beginning with a simpler case of the problem and progressing through successive cases until the solution is obtained or an alternate method of solution is discovered.

MATERIALS:

A transparency of the "To Marry or Not to Marry" problem (or a copy for each student) and one copy of worksheet 2 for each student.

INSTRUCTIONAL STRATEGY:

Step 1: Discuss the problem with the students. You might begin by talking about the origination and meaning of each symbol or the calendar dates for each sign. Before asking them to solve the problem, be sure they understand what is considered a good marriage. For example: A Leo–Leo marriage is *not* good because they are the same sign; a Leo–Cancer marriage or a Leo–Virgo marriage is *not* a good marriage because they are *adjacent* signs.

Step 2: After the students have had an opportunity to solve the problem, have some students give their answer and explain their solution.

Some of the students will probably get 108 for the answer. Their reasoning may be: for each sign, there are 3 bad marriages; this leaves 9 good marriages, and since there are 12 signs, there are 9 × 12 = 108 good marriages. Finding the number of good marriages for each sign is an excellent way to simplify the problem. However, you must be careful when you use this method of simplifying since it considers a Leo–Gemini marriage and a Gemini–Leo marriage to be different even though the signs involved are the same.

If it does not come out in the discussion, explain the following solution:

To get a better understanding of the problem and to discover a method for solving it, it might be helpful to look at a simpler version of the same problem.

Begin by considering a zodiac in which there is just one sign. Ask for the number of good marriages. (Answer 0)

Next, try a zodiac with two signs. Again, ask for the number of good marriages. (Again, it is 0.)

Continue increasing the number of signs and asking for the number of good marriages until the students recognize a pattern. Don't forget to use a table to organize the results.

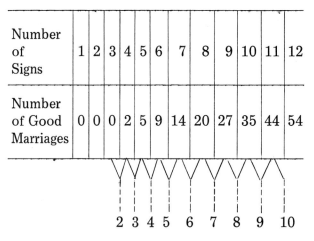

Number of Signs	1	2	3	4	5	6	7	8	9	10	11	12
Number of Good Marriages	0	0	0	2	5	9	14	20	27	35	44	54

2 3 4 5 6 7 8 9 10

After completing the solution, emphasize the following points.

1. The problem was simplified by solving a sequence of problems each of which was a simpler version of the original problem. In doing this, it really wasn't necessary to consider zodiacs with fewer than 4 signs since there are no good marriages in those cases. How-

ever, this will often happen when applying the Simplify strategy since it is generally very difficult to determine exactly where to begin.

2. The actual method of solution involved applying three other problem solving strategies: Models to represent each problem, Tables to organize the results, and Patterns to obtain the final solution. Simplifying served mainly as an aid to discovering this method.

Step 3: Assign Worksheet 2, and discuss it when it has been completed. It is very beneficial to have individual students explain their solution of problems 3 and 4. The points to be emphasized in discussion are basically the same as above. When discussing problem 3, remember that the problem can be simplified by finding the number of presents given by one family member. For this problem, this is the quickest method of simplification, and it will yield the correct solution.

For additional problems to reinforce the Simplify strategy, see the Practice Problem section of this book.

TO MARRY OR NOT TO MARRY?

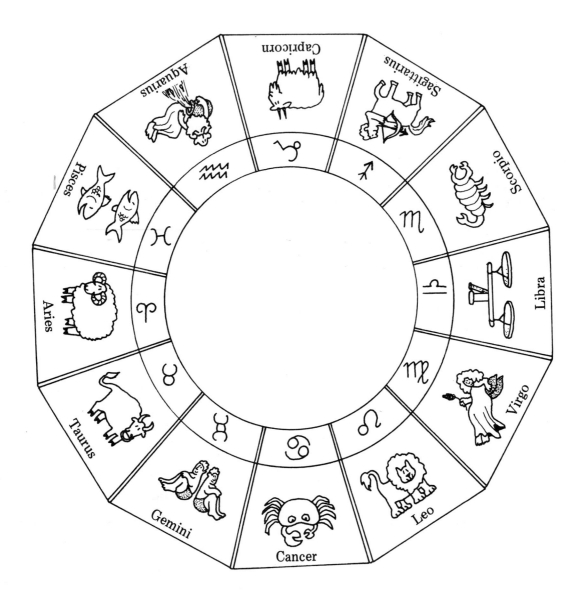

In the world of astrology, Madam Zodia considers it unwise for people born under the same sign to marry. One should also avoid marriage to persons born under a sign adjacent to one's own. Marriage between other pairs of signs are considered good.

How many pairs of signs will result in good marriages?

WORKSHEET 2—*Simplify to Solve*

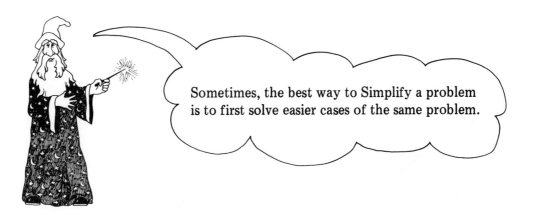

Sometimes, the best way to Simplify a problem is to first solve easier cases of the same problem.

1. Use the hints provided to solve this problem.

The nine directors of the Whacky Widget Corporation always open their annual board meetings with a special ceremony in which each director shakes hands with each of the other directors. How many hand shakes take place?

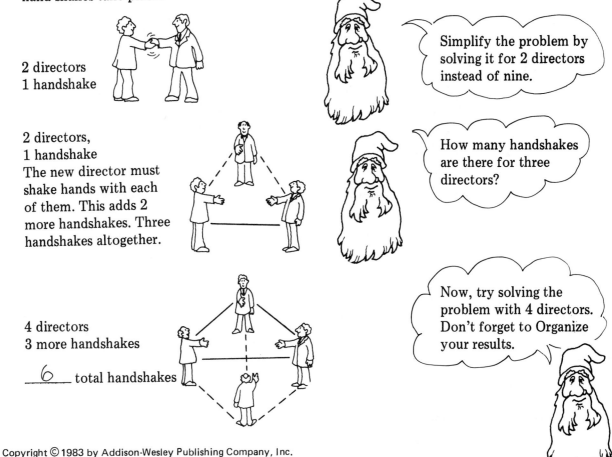

2 directors
1 handshake

Simplify the problem by solving it for 2 directors instead of nine.

2 directors,
1 handshake
The new director must shake hands with each of them. This adds 2 more handshakes. Three handshakes altogether.

How many handshakes are there for three directors?

4 directors
3 more handshakes

__6__ total handshakes

Now, try solving the problem with 4 directors. Don't forget to Organize your results.

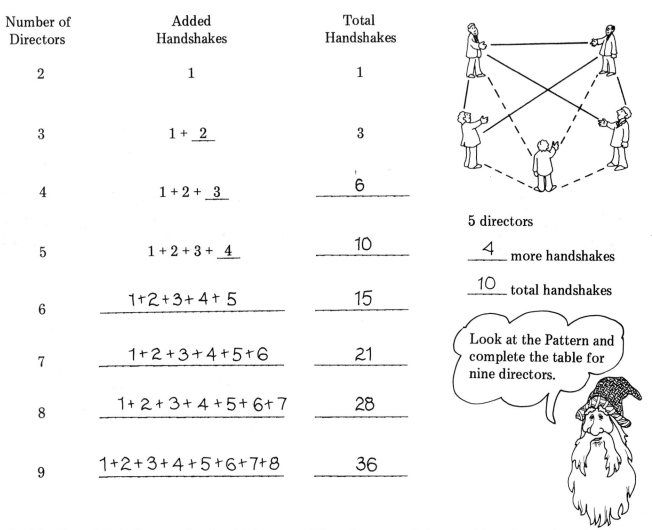

Number of Directors	Added Handshakes	Total Handshakes
2	1	1
3	1 + _2_	3
4	1 + 2 + _3_	6
5	1 + 2 + 3 + _4_	10
6	1+2+3+4+5	15
7	1+2+3+4+5+6	21
8	1 + 2 + 3 + 4 +5+ 6+ 7	28
9	1+2+3+4+5+6+7+8	36

5 directors

_4_ more handshakes

_10_ total handshakes

Look at the Pattern and complete the table for nine directors.

2. The Round Tuit Corporation has 15 directors. They also open their annual board meeting with the handshaking ceremony. How many handshakes take place?

$$36 + 9 + 10 + 11 + 12 + 13 + 14 = 105 \text{ handshakes}$$

Use the method explained in the preceding problems to solve the following:

3. It is traditional in many families at Christmas time for each family member to give a gift to each of the other members. If a family of ten followed this tradition, how many total gifts would be given?

number of family members	1	2	3	4	5	6	7	8	9	10
number of gifts	(0 x1) 0	(1 x 2) 2	(2 x3) 6	(3x4) 12	(4 x 5) 20	(5x 6) 30	(6x7) 42	(7 x 8) 56	(8 x 9) 72	(9 x 10) 90

2   4   6   8   10   12   14   16   18

4. A pie can be cut into seven pieces with three straight cuts. What is the largest number of pieces that can be made with eight straight cuts?

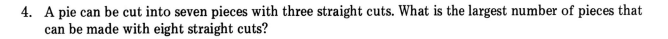

Cuts	1	2	3	4	5	6	7	8
Pieces	2	4	7	11	16	22	29	37

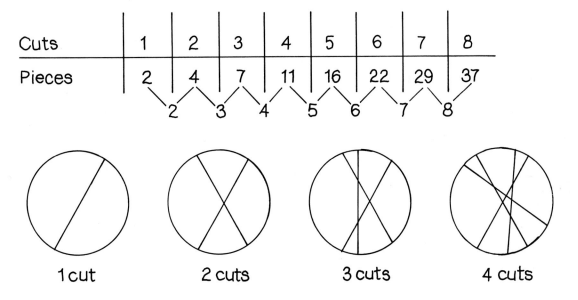

   1 cut   2 cuts   3 cuts   4 cuts

SECTION II

ACTIVITIES

ACTIVITIES

INTRODUCTION

The materials in this section are designed to physically involve students in activities which utilize one or more of the problem-solving strategies. The activities can be used to:

1. develop new mathematical concepts
2. reinforce concepts already introduced
3. maintain basic skills
4. reinforce one or more of the problem solving strategies in the context of regular course work.

The Skills Chart on page 111 indicates the correlation between each activity and the problem-solving strategies and content areas to which it is related. The chart can be used (a) to locate activities that might be included in a teaching unit for a particular content area when planning the unit; or (b) to find activities that might be used to reinforce and apply a problem-solving stratety when it is being taught.

For example, *Regular Polygons in a Row* is keyed to the Pattern strategy and the geometry strand. Thus, it could be used after the Pattern unit has been presented to provide an application of the strategy and to reinforce the procedure for developing a rule to describe a sequence. However, the activity involves finding the perimeter of polygons so it might also be used during a geometry unit to reinforce or review the concept of perimeter.

Each activity is accompanied by a set of teacher instructions. In addition to listing the content area the activity is related to, the problem-solving strategies used, and the necessary materials, the instructions also contain a brief statement of the suggested uses for the activity as well as a detailed lesson plan.

There are two important reasons for reading the teacher instructions carefully before deciding whether to use an activity.

1. Some of the activities can be used without first covering the problem-solving strategies noted. The instructions will help determine whether completion of the Introductory Units for the strategies is a prerequisite for the successful use of the activity.

2. Most of the activities can be used in more than one way. Some alternatives are listed under Suggested Use. By using the teacher instructions and some imagination, you may discover ways to use the activity which have not been suggested.

The fact that most of the activities can be used in more than one way deserves special note. For example, *Square Experiment* provides a concrete hands-on approach for introducing the concepts of prime, composite, and square numbers. However, if students have been previously introduced to these concepts but have not used the activity, it also provides an excellent review of the concepts at the beginning of a unit on prime factorization, least common multiple (LCM), and greatest common factor (GCF).

One final example: once students have been introduced to the concepts of LCM and GCF, the *Pool Factor* activity can be used to further develop the concepts. However, for those students who are proficient with the factoring concept, it also provides an excellent means to review and apply LCMs and GCFs.

SKILLS CHART

Activities:
1. The Meaty Mystery
2. How Much Is a Million
3. A Rigid Task
4. Triangle Properties I
5. Triangle Properties II
6. Kinds of Triangles
7. A Square Experiment
8. The Factor Game
9. Paper Powers
10. The Pool Factor
11. Square Fractions
12. Patterns of Repeating Decimals
13. Pico Centro
14. The Big 1
15. Equivalent Ratios
16. Regular Polygons in a Row
17. From Triangles to Polygons
18. Pentominoes
19. Integer Patterns

	1	2	3	4	5	6	7	8	9	10	11	12	13	14	15	16	17	18	19
Strands (Content Areas)																			
Whole Numbers	x	x											x						
Primes, Composites							x	x		x									
LCM, GCF										x									
Exponents, Powers									x										
Fractions: Concept											x	x							
Fractions: Operations											x	x		x					
Decimals											x	x							
Ratio-Proportion															x				
Perimeter																x		x	
Area																		x	
Triangle Properties				x	x	x													
Angles of Polygons																	x		
Identifying Polygons				x	x	x						x			x	x	x		
Integers: Operations																			x
Related Problem-Solving Strategies																			
Guess and Check	x	x					x				x	x	x	x				x	
Tables								x		x			x	x			x		
Patterns				x	x	x		x		x		x			x	x	x		x
Models				x	x	x	x	x		x		x				x	x	x	
Elimination							x						x					x	
Simplify	x	x					x					x							

THE MEATY MYSTERY

STRAND:

Whole Numbers—addition and subtraction

PROBLEM-SOLVING STRATEGY:

Guess and Check

SUGGESTED USE:

This activity provides reinforcement of addition and subtraction of whole numbers while utilizing the *Guess and Check* strategy.

MATERIALS:

Student activity page.

INSTRUCTIONAL STRATEGY:

Step 1: Distribute the student page and instruct students to read the problem. Review the examples with the class and the operation of a balance scale if students are not familiar with it. Students may then proceed to complete the problems.

THE MEATY MYSTERY

Shamrock Bones and Winston were investigating a robbery at Paoli's Pastrami Factory. In one room, Winston found a strange balance scale used to weigh the meat for the pastrami. Mr. Paoli had only four masses, 1 kg, 3 kg, 9 kg and 27 kg. He stated that he could find the mass of any whole kilogram of meat between 1 and 40 kg.

Winston said it was impossible. Shamrock said it was an elementary problem, and explained it to Winston.

How did he do it?

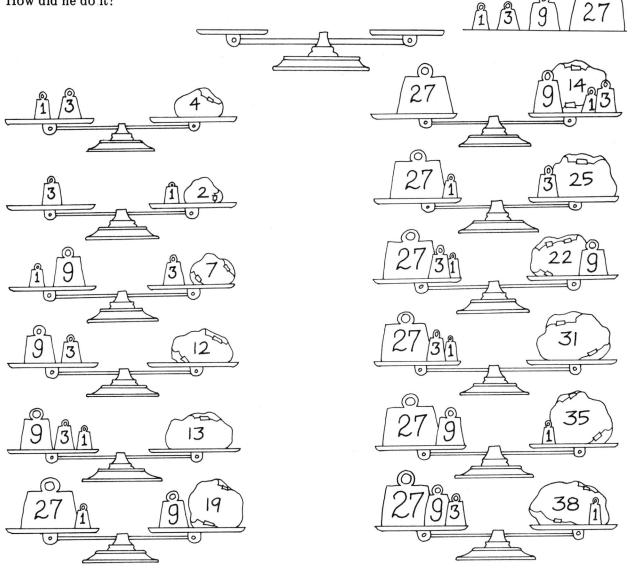

Challenge: Can you also explain to Winston how Mr. Paoli weighed the missing masses between 1 and 40?

HOW MUCH IS A MILLION?

STRAND:

Whole Numbers—estimation, large number concepts; Geometry—measurement, volume.

PROBLEM-SOLVING STRATEGIES:

Simplify, Guess and Check

SUGGESTED USE:

The first part of this activity can be used at any time, however best results will be derived if the Simplify strategy has been covered.

The follow-up section can be used after students have been introduced to the concept of volume and are familiar with the formulas for computing volume.

While the techniques developed in the first activity are used in the follow up, they could be developed in the process of doing the second portion without having done the first.

MATERIALS:

Two to four kilograms of beans, rice or some other grain, several containers of the same size, (approximately one liter works well), measuring devices such as scales, spoons, measuring cups, graduated cylinders or beakers, rulers, meter sticks or tapes, and so forth.

INSTRUCTIONAL STRATEGY:

Note: To simplify the explanation, the word "beans" has been used throughout. However, rice or any grain available works just as well.

Step 1: Divide the class into groups of three or 4.

Step 2: Lead into the activity by displaying a container which is full of beans. Ask each student to estimate the total number of beans in the container. Then, have the groups discuss the individual guesses and determine a group estimate.

Step 3: Distribute one container of beans to each group. The container should be the same size as that previously displayed. Discuss with the class the difficulty involved in counting to determine the number of beans in the container. Without suggesting a procedure for their use, point out the measuring devices that are available to help solve the problem.

Each group should develop a procedure for determining the number without counting. One person in each group should be a recorder so that an accurate account of the procedure can be kept. Each group should turn in one record of their work.

Step 4: After the class has completed the activity, allow each group to describe the procedure they used to determine their approximation and state their answer. As a bonus, extra points can be given to those groups whose number is closest to the approximation determined in advance by the teacher.

FOLLOW-UP ACTIVITY

This activity utilizes the strategies and procedures of the previous one. However, students will need to be familiar with the concept of volume and be able to determine the volume of small containers, and of the classroom.

Best results can be derived by once again allowing students to work in groups of three or four. Designate a recorder for each group and have that person turn in a record of the group's work.

Step 1: Write the following questions on the chalkboard or overhead.

1. Would one million beans fit in your classroom?
2. If you had one million beans, what would be the volume of a box needed to hold them? Give the dimensions of a box that would hold them.
3. How many millions of beans would be needed to fill your classroom?
4. How much would one million beans weigh? Could you carry them?
5. How much would one million beans cost?

Step 2: Have each student write down an estimate for each question. Allow time for the groups to discuss individual answers and determine a group estimate.

Step 3: Using the techniques learned in the first activity, have each group determine answers to the questions.

Step 4: Once the class has completed the activity, allow time for discussion of the procedures used and the answers derived. Most students have a poor concept of large numbers. It would be a good idea to provide other situations that help to develop the concept. You may wish to use such examples as:

1. How much would one million pennies weigh?
2. How large a room would be needed to hold one million soft drink cans?
3. How large a box would be needed to hold one million tops from soft drink bottles? How much would they weigh?
4. How long would it take you to count to one million?
5. Use the activity *Paper Powers*, Activities Section, page 136.

A RIGID TASK

STRAND:

Geometry—polygons.

PROBLEM SOLVING STRATEGIES:

Patterns, Models

SUGGESTED USE:

This activity provides motivation for the study of the properties of triangles. It is best used as part of an introduction to a unit on polygons.

MATERIALS:

Geostrips or D-Stix (if these are not available, use strips of tagboard (cut in several different lengths) and metal fasteners), student activity page.

INSTRUCTIONAL STRATEGY:

Step 1: Hand out the student page. Explain that changing the shape of a polygon, means changing it in a plane without changing the number of sides. A good way to test for rigidity is by laying the polygon on a desk top and trying to alter its shape without lifting any portion of the polygon off the desk.

Step 2: Have the students work in groups of three or four and complete the activity sheet. If the question arises, explain that a support is a strip that goes from one vertex to another. The students should discover that the quickest way to find the minimum number of supports is to start every support at the same vertex. However, with some students you may need to give hints that will lead them to this technique.

Step 3: When the activity sheet has been completed, you may want to discuss it briefly. The major point of the worksheet is that since triangles are the *only* rigid polygons, it would be nearly impossible to construct any rigid structure without using them (see answer key). This of course makes triangles extremely important and a study of their properties very worthwhile.

The activity also provides an opportunity to review the method for finding the general term in a linear sequence.

This activity provides an excellent introduction for the *Triangle Properties* activities. You may wish to use them at this time.

A RIGID TASK

1. Use the materials provided to make a triangle, a quadrilateral, a pentagon, and a hexagon.

2. Which one of these do you think is the most fun to play with? _____
   Why?
   Answers will vary with students.

3. Which of the polygons cannot be changed in shape? __The triangle_____

4. The triangle is called a rigid polygon because its shape cannot be changed.

   a. Can you make the quadrilateral rigid by adding supports? ____Yes_____

   b. If so, what is the minimum number of supports that you need? ____1_____

   c. Answer questions a and b for the pentagon and hexagon.

	a	b
Pentagon	yes	2
Hexagon	yes	3

5. Complete the table below. Build more polygons if necessary.

Number of Sides in the Polygon	Minimum Number of Supports Required to Make it Rigid	Number of Triangles Formed by the Supports
3	0	1
4	1	2
5	2	3
6	3	4
7	4	5
8	5	6
9	6	7
10	7	8
⋮		
n	n−3	n−2

6. The fact that triangles are the only rigid polygons makes them very important. List some situations in which triangles are used because they are rigid.

   In the construction of buildings, domes, bridges, and fence gates. In the manufacture of car frames, table leg supports, crane booms, ect.

TRIANGLE PROPERTIES I
THE SIDES

STRAND:

Geometry—Names of triangles, the triangle inequality, construction.

PROBLEM SOLVING STRATEGIES:

Models, Patterns

SUGGESTED USE:

This activity provides an excellent means for teaching the triangle inequality and the classification of triangles by the number of congruent sides. It can be used at any point in a unit on triangles, however students must know how to construct a triangle given its sides.

MATERIALS:

Student activity pages, rulers, compasses.

INSTRUCTIONAL STRATEGY:

Note: If students are not familiar with the method of using a straight edge and compass to construct a triangle when the lengths of the sides are given, it should be explained before doing this activity.

Step 1: Hand out the student pages. Explain that all the constructions are to be done on a separate sheet of paper and numbered.

Step 2: Many students will have trouble with exercise 2e because they did not use enough care in doing the construction. It is a good idea to practice this construction a few times yourself. Then, while the students are working, move about the room checking their result in 2e. When you find students who constructed a triangle in this case, go through the construction with them to show them that the result is a line segment, not a triangle.

Step 3: When the activity has been completed, a brief discussion of the results might be beneficial. The key points developed are:

1. The sum of the lengths of any two sides in a triangle is always greater than the length of the third side.
2. The definitions of scalene, isosceles, and equilateral triangles.

This activity should be followed immediately with *Triangle Properties II* and *Kinds of Triangles*.

TRIANGLE PROPERTIES I
THE SIDES

1. a. Use a ruler to construct three different triangles in which one side is 3 cm and another side is 4 cm.
   Drawings will vary.

   b. Compare your triangles with a fellow student's. What do you notice?

   They should notice that all of the triangles have different shapes.

   c. How many different triangles could you construct given the lengths of two sides?

   An infinite number.

2. In each of the following, use a ruler and compass to construct a triangle in which the sides have the lengths indicated.

   a. 4 cm, 4 cm, 3 cm

   b. 3 cm, 5 cm, 6 cm

   c. 7 cm, 3 cm, 2 cm

   d. 3 cm, 8 cm, 7 cm

   e. 8 cm, 5 cm, 3 cm
   No triangle, see drawing.
   f. 4 cm, 4 cm, 4 cm

   g. 1 cm, 2 cm, 8 cm
   No triangle, see drawing.
   h. 6 cm, 8 cm, 6 cm

   5cm)(3cm
   point of tangency

   circles don't intersect.

3. a. Which parts of exercise 2 did not result in a triangle? _c, e, g_

   b. In these cases, what is true about the sum of the lengths of the two shorter sides?
   The sum of the lengths of the two shorter sides is less than or equal to the length of the longest side.

   c. What is true about the sum of the lengths of the two shorter sides in the parts of exercise 2 that did result in a triangle?
   The sum of the lengths of the two shorter sides is greater than the length of the longer side.

   d. List four more sets of three lengths that CAN BE used to construct a triangle. Do not use more than one set in which all three lengths are equal.

   Answers will vary.

   e. List four sets that CANNOT be used to construct triangles.

   Answers will vary.

4. One way to classify triangles is by the number of congruent sides in the triangle.

a. How many congruent sides do each of the following triangles have? Measure each side if necessary.

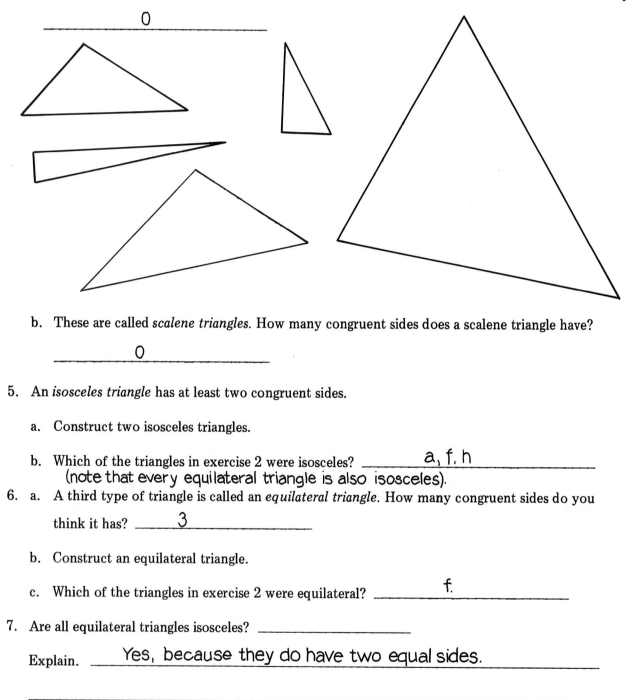

_____ 0 _____

b. These are called *scalene triangles*. How many congruent sides does a scalene triangle have?

_____ 0 _____

5. An *isosceles triangle* has at least two congruent sides.

a. Construct two isosceles triangles.

b. Which of the triangles in exercise 2 were isosceles? _____ a, f, h _____
    (note that every equilateral triangle is also isosceles).

6. a. A third type of triangle is called an *equilateral triangle*. How many congruent sides do you
        think it has? _____ 3 _____

b. Construct an equilateral triangle.

c. Which of the triangles in exercise 2 were equilateral? _____ f. _____

7. Are all equilateral triangles isosceles? _____

Explain. _____ Yes, because they do have two equal sides. _____

_____

TRIANGLE PROPERTIES II
THE ANGLES

STRAND:

Geometry—Names of triangles, the sum of the measures of the angles of a triangle, measuring angles.

PROBLEM SOLVING STRATEGIES:

Models, Patterns.

SUGGESTED USE:

This activity provides an excellent means of teaching the angle sum of a triangle and the classification of triangles according to the types of angles. It can be used at any point during a unit on triangles, however students must know the definitions of acute, right, and obtuse angles as well as how to measure an angle using a protractor.

MATERIALS:

Student activity pages, rulers, protractors.

INSTRUCTIONAL STRATEGY:

Note: If students have not already done *Triangle Properties I* you may wish to do so before doing this activity.

Step 1: Hand out the student pages. Explain that all the constructions are to be done on a separate sheet of paper and numbered. You may also find it necessary to explain a procedure for using a ruler and protractor to construct a triangle given two of the angles, however students can generally discover a method on their own.

Step 2: When the activity has been completed, discuss it with the class.

Exercises 1 and 2 develop the fact that the sum of the angles of a triangle is 180°. This can be amplified in the discussion by having each student draw a triangle on scratch paper, cut it out, cut off two of the angles, and rearrange them at the third vertex to form a line segment.

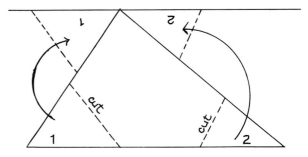

Exercise 3 develops the idea that two triangles, in which two angles of one are congruent to two angles of the other, are *similar*. This is an excellent opportunity to have students discover that the ratios of the corresponding sides in similar triangles are equal. To do this, have each student measure the sides of the triangle they drew in part 1a and use these measures to write the following ratios: shortest side to longest, shortest to middle, and middle to longest. Then have each student compare the ratios they obtained with those of a fellow student. Repeat this process for the triangle drawn in 1d.

If the original constructions were done accurately and they measure the sides accurately, they should find that the ratios are very nearly equal. Regardless of the units of measurement used, comparison of the ratios as fractions can be difficult.

For example:

$$\frac{11.8}{13.3} \text{ and } \frac{15.6}{17.6} \qquad \frac{1\frac{5}{8}}{3\frac{3}{4}} \text{ and } \frac{2\frac{7}{16}}{5\frac{5}{8}}$$

Changing the above fractions to decimals and rounding the results to three places yields

.887 and .886   .433 and .433

These decimal numbers are much easier for students to compare than the original fractions. Since this is often the case where ratios involve measurements made in real situations, we recommend that ratios be converted to decimals in order to make comparison easier.

122 Section II ACTIVITIES

Exercises 4 through 6 develop the definitions of acute, obtuse, and right traingles.

Kinds of Triangles should be done immediately to reinforce the types of triangles.

You may extend this activity to develop the formula for the sum of the interior angles of a polygon by using the activity *From Triangles to Polygons*.

TRIANGLE PROPERTIES II
THE ANGLES

1. In each of the following, use a ruler and protractor to construct a triangle which contains a pair of angles with the indicated measures. Record your results in the table.

   a. 30°, 40°   e. 130°, 80°

   b. 80°, 80°   f. 120°, 50°

   c. 60°, 60°   g. 128°, 70°

   d. 55°, 35°   h. 95°, 90°

Problem	Sum of the Given Angles	Is a Triangle Possible?	If Yes, What is the Measure of the Third Angle?
a.	70°	Yes	110°
b.	160°	Yes	20°
c.	120°	Yes	60°
d.	90°	Yes	90°
e.	210°	No	—
f.	170°	Yes	10°
g.	198°	No	—
h.	185°	No	—

2. a. List four more pairs of angles that CAN BE used to construct a triangle.

   Answers will vary.

   b. List four pairs of angles that CANNOT be used to construct a triangle.

   Answers will vary.

   c. What can you conclude about the sum of the measures of the angles of a triangle?

   The sum of the measures of the angles of a triangle is 180°.

3. a. Use a ruler and a protractor to construct two more triangles in which one angle is 30° and another is 40° as in exercise 1a.

   b. Compare your triangles with a fellow student's. What do you notice?

   All of the triangles have the same shape, but they generally have sides of different lengths.

4. Triangles can be classified by the types of angles they contain.

   a. An *obtuse triangle* is a triangle that contains one angle that is greater than 90° but less than 180°. Construct an obtuse triangle.

   b. Would it be possible to have a triangle with two obtuse angles? If yes, construct one. If no, explain why.

   No, because the sum of two obtuse angles is greater than 180°, and the sum of the measures of the angles of a triangle equals 180°.

   c. Which of the triangles that you constructed in exercise 1 were obtuse triangles? __a and f__

5. a. All of these triangles have the same special property. What is it? _____
   They all contain one right angle.
   _____

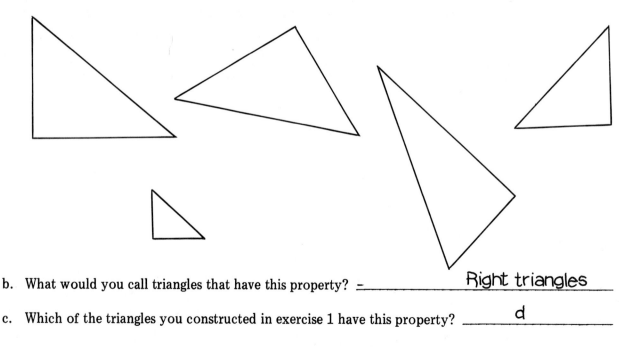

   b. What would you call triangles that have this property? – __Right triangles__

   c. Which of the triangles you constructed in exercise 1 have this property? ____d____

6. a. What do each of the following triangles have in common? If necessary, measure each angle in each triangle.

Each angle in each triangle is acute.

b. Why would triangles with this property be called *acute triangles*?

Because all of the angles are acute. Make certain the students understand that right triangles and obtuse triangles both contain 2 acute angles. Thus it isn't enough to say an acute triangle is one with one acute angle.

c. Which of the triangles you constructed in exercise 1 are acute triangles? _____ b,c _____

KINDS OF TRIANGLES

STRAND:
Geometry—classifying triangles.

PROBLEM SOLVING STRATEGY:
Models

SUGGESTED USE:
This activity is best used as a follow up to the two *Triangle Properties* activities.

MATERIALS:
Student activity pages, rulers, compasses, protractors.

INSTRUCTIONAL STRATEGY:
Step 1: Hand out the student pages and instruct the students to complete them. You may want to move about the classroom to give individualized help as needed.

Step 2: When the activity has been completed, discuss the answer to exercise 3 briefly to be certain that the students understand that since the angles of an equilateral triangle are all equal in measure the triangle is always acute.

KINDS OF TRIANGLES

1. In the preceding activities, you learned that triangles can be classified in two ways:

    a. By the number of congruent sides:

       (1) A *scalene triangle* has no congruent sides.

       (2) An *isosceles triangle* has at least two congruent sides.

       (3) An *equilateral triangle* has three congruent sides.

    b. By the type of angles:

       (1) An *obtuse triangle* has one obtuse angle.

       (2) A *right triangle* has one right angle.

       (3) An *acute triangle* has three acute angles.

It is also possible for a triangle to be classified by the number of congruent sides and the types of angles at the same time. For example, this is a right-scalene triangle. Why?

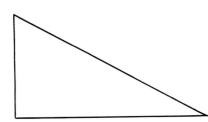

It is right because it contains one right angle
It is scalene because it does not contain any
   congruent sides.
In general, the number of congruent sides
   is not dependent on the types of angles
   in the triangle.

2. Each of the following combinations is possible. Construct one example of each type.

    a. Right-scalene

    b. Right-isosceles

c. Obtuse-scalene   d. Obtuse-isosceles

e. Acute-scalene   f. Acute-isosceles

g. Acute-equilateral

3. There are two combinations such as those above, that are impossible. Can you name them?

   _right – equilateral_____   _____obtuse – equilateral_____

4. Why are these two types impossible? _____

   _____

A SQUARE EXPERIMENT

STRAND:

Number Theory—prime, composite, square numbers, and factorization of a number.

PROBLEM SOLVING STRATEGIES:

Models, Tables, Patterns

SUGGESTED USE:

This activity provides an excellent introduction to prime, composite, and square numbers and the complete factorization of a number. It is also a valuable developmental activity for those students who have been introduced to the concepts, but have not used the activity.

MATERIALS:

Student activity pages, square chips (graph paper could be used in place of chips and students could draw the arrays).

INSTRUCTIONAL STRATEGY:

Step 1: Distribute a set of chips or graph paper and copies of the student pages. Be sure that students understand the instructions given on the activity pages. Special attention should be given to the concept of a "rectangular array" and that only the horizontal and vertical orientations of the arrays will be considered. Students must be advised that in this activity there is a

difference between ⬚⬚ and ⊟ . If they are

not familiar with placing dimensions on a rectangle, you might also explain that the figure

⬚⬚ has a base of 2 units and an altitude of

1 unit, and thus is labeled 2 × 1. The figure ⊟

is labeled 1 × 2. Allow the students to work individually or in pairs to complete the activity. Some checking with a fellow student when the work is completed might be encouraged before a general class discussion.

Step 2: The follow-up discussion of this activity will depend somewhat on the past knowledge of students with respect to factoring, primes, composites, and square numbers. This activity is an excellent introduction to these concepts. If used with students as a first exposure you may want to have them explore arrays for numbers of chips through 30. Simply have them extend Table 1. You may then wish to change the numbers given in questions 2 and 3 to some other composite and square number.

Students using this activity as a first introduction will not know the correct names to answer question 6. These should be brought out in general class discussion rather than as answers to individual questions.

An important aspect of this activity is the fact that it points out very clearly the uniqueness of 1. Many students, even those in high school and above, have the false notion that 1 is a *prime number*. The placement of 1 in column A of Table 2 clearly indicates that it is in a category all by itself and does not belong to the set of numbers described in columns B and C.

A SQUARE EXPERIMENT

Use square chips and form all of the rectangular arrays possible with each different number of chips. Record your results in the table below.

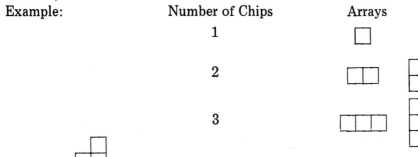

Example:

Note: is not a rectangular array.

TABLE 1

Number of Chips	Dimensions of Rectangular Arrays	Total Number of Arrays
1	1 × 1	1
2	1 × 2, 2 × 1	2
3	1 × 3, 3 × 1	2
4	1 × 4, 4 × 1, 2 × 2	3
5	1 × 5, 5 × 1	2
6	1 × 6, 6 × 1, 2 × 3, 3 × 2	4
7	1 × 7, 7 × 1	2
8	1 × 8, 8 × 1, 2 × 4, 4 × 2	4
9	1 × 9, 9 × 1, 3 × 3	3
10	1 × 10, 10 × 1, 2 × 5, 5 × 2	4
11	1 × 11, 11 × 1	2
12	1 × 12, 12 × 1, 2 × 6, 6 × 2, 3 × 4, 4 × 2	6
13	1 × 13, 13 × 1	2
14	1 × 14, 14 × 1, 2 × 7, 7 × 2	4
15	1 × 15, 15 × 1, 3 × 5, 5 × 3	4

1. Use the results from Table 1 to complete Table 2.

TABLE 2
Number of Squares that Produced

A	B	C	D
Only One Array	Only Two Arrays	More Than Two Arrays	An Odd Number of Arrays
1	2,3,5,7,11,13,.....	4,6,8,9,10,12,14,...	1,4,9,16,...

2. Suppose that you had 15 chips:

   a. How many rectangular arrays could be made? _____4_____

   b. In which column in Table 2 would you place 15? _____C_____

   c. What are the factors of 15? _____1, 3, 5, 15_____

3. a. What are the factors of 16? _____1, 2, 4, 8, 16_____

   b. How many rectangular arrays can you make with 16 chips? _____5_____

   c. In which column of Table 2 would you place 16? _____D_____

4. Look at the data in Table 1 and Table 2. How is the number of rectangular arrays related to the number of factors of any given number? The number of arrays equals the number of factors.

5. a. Why is it that the numbers in column D have an odd number of arrays? They are square numbers. One of the arrays formed is a square and when you rotate a square 90° it is unchanged.

   b. What are the next two numbers that you would place in column D? 25, 36

6. What is the mathematical name for the list of numbers in

   a. Column B? _____Prime_____

   b. Column C? _____Composite_____

   c. Column D? _____Square numbers_____

7. Which numbers can be placed in two lists? __the square numbers greater than one__ __are in both C and D. One is in A and D.__

8. Can any numbers be placed in three lists? __No__

   If so, which ones? _____

THE FACTOR GAME

STRAND:

Number Theory—factoring a number, primes and composites.

PROBLEM SOLVING STRATEGIES:

Elimination, Guess and Check

SUGGESTED USE:

After students have been introduced to factoring a number, this game reinforces the idea of identification of all factors of a given number.

MATERIALS:

Pencil and paper.

INSTRUCTIONAL STRATEGY:

The Factor Game can be played with a variety of formats, one on one, or team against team. If teams are used, they should be limited to four students to insure the participation of each student. In order to facilitate a quick and efficient use of the game, it is suggested that the teacher play a practice game with the class.

THE FACTOR GAME

1. Make a list of consecutive whole numbers 2 through n. In the sample game, let $n = 20$. For a first game, have students let $n = 20$, then change the value of n in later games and have $n = 36, 48, 64$, and so forth.

2. From the set, Player A selects a number, crosses it out, and adds it to his previous score.

3. Player B may then cross out any factors of A's selection that are not crossed out. B's score, the sum of the factors, is then added to his or her previous score.

4. Now, Player B chooses a number, crosses it out, and adds the number to his or her previous score. Player A may now cross out any factors of B's choice. A's score, the sum of the factors, is then added to his previous score.

5. Player A now selects another number and play continues until all the numbers are crossed out.

6. When all the numbers have been eliminated, the individual scores are totaled. The player with the highest total score is the winner.

A's Selection ✗

B's Selection +

Example: 2̸ 3̸ 4 5̸ 6 7̸ 8 9 10

11 12 1̸3 1̸4 1̸5 16 17 18 19 20

Scoring

	A	B	
1. A selects 15 B crosses out 3 and 5	1. 15	8	3 + 5 = 8
2. B selects 7 A receives 0	2. 0	7	
3. A selects 13 B receives 0	3. 13	0	
4. B selects 14 A crosses out 2 (7 already crossed out)	4. 2	14	

PAPER POWERS

STRAND:

Number Theory—exponents and powers.

PROBLEM SOLVING STRATEGIES:

Patterns, Tables, Simplify Models.

SUGGESTED USE:

This activity provides an introduction to the concept of exponents, exponential notation, and the powers of 2 and 3.

MATERIALS:

Sheets of paper, double page of newspaper, rulers, calculators (optional).

INSTRUCTIONAL STRATEGY:

Step 1: Distribute a sheet of paper (215 × 280 mm) to each student or have them use a sheet of scratch paper. Ask the question, "How many times do you think you can fold a sheet of paper if you fold the result in half each time?"

Illustrate the folding process.

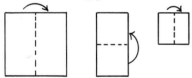

Step 2: After the estimates have been made, let the students fold the paper. Using regular note-book paper, students will probably find they can only fold seven or eight times.

Step 3: Once some maximum number of folds has been determined, some students will generally suggest that given a larger sheet of paper, more folds could be made.

Step 4: At this point, distribute a double page sheet of newspaper and a ruler to each student. Have them repeat the folding process, however, this time ask them to count the number of layers after each fold, and measure the thickness of the folds. Put the following table on the chalkboard or overhead and direct students to build such a table and use it to record their results.

Number of Folds	0	1	2	3	4	5
Number of Layers	1	2	4	8	16	32
Thickness	Answers will vary according to paper used.					

You should warn students that they will not be able to measure the thickness until they have made 4 or 5 folds. Measurements should be made to the nearest millimeter. It is not necessary to record the thickness after every fold. If the thickness is determined for 5 folds, 32 layers, then double for 64 layers, and so forth.

Step 5: Because of the difficulty of folding folded edges, students will find that the larger sheet of thinner paper does not necessarily mean more folds are possible.

Observing the table, note that in the process of making the eighth fold, one must be able to fold 128 ($2^7 = 128$) sheets of paper. Some students will claim that it is possible to do this. An example might be the folding of a telephone book or the like.

A fact that must be considered is the pattern of the diminishing area of the paper. After eight folds, the area of the paper to be folded is 1/256 of the area of the original sheet. If we were to begin with a square sheet 10 m on a side, after eight folds the stack of paper would have 256 layers and be a square approximately 60 cm on a side.

To develop the power of 3, repeat the experiment making a double fold in the paper at each step.

Step 6: Once students have determined the pattern, fill in the correct values in the table which you put on the board. Ask students how the numbers in the "Number of Layers" row are determined. Most will recognize that each entry is twice the preceding entry.

The use of exponentail notation can then be developed easily by using the following table.

Folds	Layers	Expanded Notation		Exponential Notation
0	1	$= 1$	$=$	2^0
1	2	$1 \times 2 = 2$	$=$	2^1
2	4	$2 \times 2 = 2 \times 2$	$=$	2^2
3	8	$4 \times 2 = 2 \times 2 \times 2$	$=$	2^3
4	16	$8 \times 2 = 2 \times 2 \times 2 \times 2$	$=$	2^4
.	.	. . . . .		.
.	.	. . . . .		.
.	.	. . . . .		.
n		$\times 2 = 2 \times 2 \times 2 \times 2 \times \cdots 2$	$=$	2^n

n factors of 2

Once you have developed the exponential notation for $n \geqslant 1$, use the table to illustrate the fact that $2^0 = 1$. Once again, we find a pattern, and if the pattern is to be consistent, then there is only one possible answer for 2^0.

Extension: If you are using this activity with students who have previously been exposed to exponents and powers, use the table to introduce the concept of negative exponents. Look at the pattern in the "Layers" column in reverse order. (that is, 16, 8, 4, 2, $\cdots$) Ask how the numbers are related. Since we are reversing the pattern, we use the *inverse operation* of multiplication, division.

Since we know the pattern, each term is equal to the previous term divided by two, then

$$2^{-1} = 2^0 \div 2 = 1 \div 2 = \frac{1}{2} = \frac{1}{2^1}$$

$$2^{-2} = 2^{-1} \div 2 = \frac{1}{2} \div 2 = \frac{1}{4} = \frac{1}{2^2}$$

THE POOL FACTOR

STRAND:

Number Theory—least common multiple and greatest common factor.

PROBLEM SOLVING STRATEGIES:

Models, Tables, Patterns

SUGGESTED USE:

After students have developed the concepts of LCM and GCF, this activity provides an excellent review of these concepts while utilizing the strategies listed above.

MATERIALS:

Graph paper, straight edge, and student activity pages.

INSTRUCTIONAL STRATEGY:

Step 1: Distribute a copy of the student pages and graph paper. Review the example with the class so that they clearly understand the terminology. It is important that the class realizes that the initial hit of the ball at pocket A counts as one of the hits.

Instruct students to draw a model of the pool tables described in the Table and trace the path of the ball. Emphasize that the ball must only pass through the corners of the squares.

Once they have completed the blanks in the Table for the information given, they should try other values for the base and the altitude, construct additional Models, and trace the path of the ball. Data derived from each drawing should be entered in the Table.

Some students may soon recognize that the Number of Hits and Number of Squares can be easily derived when the values of the base and altitude are relatively prime. They may then draw models utilizing only relatively prime values and state an incorrect conclusion. If so, tell them to try some other values which are not relatively prime. A hint toward the solution would be to suggest that they use numbers which are multiples

of a set already used. For example, if they have used 4 and 7, suggest they try 8 and 14.

The Number of Hits = (Base + Altitude) ÷ (GCF of B and A)

The Number of Squares = LCM of B and A.

Step 2: There is a simple extension of this problem which you may wish to consider for some of the better students. That is, ask the students to determine into which pocket the ball will finally fall. If you plan to do this, have the students put an additional column on their data table as shown.

Example:

Base	Altitude	Number of Hits	Number of Squares	Final Pocket

In order to determine the Final Pocket, let
X = Altitude ÷ (GCF of A and B)
Y = Base ÷ (GCF of A and B)

Final Pocket	X	Y
A	The ball will never fall in pocket A.	
B	odd	even
C	odd	odd
D	even	odd

Example:
Base = 6 and Altitude = 4
GCF of 6 and 4 = 2
$X = 4 ÷ 2 = 2$
$Y = 6 ÷ 2 = 3$
Final pocket is D.

THE POOL FACTOR

While investigating a jewelery robbery at the Parrington mansion, Detective Shamrock Bones became distracted from the case while looking for clues in the Billiard Room. He found several tables of various sizes, each having four pockets and a square grid on it as shown below.

On the wall he found this sign.

The Pool Factor

Rules of the Game

1. Place a ball on the x in front of pocket A.

2. Shoot the ball through the dot shown on the table. By doing so, the ball will always rebound at an angle of 45° when it hits a side cushion.

3. Count the number of squares that the ball travels through.

4. Count the number of times the ball hits the sides of the table. Be sure to count the initial hit of the cue against the ball and the hit as the ball falls in the pocket.

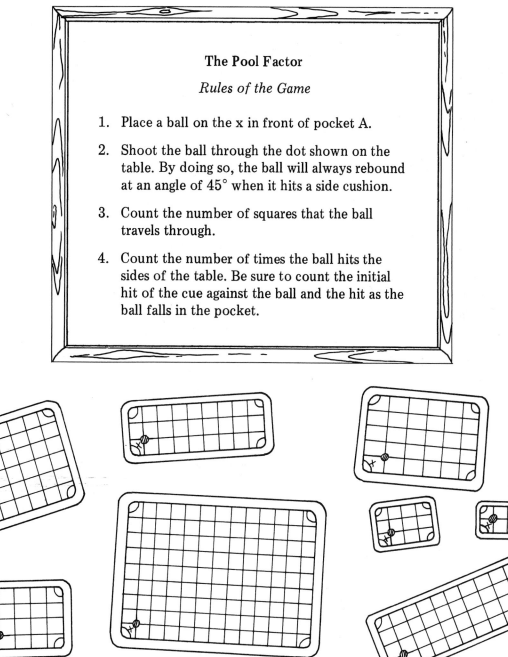

Bones became so interested in the pool table game that he forgot about the robbery case. See if you can help him solve The POOL FACTOR. Use graph paper to construct models of pool tables with the measurements given in the table. If necessary, extend the table by drawing additional pool tables with other measurements until you discover a pattern that you can use to determine the Number of Hits and Number of Squares when given any measurements for the base and altitude.

Example:

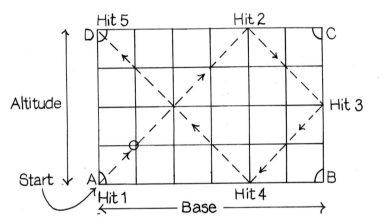

Base	Altitude	Number of Hits	Number of Squares
6	4	5	12
3	5	8	15
5	4	9	20
3	2	5	6
8	4	3	8

SQUARE FRACTIONS

STRAND:

Fractions—concept of a fraction, addition, subtraction and multiplication of fractions; Geometry—classifying triangles and quadrilaterals, similarity, and congruence.

PROBLEM SOLVING STRATEGIES:

Models, Simplify, Guess and Check.

SUGGESTED USE:

This activity provides an excellent means to develop the concept of a fraction through modeling. Sections of the activity can be used to illustrate multiplication of fractions, and it can be extended to show addition and subtraction. When used in conjunction with a section on geometry, the activity can serve as a means of reinforcing the names and properties of some triangles and quadrilaterals, and the concept of congruence. Sections may also be used to introduce the concept of similarity.

MATERIALS:

Square sheets of paper, 20 cm to 30 cm square (colored construction paper works well), student activity pages (if self-directed), scissors are optional.

INSTRUCTIONAL STRATEGY:

These pages can be used as a self-directed activity by the students or as a teacher-led class activity.

1. Student Activity

    Step 1: Distribute a square sheet of construction paper, scissors, and the student pages. Direct students to follow the instructions carefully and complete the sheets. Allow them to assist each other if necessary.

    Step 2: Upon completion, you can collect the student sheets, but have students retain the seven pieces they cut from the square. You may wish to explore additional questions not on these sheets (see step 2 below) and also utilize the pieces to illustrate a variety of sums and differences with fractions.

    Step 3: Assign the following: Put the seven pieces back together to form the original square.

2. Teacher-led Activity

    Step 1: Distribute a square sheet of construction paper and scissors.

    Step 2: Use the questions on the student pages as a script and lead the students through the activity. As you proceed through the activity, demonstrate each of the folding and cutting procedures to the class to be certain they understand the procedures and so that you have an example of each piece. As you ask the various questions, hold up the pieces being used. You may wish to include other similar questions not included here.

    When dealing with the similarity between #3 and #1 in question 3b, it may be valuable to have students verify the fact. The angles can be matched to determine their equality. Have the students measure the lengths of the sides to show that they are proportional.

    If students are not familiar with similarity this is an excellent method of introduction. The activity also provides an opportunity to compare the difference between congruence and similarity of polygons.

    Question 3c, part 1, provides an opportunity to illustrate multiplication of fractions with models. Since #3 is one-half of #1, and #1 is one-half of A, then #3 is 1/4 of A, illustrating

$$\frac{1}{2} \times \frac{1}{2} = \frac{1}{4}.$$

Many other examples of multiplication are contained in these questions and should be explored.

Be sure to take advantage of the relationship between figures 3, 5, and 7. While these figures are different in size and shape, they are equal in area. When students answer that 3 and 5 are equal, ask how it is possible for two figures to have different numbers of sides, measures of angles, and shape, however still be equal. This is a good example of the concept of different shape but equal area. You may also use the example to discuss the difference between "congruence" and "equal." The word "equal" refers to one measure of the polygons, in this case area. However, "congruence" implies much more.

After you have completed the activity, be sure to ask students to reconstruct the original square. Don't be surprised if, after several futile attempts, some students state that this cannot be done. Even some junior high students have yet to fully develop the concept of conservation of area.

Extension: You may also wish to use the pieces from this activity to illustrate addition of fractions.

Consider #5 + Trapezoid D = Trapezoid C.

If we relate each figure to the original square, we have

$$\frac{1}{8} + \frac{3}{16} = \frac{5}{16}.$$

You can use the relationship between #6 and #5 to easily show that

$$\frac{1}{8} = \frac{2}{16}.$$

Many other such problems can be developed by relating the pieces to triangle A or the original square. Students can generate their own problems by putting two or more pieces together to form a new shape. After relating each piece as a fraction of the new shape, other such addition problems can be developed.

Subtraction can be illustrated by reversing the above procedure.

Like the *Pentomino* activity, this one helps to develop a student's spacial perception. Many other activities using these seven pieces can be found in publications involving Tangrams.

SQUARE FRACTIONS

Follow the folding and cutting directions carefully. If scissors are not used, make a sharp crease in the paper, and tear along the crease. Answer each question as you proceed through the activity.

1. Fold the square on the diagonal and cut along the fold:

    a. What are the resulting polygons?

    Right triangles   _Isosceles triangles_

    b. How are the two polygons realted?

    Equal in area and Congruent

    c. Each polygon is what fraction of the original square? __1/2__

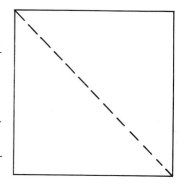

2. Select one of the triangles and fold it so that two congruent polygons result. Cut along the fold and label the polygons 1 and 2 as shown.

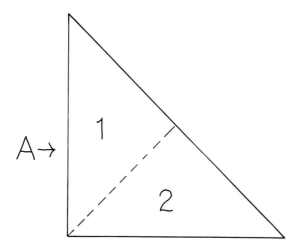

Note: The large triangle will be referred to later as triangle A.

    a. What are the resulting polygons?

    Right triangles   _Isosceles triangles_

    b. How are the two polygons related? _Equal in area and Congruent_

    c. Triangle 1 is what fraction of triangle A? __1/2__

    d. Triangle 1 is what fraction of the original square? __1/4__

3. Locate the midpoint of the longest side of the remaining large triangle. Fold the vertex of the right angle to the midpoint of the longest side and cut along the fold. Mark the triangle 3.

   a. What are the resulting polygons?

   Right-Isosceles triangle   Isosceles trapezoid

   b. How is triangle 3 related to:

   1. triangle 1? __Similar__   2. triangle A? __Similar__

   c. Triangle 3 is what fractional part of:

   1. triangle 1? __1/2__   2. triangle A? __1/4__

   3. the original square? __1/8__   4. the isosceles trapezoid? __1/3__

4. Using the isosceles trapezoid, fold one of the vertices of the long side to the midpoint and cut along the fold. Mark the triangle 4.

   Note: The isosceles trapezoid is trapezoid B. The shaded section is C.

   a. What are the resulting polygons?

   Right-Isosceles triangle   trapezoid

   b. How is triangle 4 related to:

   1. triangle 3? __Similar__   2. triangle 1? __Similar__

   3. triangle A? __Similar__

c. Triangle 4 is what fraction of:

1. triangle 3? __1/2__   2. triangle 1? __1/4__

3. triangle A? __1/8__   4. trapezoid C? __1/5__

5. trapezoid B? __1/6__   6. the original square? __1/16__

5. Using trapezoid C match the endpoints of the shortest of the parallel sides and fold. Cut along the fold and mark 5 as shown.

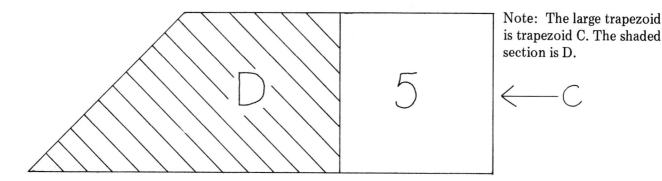

Note: The large trapezoid is trapezoid C. The shaded section is D.

a. What are the resulting polygons?

___Square___   ___Trapezoid___

b. Square 5 is what fractional part of:

1. trapezoid C? __2/5__   2. trapezoid D? __2/3__

3. triangle 3? __1/1__   4. trapezoid B? __1/3__

5. triangle 4? __2/1__   6. triangle 1? __1/2__

7. triangle A? __1/4__   8. the original square? __1/8__

c. C is what fraction of:

1. trapezoid D? __5/3__   2. square 5? __5/2__

3. the original square? __5/16__

6. Using the trapezoid that is left, fold as shown, matching opposite corners. Cut along the fold and mark 6 and 7 as shown.

Note: The trapezoid shown here is trapezoid D.

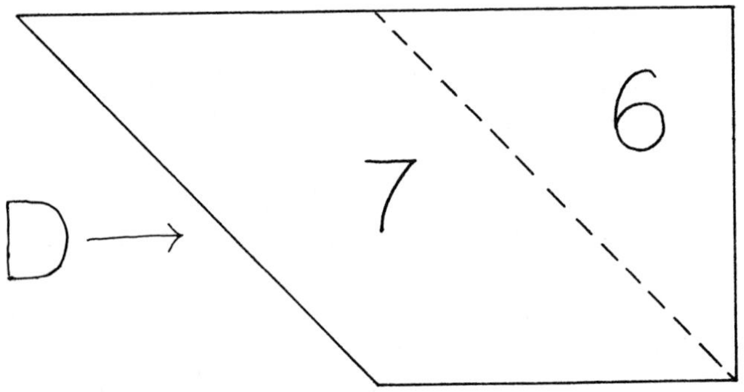

a. What are the resulting polygons?

Isosceles - Right triangle

Parallelogram

b. How is triangle 6 related to:

1. triangle 4? __Congruent__   2. triangle 3? __Similar__

3. triangle A? __Similar__

c. Triangle 6 is what fraction of:

1. trapezoid D? __1/3__   2. trapezoid C? __1/5__

3. parallelogram 7? __1/2__   4. triangle 3? __1/2__

5. triangle 1? __1/4__   6. square 5? __1/2__

7. trapezoid B? __1/6__   8. traingle A? __1/8__

9. the original square? __1/16__

7. Parallelogram 7 is what fraction of:

a. trapezoid D? ___2/3___

b. triangle 3? ___1/1___

c. trapezoid C? ___2/5___

d. trapezoid B? ___1/3___

e. triangle 4? ___2/1___

f. square 5? ___1/1___

g. triangle 1? ___1/2___

h. triangle A? ___1/4___

i. the original square? ___1/8___

PATTERNS OF REPEATING DECIMALS

STRAND:
Decimals—changing fractions to decimals.

PROBLEM SOLVING STRATEGIES:
Patterns, Guess and Check.

SUGGESTED USE:
After students have covered the concept of changing a fraction to a decimal, this activity provides an opportunity for them to observe patterns in repeating decimals and predict the decimal equivalent for fractions whose denominators contain only 9s.

MATERIALS:
Copies of student activity pages, calculators.

INSTRUCTIONAL STRATEGY:
Step 1: Distribute calculators and student pages. Instruct students to follow instructions and complete the activity. Direct their attention to the examples showing a correct method of writing a repeating decimal. Emphasize that they write only the digits necessary to indicate the repeating pattern.

Step 2: After the students have completed the activity, have several state the rule which they developed to describe the decimal equivalent for fractions whose denominators contain only 9s. Having discussed some of these rules with the class, give several examples of such fractions and ask for the correct decimal equivalent.

The question concerning the decimal equivalent for 9/9 is asked specifically to present the idea that $.\overline{9} = 1$. If the pattern of repeating digits is to continue as shown throughout all of this activity, then

$$\frac{9}{9}, \ \frac{99}{99}, \ \frac{999}{999},$$

all have a decimal equivalent $.\overline{9}$. Since the simple division results in 1, we see that $.\overline{9} = 1$.

The idea that $.\overline{9} = 1$ is one that students have a very difficult time accepting. Some other means of explaining this concept in light of the results of this activity are as follows:

a.
$$\frac{4}{9} = .\overline{4}$$
$$+\frac{5}{9} = .\overline{5}$$
$$\overline{\quad}$$
$$\frac{9}{9} = .\overline{9}$$
$$\therefore 1 = .\overline{9}$$

b. $3 \times \dfrac{1}{3} = 1$

$$\frac{1}{3} = .\overline{3}$$

$$3 \times \frac{1}{3} = 3 \times (.\overline{3})$$

Since $3 \times (.\overline{3}) = .\overline{9}$

$$\therefore .\overline{9} = 1$$

c.
$$\frac{1}{3} = .\overline{3}$$
$$+\frac{2}{3} = .\overline{6}$$
$$\overline{\quad}$$
$$\frac{3}{3} = .\overline{9}$$
$$\therefore 1 = .\overline{9}$$

For better students you may wish to extend this idea and explain the equivalence using an algebraic proof.

PATTERNS OF REPEATING DECIMALS

In order to change a fraction to a decimal, divide the numerator by the denominator. To correctly write a repeating decimal:

1. Put a bar over those digits that repeat.
2. Write only those digits necessary to show the repeating pattern.

Example:

.428428428 ⋯ should be written $.\overline{428}$.

.1676767 ⋯ should be written $.1\overline{67}$.

Use your calculator to change the following fractions to decimals. Look for patterns in the digits of the decimals, you may find a way to write the answer without doing the division.

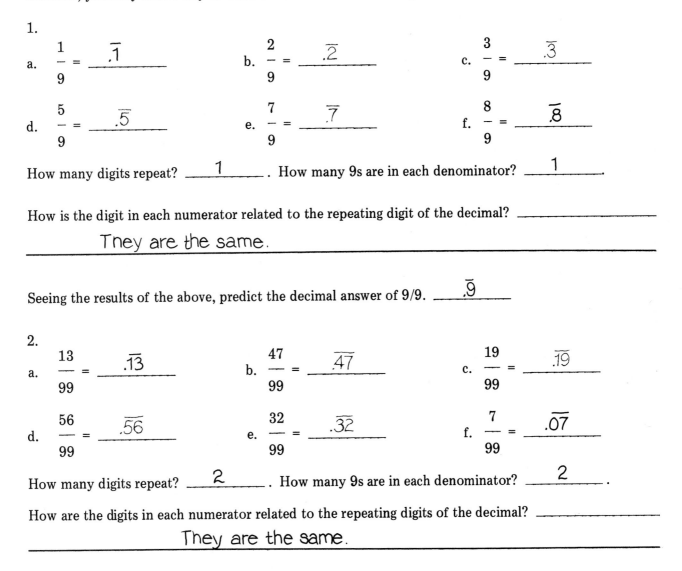

1.

a. $\dfrac{1}{9}$ = _____ $.\overline{1}$

b. $\dfrac{2}{9}$ = _____ $.\overline{2}$

c. $\dfrac{3}{9}$ = _____ $.\overline{3}$

d. $\dfrac{5}{9}$ = _____ $.\overline{5}$

e. $\dfrac{7}{9}$ = _____ $.\overline{7}$

f. $\dfrac{8}{9}$ = _____ $.\overline{8}$

How many digits repeat? __1__ . How many 9s are in each denominator? __1__ .

How is the digit in each numerator related to the repeating digit of the decimal? _____

____ They are the same. ____

Seeing the results of the above, predict the decimal answer of 9/9. __$.\overline{9}$__

2.

a. $\dfrac{13}{99}$ = _____ $.\overline{13}$

b. $\dfrac{47}{99}$ = _____ $.\overline{47}$

c. $\dfrac{19}{99}$ = _____ $.\overline{19}$

d. $\dfrac{56}{99}$ = _____ $.\overline{56}$

e. $\dfrac{32}{99}$ = _____ $.\overline{32}$

f. $\dfrac{7}{99}$ = _____ $.\overline{07}$

How many digits repeat? __2__ . How many 9s are in each denominator? __2__ .

How are the digits in each numerator related to the repeating digits of the decimal? _____

____ They are the same. ____

Copyright © 1983 by Addison-Wesley Publishing Company, Inc.

3.

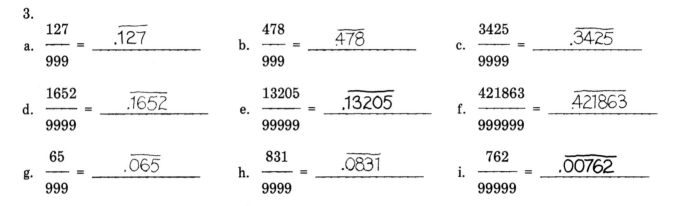

a. $\dfrac{127}{999}$ = $.\overline{127}$ b. $\dfrac{478}{999}$ = $.\overline{478}$ c. $\dfrac{3425}{9999}$ = $.\overline{3425}$

d. $\dfrac{1652}{9999}$ = $.\overline{1652}$ e. $\dfrac{13205}{99999}$ = $.\overline{13205}$ f. $\dfrac{421863}{999999}$ = $.\overline{421863}$

g. $\dfrac{65}{999}$ = $.\overline{065}$ h. $\dfrac{831}{9999}$ = $.\overline{0831}$ i. $\dfrac{762}{99999}$ = $.\overline{00762}$

How does the number of 9s in each denominator relate to the number of repeating digits in the decimal?

The number of 9 s is the same as the number of repeating digits in the decimal.

How do the digits in each numerator relate to the repeating digits in the decimal?

The digits in the numerator are the same as the repeating digits.

Having observed the pattern of repeating digits in each of the decimals, state a general rule which describes the decimal equivalent of a fraction whose denominator contains only 9s.

The repeating digits in the decimal are the same as the digits in the numerator.

The number of repeating digits in the decimal is the same as the number of 9s in the denominator.

PICO CENTRO

STRAND:

Whole numbers

PROBLEM SOLVING STRATEGIES:

Elimination, Guess and Check

SUGGESTED USE:

This activity can be used after the Elimination strategy has been covered. It provides an excellent reinforcement of the strategy, is quick and easy to use with a class, and can be utilized throughout the year for as little or as much time as desired.

INSTRUCTIONAL STRATEGY:

Step 1: Divide the class into groups of three or four. Tell the students that you are thinking of a three-digit number, and they are to determine the number by making guesses and using Elimination. Begin with a number that contains three different digits.

Step 2: Each group is to make its guesses on a sheet of paper. The teacher, or a student leader, will move around the room and tell each group how many Picos and how many Centros each guess contains.

Pico means the number of correct digits in the guess.

Centro means the number of these digits that are in the correct place.

Example: Teacher's number—394

If the first guess is 347, you would reply 2—Pico, 1—Centro, since two of the digits (3, 4) are correct, and one of these digits, (3) is also in the correct place.

Correct Number: 394

Guess	Teacher's Response
1: 347	2 Pico, 1 Centro
2: 371	1 Pico, 1 Centro
3: 304	2 Pico, 2 Centro
4: 395	2 Pico, 2 Centro
5: 394	3 Pico, 3 Centro You have the number.

A group may make more than one guess at a time, however this is not the best strategy, since they are not using information gained from one guess to make others. The group that determines the number using the least number of guesses is the winner. The first team to find the number may not have the fewest guesses, so they should not announce the answer until the teacher declares a winner.

Alternatives:

a. Use a four- or five-digit number.

b. Use a digit more than once in the number.

The Big 1

STRAND:

Fractions—addition, multiplication and division.

PROBLEM SOLVING STRATEGY:

Guess and Check.

SUGGESTED USE:

The different variations of the activity can be used after the needed operations with fractions have been covered.

MATERIALS:

Paper and pencil.

INSTRUCTIONAL STRATEGY:

Game 1 (×, ÷)

Directions

In this variation, students compete with each other to find the greatest number of ways to get 1 as the answer when three fractions are used in one of the following ways:

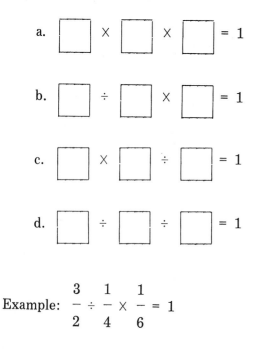

a. $\boxed{} \times \boxed{} \times \boxed{} = 1$

b. $\boxed{} \div \boxed{} \times \boxed{} = 1$

c. $\boxed{} \times \boxed{} \div \boxed{} = 1$

d. $\boxed{} \div \boxed{} \div \boxed{} = 1$

Example: $\dfrac{3}{2} \div \dfrac{1}{4} \times \dfrac{1}{6} = 1$

$$\frac{2}{3} \times \frac{1}{4} \div \frac{1}{6} = 1$$

A fraction of the form a/a, a ≠ 0 is NOT allowed and a fraction may NOT be used twice in one problem.

SUGGESTIONS:

Step 1: Write the four equations on the board or overhead and explain two examples such as those given. Tell the students that they are to use those two equations in the first race, and that they *must* alternate their use.

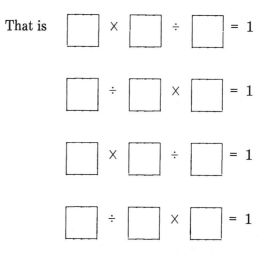

That is $\boxed{} \times \boxed{} \div \boxed{} = 1$

$\boxed{} \div \boxed{} \times \boxed{} = 1$

$\boxed{} \times \boxed{} \div \boxed{} = 1$

$\boxed{} \div \boxed{} \times \boxed{} = 1$

A great motivational tool for this activity is a recording of the "Lone Ranger" theme from the *William Tell Overture*. After all instructions have been given, say "Ready—Go!!" and start the music.

Step 2: At the end of three or four minutes, stop the music. Ask how many students wrote more than 15 equations, 10 equations, 5 equations? Have students exchange papers in order to check the work, but have those people who had approximately the same number of equations exchange with each other.

Step 3: After correction, write two different equations on the board and run the race again. If you started with four minutes, reduce the time in later races. Have students keep score in each race, one point for each correct equation written. Total score is the sum of scores for the individual races. At the end of the period, grade points can be awarded according to a student's total score.

It generally takes two or three races before students find that there is an easy way to write many equations. You will quickly have students recognize that in the equation □ × □ ÷ □ = 1, one can put any fractions in the first two boxes, get an answer, and then put the answer in the third box. They are rediscovering the concept that any number divided by itself is one.

In the equation, □ ÷ □ × □ = 1, they again find that any fractions can be put in the first two boxes. Once the answer is determined, one only needs to place the *reciprocal* of the result in the last box. This reinforces the concept of multiplicative inverses.

In the case of those expressions using all multiplication or division, students quickly start putting together combinations of numbers in the numerators and denominators, such as

$$\frac{1}{3} \times \frac{3}{5} \times \frac{5}{1} = 1$$

$$\frac{4}{5} \times \frac{2}{3} \times \frac{15}{8} = 1$$

As these come out, allow students to explain them. Run the race again, so that all can practice using the new ideas learned in the discussion.

The game may be varied by requiring:

1. The use of three or four equations
2. The use of four fractions
3. A number other than ONE as the answer, or
4. A combination of these.

Game 2 (+)

Directions

In this variation, students attempt to find the greatest number of ways to get ONE as the sum of three fractions.

Example:
$$\frac{1}{2} + \frac{1}{3} + \frac{1}{6} = 1$$

$$\frac{1}{5} + \frac{1}{3} + \frac{7}{15} = 1$$

In any equation, a fraction may NOT be used twice and a number may be used as a denominator only once.

Suggestions for play and variations are the same as for Game 1.

EQUIVALENT RATIOS

STRAND:

Ratio and Proportion—equivalence, solving for the unknown term in a proportion; Fractions—comparison.

PROBLEM SOLVING STRATEGY:

Patterns

SUGGESTED USE:

This activity can be used to introduce the cross multiplication method of solving a proportion. The activity can be easily extended to develop a method for comparing fractions.

MATERIALS:

Student activity pages.

INSTRUCTIONAL STRATEGY:

Step 1: Hand out the student pages and instruct the students to complete them .

Step 2: Discuss the activity when it has been completed. The points to emphasize are:

> Problem 2: The products are formed by multiplying the numerator of each fraction by the denominator of the other fraction.
>
> Problem 3: If the products are equal, then the ratios are equal. If the products aren't equal, the ratios aren't equal either.
>
> Problem 5: This shows the cross-product method of solving a proportion:

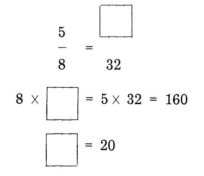

The activity can be followed up immediately with an assignment of similar problems from your textbook.

Step 3: This activity can be easily extended to develop a quick method for comparing fractions. All that need be observed is that each product is written underneath the fraction containing the numerator used in the product. The larger product appears underneath the larger fraction. The following example contrasts this method of comparing fractions with the conventional method of converting to a common denominator which appears on the right.

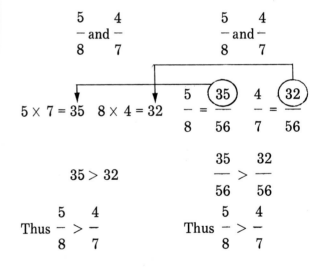

EQUIVALENT RATIOS

1. Circle the pairs in which the two given ratios are equal.

(a.) $\frac{1}{2}$ and $\frac{3}{6}$ b. $\frac{2}{4}$ and $\frac{1}{3}$ c. $\frac{2}{3}$ and $\frac{4}{5}$ d. $\frac{2}{3}$ and $\frac{5}{6}$

(e.) $\frac{3}{4}$ and $\frac{30}{40}$ f. $\frac{2}{5}$ and $\frac{3}{4}$ (g.) $\frac{4}{5}$ and $\frac{8}{10}$ h. $\frac{1}{3}$ and $\frac{9}{10}$

(i.) $\frac{3}{4}$ and $\frac{6}{8}$ (j.) $\frac{5}{6}$ and $\frac{10}{12}$ (k.) $\frac{1}{2}$ and $\frac{5}{10}$ l. $\frac{4}{6}$ and $\frac{2}{5}$

2. For each pair of ratios in exercise 1, find the pairs of products as shown in this example:

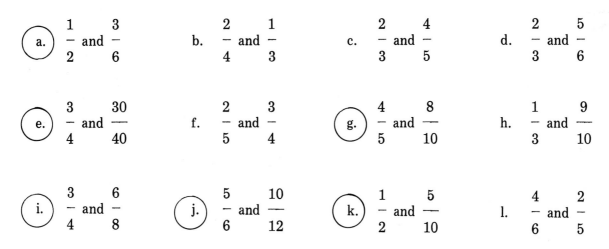

$$\frac{2}{3} \quad \text{and} \quad \frac{6}{9}$$

$$2 \times 9 = 18 \qquad 3 \times 6 = 18$$

a. $\frac{1}{2}$ and $\frac{3}{6}$ b. $\frac{2}{4}$ and $\frac{1}{3}$

$1 \times 6 = \underline{6}$ $2 \times 3 = \underline{6}$ $2 \times 3 = \underline{6}$ $4 \times 1 = \underline{4}$

c. $\frac{2}{3}$ and $\frac{4}{5}$ d. $\frac{2}{3}$ and $\frac{5}{6}$

$2 \times 5 = \underline{10}$ $3 \times 4 = \underline{12}$ $\underline{2} \times 6 = \underline{12}$ $3 \times \underline{5} = \underline{15}$

e. $\frac{3}{4}$ and $\frac{30}{40}$ f. $\frac{2}{5}$ and $\frac{3}{4}$

$\underline{3} \times \underline{40} = \underline{120}$ $\underline{4} \times \underline{30} = \underline{120}$ $2 \times 4 = 8$ $5 \times 3 = 15$

g.　$\dfrac{4}{5}$　and　$\dfrac{8}{10}$　　　h.　$\dfrac{1}{3}$　and　$\dfrac{9}{10}$

4 x 10 = 40　　5 x 8 = 40　　　　1 x 10 = 10　　3 x 9 = 27

i.　$\dfrac{3}{4}$　and　$\dfrac{6}{8}$　　　j.　$\dfrac{5}{6}$　and　$\dfrac{10}{12}$

3 x 8 = 24　　4 x 6 = 24　　　　5 x 12 = 60　　6 x 10 = 60

k.　$\dfrac{1}{2}$　and　$\dfrac{5}{10}$　　　l.　$\dfrac{4}{6}$　and　$\dfrac{2}{5}$

1 x 10 = 10　　2 x 5 = 10　　　　4 x 5 = 20　　6 x 2 = 12

3. What did you notice about the products in the problems which have equal ratios?

In the problems which have equal ratios, the products were equal.

In the problems which do not have equal ratios?

In the problems which do not have equal ratios, the products are unequal.

4. Use this method to find which of the following pairs of ratios are equal.

a.　$\dfrac{6}{3}$ and $\dfrac{16}{9}$　6 x 9 = 54　　　b.　$\dfrac{5}{7}$ and $\dfrac{7}{9}$　5 x 9 = 45　　　c.　$\dfrac{9}{6}$ and $\dfrac{6}{4}$　9 x 4 = 36
　　　　　　　　　3 x 16 = 48　　　　　　　　　　7 x 7 = 49　　　　　　　　　　6 x 6 = 36
　　　　　　　　　not equal　　　　　　　　　　　not equal　　　　　　　　　　equal

Copyright © 1983 by Addison-Wesley Publishing Company, Inc.

5. How would you use this method to help find the missing number in each of the following equations?

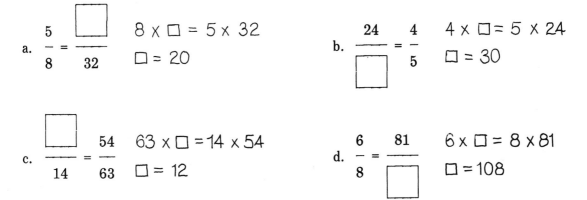

a. $\dfrac{5}{8} = \dfrac{\boxed{}}{32}$ $8 \times \square = 5 \times 32$
$\square = 20$

b. $\dfrac{24}{\boxed{}} = \dfrac{4}{5}$ $4 \times \square = 5 \times 24$
$\square = 30$

c. $\dfrac{\boxed{}}{14} = \dfrac{54}{63}$ $63 \times \square = 14 \times 54$
$\square = 12$

d. $\dfrac{6}{8} = \dfrac{81}{\boxed{}}$ $6 \times \square = 8 \times 81$
$\square = 108$

REGULAR POLYGONS IN A ROW

STRAND:

Geometry—perimeter of polygons.

PROBLEM SOLVING STRATEGIES:

Patterns, Models, Tables.

SUGGESTED USE:

This activity can be used after students have been introduced to the concept of perimeter. The unit on Patterns should be completed before using the activity.

MATERIALS:

Student activity pages.

INSTRUCTIONAL STRATEGY:

Step 1:   Distribute the student pages and instruct students to complete them. Point out that Tables are constructed for the first two polygons, trian- triangles and squares. They should construct simi- lar tables for the remaining polygons.

All of the polygons in this activity are *regular*, that is; *equilateral* and *equiangular*. In each case where more than one figure is used, they are placed end to end so that two polygons join along one complete side.

In the last table, it may be necessary to explain that a (n)gon is a polygon with n sides.

REGULAR POLYGONS IN A ROW

Fill in each blank with the correct answer. Draw a Model for the figures not given and construct a Table so that you will be able to determine a Pattern.

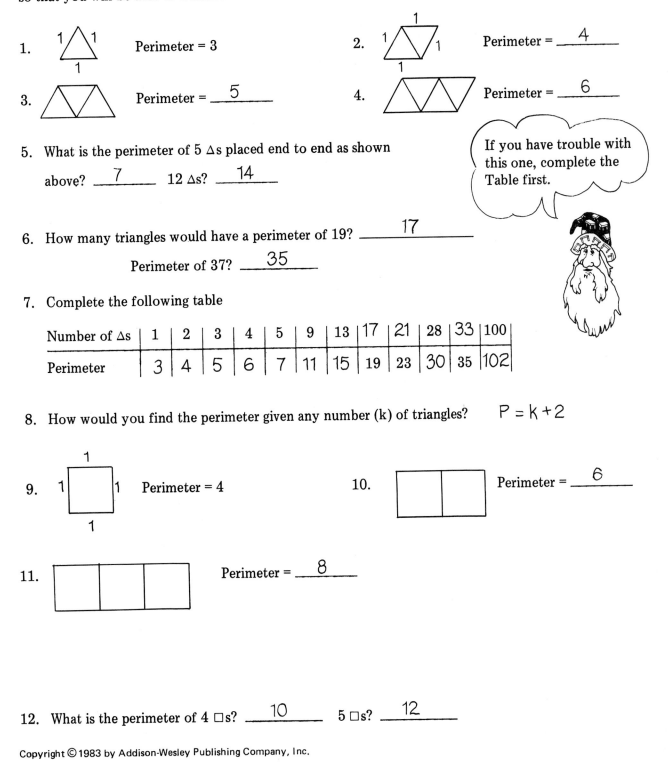

1. Perimeter = 3

2. Perimeter = __4__

3. Perimeter = __5__

4. Perimeter = __6__

5. What is the perimeter of 5 △s placed end to end as shown

    above? ___7___ 12 △s? ___14___

    If you have trouble with this one, complete the Table first.

6. How many triangles would have a perimeter of 19? ___17___

    Perimeter of 37? ___35___

7. Complete the following table

Number of △s	1	2	3	4	5	9	13	17	21	28	33	100
Perimeter	3	4	5	6	7	11	15	19	23	30	35	102

8. How would you find the perimeter given any number (k) of triangles? $P = k + 2$

9. Perimeter = 4

10. Perimeter = __6__

11. Perimeter = __8__

12. What is the perimeter of 4 □s? ___10___ 5 □s? ___12___

13. Complete the following table to help you answer the questions below.

Number of □s	1	2	3	4	5	6	7	8		100
Perimeter	4	6	8	10	12	14	16	18		202

14. What is the perimeter of 11 □s? ___24___   19 □s? ___40___

15. How many squares would have a perimeter of 26? ___12___   Perimeter of 40? ___19___

16. How would you find the perimeter given any number (k) of squares? $P = 2k + 2$

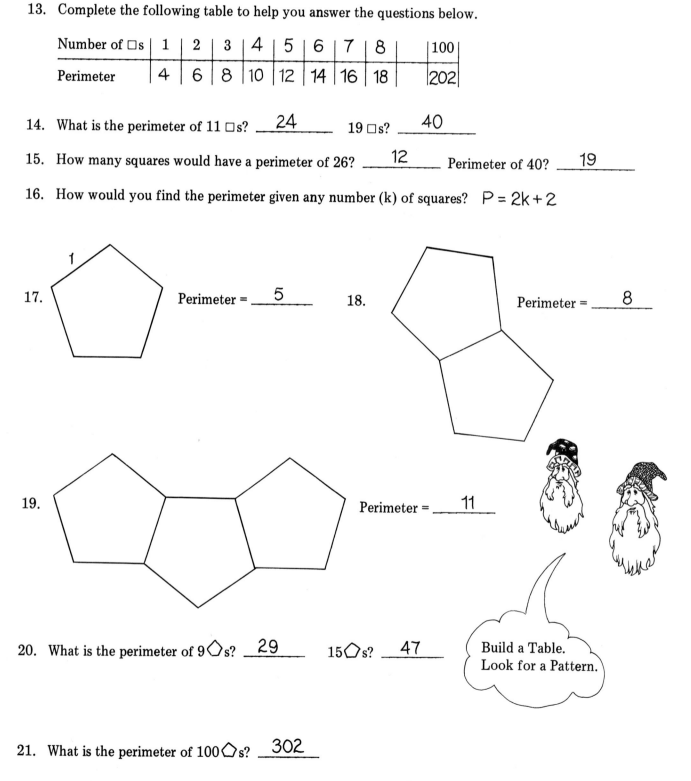

17.   Perimeter = ___5___   18.   Perimeter = ___8___

19.   Perimeter = ___11___

20. What is the perimeter of 9 ⬠s? ___29___   15 ⬠s? ___47___

Build a Table.
Look for a Pattern.

21. What is the perimeter of 100 ⬠s? ___302___

22. How would you find the perimeter given any number (k) of pentagons?

$$P = 3k + 2$$

23. Now that you have developed a method for determining the perimeter of some regular polygons placed end to end, use the above procedure to find the following:

a. The perimeter given any number (k) of hexagons? (6 sides) $P = 4k + 2$

b. The perimeter given any number (k) of heptagons? (7 sides) $P = 5k + 2$

c. The perimeter given any number (k) of octagons? (8 sides) $P = 6k + 2$

24. Complete the table below with the rule you developed to determine the perimeters given any number (k) of polygons placed end to end.

Regular Polygons	Number of Sides in Each Polygon	Rule
Triangles	3	$k + 2$
Squares	4	$2k + 2$
Pentagons	5	$3k + 2$
Hexagons	6	$4k + 2$
Heptagons	7	$5k + 2$
Octagons	8	$6k + 2$
⋮		
n(gon)	n	$(n-2)k + 2$

FROM TRIANGLES TO POLYGONS

STRAND:

Geometry—sum of the interior angles of a polygon, number of diagonals in a polygon.

PROBLEM SOLVING STRATEGIES:

Patterns, Models.

SUGGESTED USE:

This activity develops the formula for the sum of the interior angles of a polygon. It is an excellent followup to A *Rigid Task* and *Triangle Properties* II activities. However, it can be used at anytime after the student has learned that the sum of the measures of the angles of a triangle is 180°, and the Patterns strategy has been covered.

MATERIALS:

Student activity page, rulers, protractors.

INSTRUCTIONAL STRATEGY:

Step 1: Hand out the student page and instruct the students to complete it. Most students quickly recognize that if they multiply the number of triangles by 180, they can determine the sum of the interior angles. They should be encouraged to check some of their sums by measuring the interior angles.

Step 2: When the activity has been completed, the results should be discussed with the class. During the discussion the students should be asked to find the formula for the sum of the interior angles using the method developed in the Patterns introduction. When they do, they get $180n - 360$. The distributive law should be applied to this formula to get $180(n - 2)$, which is the formula obtained by the method described in step 1. This step is very important, because some students may have written the latter formula without the parenthesis. This emphasizes that $180n - 2 \neq 180(n - 2)$.

Step 3: As a followup, you may want to have the students add a column to the table and find the total number of diagonals in a polygon (see answer key). Since this is not a linear sequence, you may not want them to find the formula for the nth term. However they can use the methods developed in the Patterns introduction to extend the sequence to eleven terms. If you have taught the introductory lessons for the Simplify strategy, some students will probably recognize that this is another way of stating the "handshake problem" from Lesson 2 of Unit 6.

FROM TRIANGLES TO POLYGONS

Study the example and complete the table.

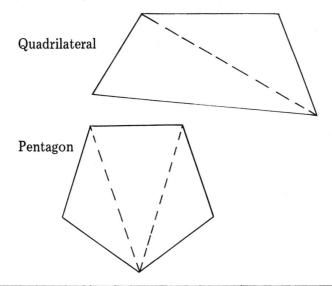

Quadrilateral

4 sides
1 diagonal from a vertex
2 triangles

Pentagon

5 sides
2 diagonals from a vertex
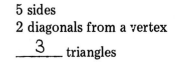
___3___ triangles

Polygon	Number of Sides	Number of Diagonals from One Vertex	Number of Triangles Formed by the Diagonals From One Vertex	Sum of the Interior Angles of the Polygon	Total Diagonals
Triangle	3	0	1	180	0
Quadrilateral	4	1	2	360	2
Pentagon	5	2	3	540	5
Hexagon	6	3	4	720	9
Heptagon	7	4	5	900	14
Octagon	8	5	6	1080	20
Nonagon	9	6	7	1260	27
Decagon	10	7	8	1440	35
Dodecagon	12	9	10	1800	54
$\vdots$					
N gon	n	n−3	n−2	(n−2) 180	$\frac{n(n-3)}{2}$

PENTOMINOES

STRAND:

Geometry—spatial perception, perimeter, area, similarity, reflections, rotations, and translations.

PROBLEM SOLVING STRATEGIES:

Models, Guess and Check, Elimination

SUGGESTED USE:

These activities reinforce the fundamental concepts of area and perimeter, and help to develop spatial perception. Since they do not require the use of formulas, they can be used either as part of an introduction to the concepts of area and perimeter, or as a review of these concepts. These activities are best used after the Make a Model strategy has been covered since the students construct the twelve pentomino pieces in the introduction to that strategy. There are three separate activities. You may use any or all of them as desired.

MATERIALS:

Student activity pages, pentomino sheet, pentomino cover-up gameboards, graph paper, tagboard, glue, scissors. (If possible, copy the cover-up gameboards and the pentomino sheet on tagboard. This will save time and eliminate the need for glueing.)

INSTRUCTIONAL STRATEGY:

Note: A polyomino is any arrangement of n squares in which every square borders at least one other square along a full side, and no square borders another square along only a portion of a side.

PENTOMINOES AND RECTANGLES

Step 1: Review the following facts concerning polyominoes. In each case, emphasize how the area and perimeter can be obtained by counting. In c and d you may want to allow members of the class to take turns drawing arrangements on the board. This provides practice in identifying arrangements that may be reflections or rotations of ones already drawn.

   a. There is only one monomino, □. Its area is one and its perimeter is four.

   b. There is only one domino, ▭. Its area is two and its perimeter is six. Be sure to point out that other arrangements which are a rotation or a reflection of this, such as ▯, are not considered to be different arrangements. Also, arrangements such as ⌐ and ⌐ cannot be used because the squares do not border each other along a full side.

   c. There are two triominoes, ▭ and ⌐. Both have an area of three and a perimeter of eight.

   d. There are five tetrominoes, ⊞, ⊞, ⊞, ⊞, and ▭. All have an area of four. The perimeter is ten, except for the square, where it is eight.

   e. There are twelve pentominoes. They were developed in the Models Introduction. You may or may not wish to take the time to review them here.

Step 2: Give each student a copy of the Pentominoes sheet. If the sheet was not copied on tagboard, have the students glue the sheet to tagboard before cutting out the pieces. You may also want to provide each student with an envelope in which to keep their pieces.

Step 3: Hand out the Pentominoes and Rectangles student page. Go through the example

with the students emphasizing how to record the solution and find the dimensions, perimeter, and area. Then have the students find solutions for the two rectangles that can be made with four pentominoes and discuss the solutions with the class.

Step 4: You should not expect students to find all of the possible solutions in a short time. You might have students discover as many solutions as they can in an assigned time and then allow extra credit for additional solutions found during spare time.

If your students are proficient with the formula for the area of a rectangle, you may want to use the following approach before completing the activity page.

Ask the students to list all the possible dimensions of the rectangles for each number of pentominoes. Since each pentomino has an area of five, the areas of possible rectangles will be the multiples of five, 5–60 inclusive, and the dimensions are the factors of each area. For example, if all 12 pentominoes are used, the area of the rectangle must be 60, and the possible dimensions are 1×60, 2×30, 3×20, 4×15, 5×12 and 6×10.

Narrow this list of possibilities using Elimination.

   a. Since there is only one piece with a height of 1, the only possible rectangle with a dimension of 1 is the 1×5.

   b. There are only six possible pieces that can be used to construct a $2 \times n$ rectangle. Of these, the ⊞ cannot be used. Therefore, it is not possible to construct a rectangle with dimensions $2 \times n$ with more than five pieces.

   c. The 2×5 rectangle is impossible because it requires two congruent pieces.

Rectangles having all the remaining dimensions can be constructed using the pentomino pieces.

Step 5: After you collect the solutions, explain why it is impossible to construct a rectangle using just two pieces. If your students are not familiar with the formula for the area of a rectangle, develop it by asking them how the dimen-sions and the area are related. The form used in writing the dimensions provides the clue for the answer. A formula for perimeter can be developed in a similar fashion by asking how the dimensions are related to the perimeter. Students may discover that they can determine the perimeter by replacing the $\times$ in the dimensions by +, and multiplying the result by two.

PENTOMINOES

Cut out each of the figures.

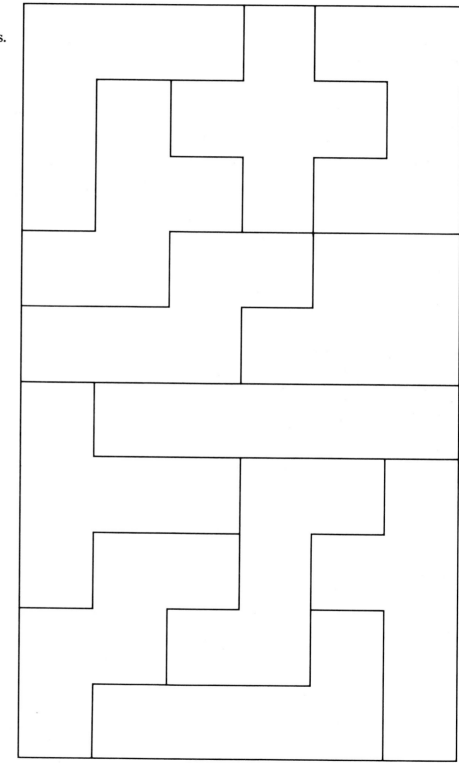

PENTOMINOES AND RECTANGLES

Study the example and complete the table. Look for rectangles with different dimensions in each case. Sketch your solutions on graph paper.

Number of Pentominoes

3

Record of Solution

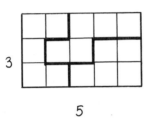

3

5

Dimensions 3 × 5

Area   15

Perimeter 16

Number of Pentominoes	Can You Make a Rectangle?	Dimensions	Area	Perimeter
1	Yes	1 x 5	5	12
2	No	—	—	—
3	Yes	3 x 5	15	16
4	Yes	2 x 10, 4 x 5	20	24, 18
5	Yes	5 x 5	25	20
6	Yes	3 x 10, 5 x 6	30	26, 22
7	Yes	5 x 7	35	24
8	Yes	4 x 10, 5 x 8	40	28, 26
9	Yes	3 x 15, 5 x 9	45	36, 28
10	Yes	5 x 10	50	30
11	Yes	5 x 11	55	32
12	Yes	3 x 20 4 x 15 5 x 12 6 x 10	60	46 38 34 32

PENTOMINO TRIPLICATION

Step 1: Hand out the student pages, and instruct the students to complete them.

Step 2: When the students have completed the activity, discuss the fact that when the linear dimensions of an object are tripled, the area increases nine times. You may want to extend the activity by considering what happens to the area when the linear dimensions are doubled, halved, and so forth. This is an excellent opportunity to review exponents.

At a later date, after the students have covered volume, you may wish to review these results and extend them to include volume. You may also want to have a science teacher discuss the role that these relationships play in the specialization of organisms at that time.

See: J. B. S. Haldane, "On Being the Right Size," *The World of Mathematics*, Vol. II.

PENTOMINO TRIPLICATION

1. a. Fill in figure A with one pentomino piece.
    b. Fill in figure B with nine of the remaining pieces.

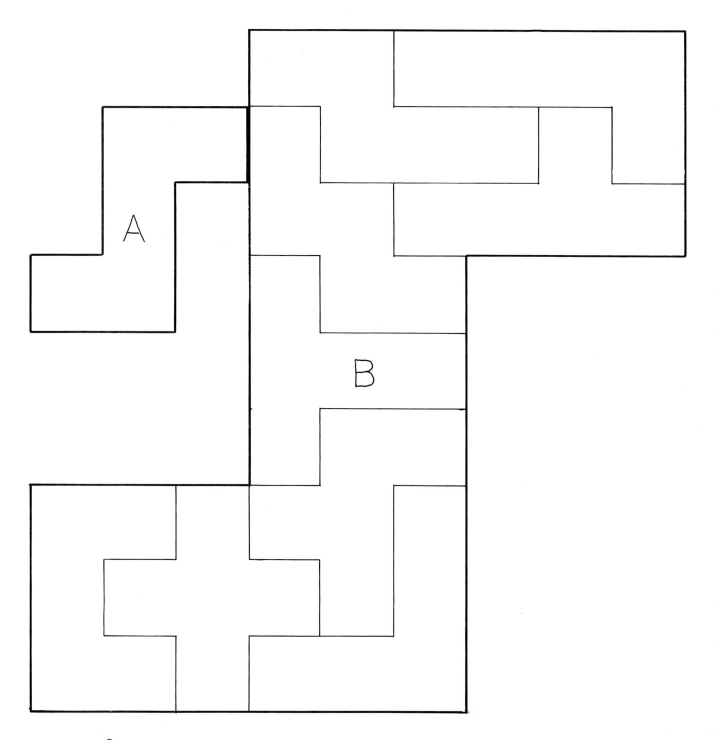

2. a. Select any pentomino.
    b. As in exercise 1, use nine of the remaining pentominoes to make an enlargement of the pentomino you selected. Record your solution on graph paper.

3. a. How does the area of the enlargement compare with the area of the single pentomino?

    The area of the enlargement is nine times the area of the original piece.

    b. How do the dimensions of the enlargement compare with the dimensions of the single pentomino?

    The dimensions of the enlargement are three times the dimensions of the single piece.

4. Which pentominoes can you enlarge in this fashion?

    All of them.

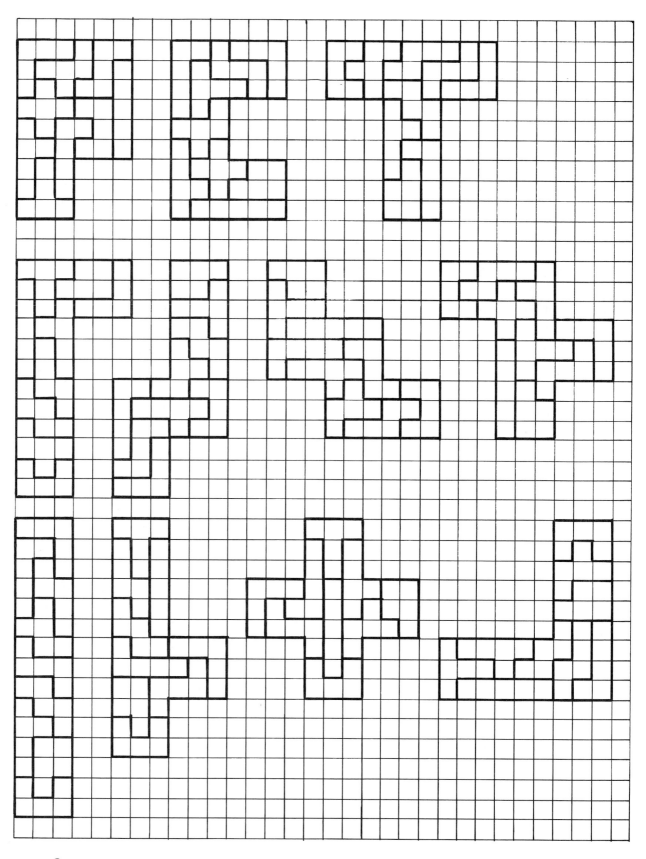

PENTOMINO COVER UP

Cover Up is a strategy game for two players. Two different gameboards are included, however the rules are the same for each. Gameboard II is a slightly more challenging game.

Rules:

1. Place the set of twelve pentominoes in a "pile."
2. Each player draws in turn from the pile to form his own set of pentominoes.
3. Each player in turn plays one of his pentominoes anywhere on the playing board.
4. Play continues until a player cannot place a pentomino on the board.
5. The winner is the last person to play.

Variations:

1. Gameboard I: Black out either the four corner squares or the four center squares and play on the remaining 60 squares.

2. Gameboard II: Black out the center square and play on the remaining 60 squares.

3. In either game: Change the winner to the player with the least number of pentominoes left after it is impossible for any player to place another piece on the board. If this variation is used, there will be several tie games until the players determine the strategy of blocking off a space where the only piece that will fit is one of theirs.

PENTOMINO COVER UP
GAME BOARD I

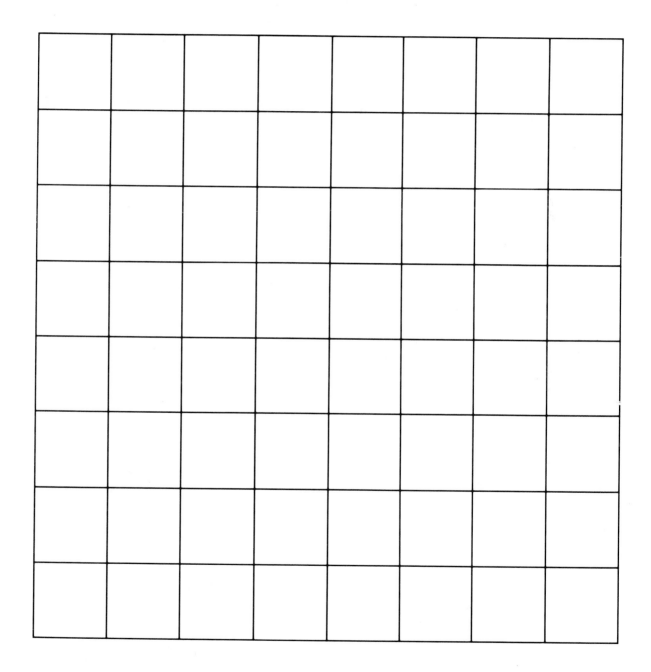

PENTOMINO COVER UP
GAME BOARD II

INTEGER PATTERNS

STRAND:
Integers—addition, subtraction, commutative property of addition.

PROBLEM SOLVING STRATEGY:
Patterns

SUGGESTED USE:
This activity develops the algorithm for addition of integers, and can be extended to develop the algorithm for subtraction. Before doing the activity, students must be familiar with the concept of an integer, the ordering of integers, and the commutative property of addition.

MATERIALS:
Student activity pages.

INSTRUCTIONAL STRATEGY:
Step 1: Hand out the student pages and instruct the students to complete them.

Step 2: After the activity has been completed, it should be discussed with the class. Problems that need special emphasis are:

Problem 2: Some students will use incorrect terminology when answering the question. For example, they might state the rule for adding a positive and a negative number as:
Subtract the "smaller" number from the "larger" one. The sign of the answer is the sign of the "larger" number.
By "smaller" number and "larger" number they really mean the number with the smaller absolute value and the number with the larger absolute value respectively. The use of correct terminology is important. However, students who expressed the rule in this fashion have achieved the goal of the worksheet, which is to discover an algorithm for addition of integers that they will remem-

ber. Thus, it might be advisable to delay correcting the terminology until they are comfortable with applying the algorithm.

Problem 4: Some students may be uncomfortable with the results they obtained. To show that the answers are consistent with their previously acquired knowledge, explain the results in this problem using a number line and the rule for addition on it, or use real-life examples such as:
If your checking account is $5 overdrawn and you deposit $10, what is your new balance?

Problem 6: Check to see that the patterns have been extended correctly to obtain the next five problems, and that the students recognize that the sum is always negative. At this point, students should be able to state a complete algorithm for addition. It should be discussed briefly and used to find the sums in exercise 7.

Step 3: After completing the activity, you may want to make an assignment from your textbook on addition of integers.

Step 4: An algorithm for subtraction of integers can be developed by considering the patterns in the following lists:

I	II
$5 - 0 = $ _____	$4 - 5 = $ _____
$5 - 1 = $ _____	$3 - 5 = $ _____
$5 - 2 = $ _____	$2 - 5 = $ _____
$5 - 3 = $ _____	$1 - 5 = $ _____
$5 - 4 = $ _____	$0 - 5 = $ _____
$5 - 5 = $ _____	$-1 - 5 = $ _____

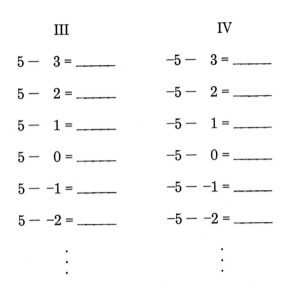

III	IV
5 − 3 = _____	−5 − 3 = _____
5 − 2 = _____	−5 − 2 = _____
5 − 1 = _____	−5 − 1 = _____
5 − 0 = _____	−5 − 0 = _____
5 − −1 = _____	−5 − −1 = _____
5 − −2 = _____	−5 − −2 = _____

Begin by writing the problems in I on the board and having the students find the differences and extend the list. Verify the results by using a number line or real-life examples.

Step 5: Now write the related addition problems next to each subtraction problem. For example, 5 − 3 = 2, 5 + −3 = 2. Ask students to explain how the problems are related.

Step 6: Repeat steps 4 and 5 using the problems in II. When you are finished, the students should be able to extend sets III and IV by using the related addition problems. When they are done, review their results and ask the students to state a rule for subtraction of integers.

Step 7: Follow up the activity with an assignment on addition and subtraction of integers in your textbook.

A similar pattern approach can be used to develop the rules for multiplication and division of integers.

INTEGER PATTERNS

1. Complete the list of problems by looking for patterns.

2. Use the completed list to help answer the following questions.

   When is the sum of a positive number and a negative number

   a. positive?

   When the absolute value of the negative number is less than the positive number.

   b. zero?

   When the absolute value of the negative number equals the positive number.

   c. negative?

   When the absolute value of the negative number is greater than the positive number.

   d. Write a rule for adding a positive and a negative number.

   To find the sum of a positive and a negative number subtract the smaller absolute value from the larger. The sign of the answer is the sign of the number with the greater absolute value.

5 + 5	=	10
5 + 4	=	9
5 + 3	=	8
5 + 2	=	7
5 + 1	=	6
5 + 0	=	5
5 + ⁻1	=	4
5 + ⁻2	=	3
5 + ⁻3	=	2
5 + ⁻4	=	1
5 + ⁻5	=	0
5 + ⁻6	=	⁻1
5 + ⁻7	=	⁻2
5 + ⁻8	=	⁻3
5 + ⁻9	=	⁻4
5 + ⁻10	=	⁻5

3. Use your results from exercise 2 to find these sums.

   a. 10 + ⁻5 = __5__   b. 6 + ⁻5 = __1__   c. 4 + ⁻5 = __⁻1__   d. 1 + ⁻5 = __⁻4__

4. Addition is a commutative operation. That is, a + b = b + a for all numbers a and b. Use the commutative property of addition and your answers in exercise 3 to find the following sums.

   a. ⁻5 + 10 = 10 + ⁻5 = __5__

   b. ⁻5 + 6 = __6+⁻5__ = __1__

   c. ⁻5 + 4 = __4+⁻5__ = __⁻1__

   d. ⁻5 + 1 = __1+⁻5__ = __⁻4__

5. Use the results of exercise 2 and the commutative property to complete the problems in this list.

6. Write the next five problems in the list by looking for patterns in the numbers.

Is the sum of the two negative numbers positive or negative? __negative__

Write a rule for adding two negative numbers.

The sum of two negative numbers is the negative of the sum of their absolute values.

—5 + 10 = __5__

—5 + 9 = __4__

—5 + 8 = __3__

—5 + 7 = __2__

—5 + 6 = __1__

—5 + 5 = __0__

—5 + 4 = __$^-$1__

—5 + 3 = __$^-$2__

—5 + 2 = __$^-$3__

—5 + 1 = __$^-$4__

__$^-$5__ + __0__ = __$^-$5__

__$^-$5__ + __$^-$1__ = __$^-$6__

__$^-$5__ + __$^-$2__ = __$^-$7__

__$^-$5__ + __$^-$3__ = __$^-$8__

__$^-$5__ + __$^-$4__ = __$^-$9__

7. Use your results from exercises 2 and 6 to find these sums:

a. 18 + —6 = __12__

b. —6 + —8 = __$^-$14__

c. —11 + 7 = __$^-$4__

d. —6 + 18 = __12__

e. 12 + —15 = __$^-$3__

f. —11 + —13 = __$^-$24__

SECTION III

PRACTICE PROBLEMS

INTRODUCTION

The Practice Problems section contains a variety of problems that can be used to:

1. provide additional practice with a problem-solving strategy when it is being introduced.
2. review and reinforce a strategy after it has been introduced.
3. provide enrichment material for supplementary work throughout the year.
4. evaluate student progress and achievement.

The solution of most meaningful problems generally involves the application of more than one problem-solving strategy. *However, we have keyed the problems on each page to a single strategy which we perceive to be the major one employed in solving the problem.* The problems are also leveled according to difficulty, the last problem on a page being the most difficult. Both the keying and the leveling are results of our use of these and similar problems over a period of five years with junior high students and our observation of the strategies they employed and the degrees of difficulty they encountered in solving them.

While on most of the pages all of the problems involve the same major strategy, the problems on pages 195 and 207 each involve a different strategy. Page 195 contains one Guess and Check problem, two Tables problems, and two Patterns problems. Page 207 contains one problem involving each of the six strategies. The problems on these two pages have not been ordered according to difficulty.

There are two reasons for including these two pages. First, if the teacher so desires, they may be used after completion of the third and the sixth Introductory Units as tests to evaluate student progress. However, the main reason for including them is concerned with pedagogy. A major difficulty that students face in solving a problem is choosing an appropriate strategy to use. Once some of the Introductory Units have been completed, we suggest that you select problems involving a variety of strategies to construct worksheets like pages 195 and 207 rather than duplicate a page that involves just one strategy. By doing the latter, one may tend to mirror the example of many textbooks in which the word problems that constitute the problem-solving strand are placed at the end of a computational segment and all involve the algorithm just completed. That is, if multiplication of whole numbers has just been covered, then all of the word problems which follow involve multiplication.

1. Place the numbers 1, 2, 3, 4, 5, 6 in the circles in such a way that each side of the triangle adds up to 10, 11, 12.

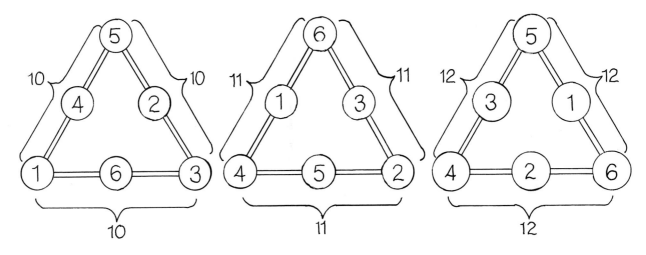

2. A math book is lying open on a desk. To what pages is it opened if the product of the facing pages is 8556?

Pages 92 and 93.

3. The difference between two numbers is 75. If the larger number is divided by the smaller number, the quotient is 6 and the remainder is 5. What are the two numbers?

l	89
s	14
l-s	75
l ÷ s	6 R5

4. Gina and Tom raise cats and birds. They counted all the heads and got 10. They counted all the feet and got 34. How many birds and cats do they have?

b	5	4	③
c	5	6	⑦
b+c	10	10	10

b x 2	10	8	6
c x 4	20	24	28
Total	30	32	34

3 birds
7 cats

5. Adult tickets to the Boya 1 Theater cost $2.00 more than student tickets. The total receipts from 100 students and 200 adults were $850.00. What was the cost of the student ticket?

student ticket	$2	$1.50
adult ticket	$4	$3.50
100 x student	$200	$150
200 x adult	$800	$700
Total	$1000	$850

1. The mile relay team of Central High consists of four runners; Speedy, Flash, Dasher, and Stumbles. Each runner runs one-quarter of a mile in the order listed. As they race, each member runs his quarter mile two seconds faster than the previous runner. If they run the mile in 3 minutes and 40 seconds, what is the time for each runner's lap?

Speedy	60	59	58
Flash	58	57	56
Dasher	56	55	54
Stumbles	54	53	52
Total time	228	224	220

58 —answers

3 min, 40 sec = 220 sec.

2. The difference between two numbers is 37, their sum is 215. What are the numbers?

1	125	126
s	90	89
1+s	215	215
1−s	35	37

126 — answers 126 and 89

3. A farmer went to market and sold 62 chickens. He sold the hens for $1.50 each and the roosters for $0.75 each; his total receipts were $61.50. How many hens and roosters did he sell?

hens	32	30	20
roosters	30	32	42
1.50 x hens	48.00	45.00	30.00
.75 x roosters	22.50	24.00	31.50
Total receipts	70.50	69.00	61.50

20 —— answers 20 hens
42 roosters

4. Three girls received a quarter each to spend for candy. The candy store contained lollipops at 3 for a nickel, licorice sticks at 4 for a nickel, and cinnamon bears at one cent each. Each girl ended up with a different selection of candy, but each spent her entire quarter. Each girl received exactly 20 pieces of candy. What were their selections?

One bought 20 pieces of licorice for 25¢.
One bought 12 pieces of licorice for 15¢, 3 lollipops for 5¢, and 5 cinnamon bears for 5¢.
One bought 4 pieces of licorice for 5¢, 6 lollipops for 10¢, and 10 cinnamon bears for 10¢.

1. Roofing nails sell for $0.60 per pound.

Pounds of Nails	1	2	5	6	½			
Cost	0.60	1.20	3.00	3.60	0.30			

a. What is the cost of 11 pounds? ___$6.60___.

b. If you have only $0.30, how many pounds of nails can you buy? ___½ lb.___.

c. How many pounds can you buy for $12.00? ___20 lbs.___.

d. If you have $0.75, how many pounds can you buy? ___¾ lb.___.

2. With five minutes left to play in the championship game between the Cougars and the Huskies, the Cougars were leading by 16 points. In the last five minutes, the Cougars scored 6 points per minute and the Huskies scored 9 points per minute. Who won the game and by how much?

Cougars win by 1 point

Minutes	1	2	3	4	5	
Cougars	6	12	18	24	30	30+16=46
Huskies	9	18	27	36	45	

3. A drippy water faucet will fill a 100 ml cup in 10 minutes. Make a table and answer the following:

Time	10 min	20 min	5 min	100min	1 hr			
Water Wasted	100 ml	200 ml	50ml	1 L	600mL			

a. How much water is wasted in 1 day? ___14.4 L.___.

b. How long does it take to waste 10 liters of water? ___1000 min.   16 hrs. 40 min.___.

c. How much water is wasted in one week? ___100.8 L.___.

d. How long does it take to waste 1 kiloliter of water? ___100,000 min   1666 hrs, 40 min.___

4. George has $3.71 in pennies, nickels, dimes, and quarters in his pocket. He has twice as many dimes as nickels, two more nickels than quarters, and three fewer pennies than three times the number of nickels. How many of each kind of coin does he have?

Answer: 8 nickels, 6 quarters
16 dimes, 21 pennies

Nickels	5 = 25	7 = 35	8 = .40
Dimes	10 = 50	14 = 1.40	16 = 1.60
Quarters	3 = 75	5 = 1.25	6 = 1.50
Pennies	12 = 12	18 = .18	21 = .21
Total value	$1.62	$3.18	$3.71

1. The stockholders receive an 8% dividend.

Stock Value	$100	$200	$50	$300	$500	$700		
Dividend	$8	$16	$4	$24	$40	$56		

a. If you own $500 in stock, what is your dividend? ____$40____ .

b. If you own $750 in stock, what is your dividend? ____$60____ .
   add dividends for $700 and $50.

c. You receive a $72 dividend, what is the value of your stock? ____$900____ .

2. Terry has five objects, all having a different weight from 1 through 5 kg. If she weighs them three at a time, what is the largest possible number of different weights she can have?

1,2,3 – 6   1,4,5 – 10
1,2,4 – 7   2,3,4 – 9   7 different total weights.
1,2,5 – 8   2,3,5 – 10
1,3,4 – 8   2,4,5 – 11
1,3,5 – 9   3,4,5 – 12

3. A cashier found that he was often asked to give change for a dollar to people who had made no purchases but wanted 20 cents for a telephone call. He started thinking one day about the number of ways he could make change. If he gave no more than four of any coin, in how many different ways could he give change for a dollar to people who wanted to make a telephone call?

Nickels	1	2	4	3	1	3	2	4
Dimes	2	4	3	1	2	1	4	3
Quarters	1			1	3	3	2	2
Half Dollars	1	1	1	1				

8 ways

4. While attending "The Great Mandini" magic show, Brett was asked to come on stage to be part of the program. When asked how much change he had, Brett said he had 55¢ in dimes and nickels. Mandini said he would change all the nickels to dimes and the dimes to nickels. After the change was made, Brett counted his money and had 65¢. How many nickels and dimes did Brett have before he went on stage?

Before the change 55¢ {	Dimes	1	2	3
	Nickels	9	7	5
After the change {	Dimes	9	7	5
	Nickels	1	2	3
	New total	95	80	65

Brett had 3 dimes and 5 nickels

1. Two clocks show the correct time to be one o'clock. One clock is running properly; the other is also running at the correct rate, but backwards. When is the next time that both clocks will show the same time?

Clock 1	1	2	3	4	5	6	7
Clock 2	1	12	11	10	9	8	7

7 o'clock

2. Colleen is going to buy a new car. The local dealer has cars with exterior colors of black, white, and turquoise.

The same colors are available for the interiors, however, the interior color is always the same as, or lighter than the exterior color.

Pin stripes are found only on cars with a black exterior.

How many styles are available?
9

Exterior	B	B	B	B	B	B	T	T	W
Interior	B	T	W	B	T	W	T	W	W
Pin Stripe				P	P	P			

3.

SPECIAL!!!

Assorted Greeting Cards

15¢ each

$1.50 — Box of 12 Cards

Cards	1	5	10	12	24		
Boxes	0	0	0	1	2		
Cost	$0.15	$0.75	$1.50	$1.50	$3.00		

a. What is the cost of 3 boxes? _$4.50_

b. What is the least cost for 30 cards? _$3.90_

11 cards – $1.65

c. Which costs more — 12 cards or 11 cards? _11 cards_

12 cards – $1.50/box

d. Eileen spent $7.20 for cards. What is the greatest number of cards she could buy? _56 cards._

4 boxes   48 cards $6.00, 8 cards $1.20

4. Joan buys 3 skirts, 4 blouses, and 3 sweaters. She intends to wear them in various combinations. The blue skirt doesn't go with the green sweater, but otherwise any combination of the three garments is attractive. How many different combinations can Joan make that include a skirt, a blouse, and a sweater?

Total combinations = 36 [3 x 4 x 3] However, the blue skirt and green sweater can be worn with 4 blouses. 36 − 4 = 32
32 different combinations.

1. Two planes leave Denver at the same time from adjoining runways; one flies west to San Francisco, the other east to Baltimore. The westbound plane travels at 400 km/hr, and the other at 450 km/hr. When will the planes be 3825 km apart?

Hours	1	2	4	½	4½
East	450	900	1800	225	
West	400	800	1600	200	
Total	850	1700	3400	425	3825

2. Number 1 apples sell for $5.00 a bushel and number 2 apples sell for $4.00 a bushel. If the value of a crop of 100 bushels is $460.00, how many bushels are number 1 apples and how many bushels are number 2 apples?

No.1	50 = $250	40 = 200	60 = 300
No. 2	50 = $200	60 = 240	40 = 160
Total	= $450	= 440	= 460

60 bu = No 1 apples

40 bu = No 2 apples

3. If 3 people can complete 1/2 of a job in 20 days, how long would it take 12 people to do the complete job?

People	3	3	6	12
Job	½	1	1	1
Days	20	40	20	10

10 days

4. Three boxes labeled A, B, and C all contain a number of beans. The sum of the number of beans in A and B is 385. The difference between the numbers of beans in B and C is 65. The sum of the numbers of beans in A and C is 320. The difference between the numbers of beans in A and C is 70. Use this information to determine how many beans are in each box.

A	300	250	200	190	195
B	85	135	185	195	190
C	20	70	120	130	125

A = 195

B = 190

C = 125

1. Joe Gardener is a greenhouse operator. Each spring, he plants cucumbers, peppers, and tomatoes. He plants 50 rows, each row containing 100 plants according to the following scheme:

1st Row — 100 cucumber plants

2nd Row — 98 cucumber plants, 2 pepper plants

3rd Row — 96 cucumber plants, 3 pepper plants, 1 tomato plant

4th Row — 94 cucumber plants, 4 pepper plants, 2 tomato plants

5th Row — 92 cucumber plants, 5 pepper plants, 3 tomato plants

6th Row — __90__ cucumber plants, __6__ pepper plants, __4__ tomato plants

7th Row — __88__ cucumber plants, __7__ pepper plants, __5__ tomato plants

8th Row — __86__ cucumber plants, __8__ pepper plants, __6__ tomato plants

How many of each type of plant are in the:

a. 10th Row? __82 cucumbers   10 peppers   8 tomatoes__

b. 15th Row? __72 "   15 "   13 "__

c. 28th Row? __46 "   28 "   26 "__

d. 50th Row? __2 "   50 "   48 "__

2. At 3:20 p.m., a jeweler set three antique clocks to the correct time. The next afternoon at 3:20, she found that one clock was correct, one was 2 minutes slow and one was 2 minutes fast. At those rates, how long will it take before all three clocks show 3:20 again?

The clocks gain or lose 1 hour each 30 days. They would usually show 3:20 again in 12 hours, therefore it will take 360 days.

PERIMETER PATTERNS 1

Stack rectangles end to end only.

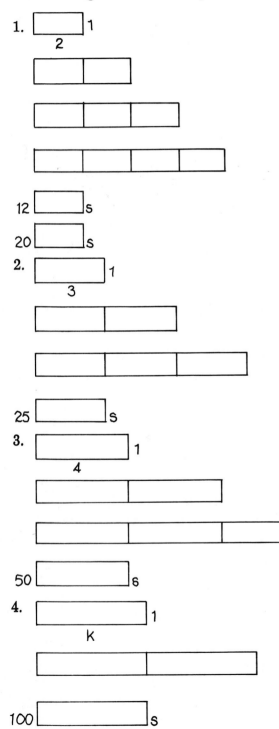

perimeter = _____ 6

perimeter = _____ 10

perimeter = _____ 14

perimeter = _____ 18

perimeter = _____ 50

perimeter = _____ 82

perimeter = _____ 8

perimeter = _____ 14

perimeter = _____ 20

perimeter = _____ 152

perimeter = _____ 10

perimeter = _____ 18

perimeter = _____ 26

perimeter = _____ 402

perimeter = _____ 2k + 2

perimeter = _____ 4k + 2

perimeter = _____ 2k(100) + 2

PERIMETER PATTERNS 2

Stack rectangles end to end only.

1.

perimeter = __10__

perimeter = __16__

perimeter = __22__

perimeter = __604__

2.

perimeter = __12__

perimeter = __20__

perimeter = __4004__

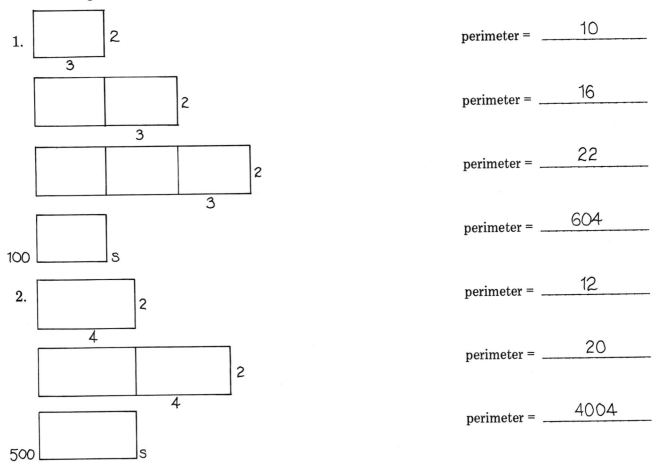

3. Can you write a rule that could be used to find the perimeter of each of the following for any number (n) of rectangles?

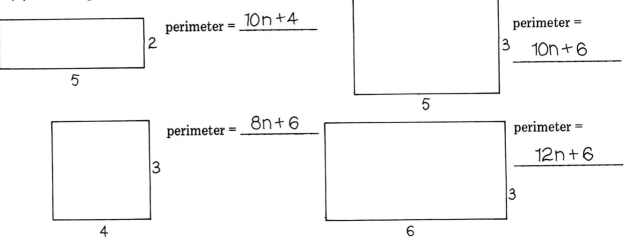

perimeter = __10n + 4__

perimeter = __10n + 6__

perimeter = __8n + 6__

perimeter = __12n + 6__

Copyright © 1983 by Addison-Wesley Publishing Company, Inc.

1.

```
                                                          x x x x x x
                                                          x x x x x x
                                    x x x x x             x x x x x x
                                    x x x x x             x x x x x x
                       x x x x      x x x x x             x x x x x x
                       x x x x      x x x x x             x x x x x x
            x x x      x x x x      x x x x x             x x x x x x
            x x x      x x x x      x x x x x             x x x x x x
   x x      x x x      x x x x      x x x x x             x x x x x x
   x x,     x x x,     x x x x,     x x x x x,            x x x x x x
```

1	2	3	4	Draw the fifth picture

Describe the fiftieth picture. ___ 51 across, 100 up ___

2. A raft on the Yellowstone Boat Float can hold 270 liters of water before sinking. During the float last year, Randy hit a rock and the raft began to leak. It gained 10 liters of water the first kilometer, 15 liters the second kilometer, 20 liters the third, and so on. How far could it travel before sinking?

Kilometers	1	2	3	4	5	6	7	8	9
Liters gained	10	15	20	25	30	35	40	45	50
Total	10	25	45	70	100	135	175	220	270

9 km

3. Good news travels fast. For instance, Jan Smith received a new car from her parents. Being excited, she immediately told two friends who, ten minutes later, each repeated the news to two other friends. Ten minutes later, these four friends each told two others. If the news continues to spread in this fashion, how many friends know about Jan's new car after 80 minutes?

Time	0	10	20	30	40	50	60	70	80
People told	2	4	8	16	32	64	128	256	512
Total	2	6	14	30	62	126	254	510	1022

1022 people

4. One afternoon, the Royal Duck Squadron was resting on the Palace lawn. The Head Quack dismissed them to the Royal Pond in the following manner. At 1:00 p.m. one duck was dismissed. Every 10 minutes after, two times the number that had already left were dismissed. If there were 243 ducks, and it took ten minutes to get to the Pond, at what time were all the ducks in the Pond?

Time	1	1:10	1:20	1:30	1:40	1:50	2
Ducks dismissed	1	2	6	18	54	162	
Ducks in pond	0	1	3	9	27	81	243

2 p.m.

1. Which number between 1 and 150 when multiplied times itself results in a product which is closest to 300?

$$17^2 = 289 \quad 18^2 = 324 \quad \text{Answer} = 17$$

2. Joe charges $3.50 to mow a lawn. His expenses for gas and repairs average $0.60 per lawn.

Lawns Mowed	1	2	3	4	5		
Income	3.50	7.00	10.50	14.00	17.50		
Expenses	.60	1.20	1.80	2.40	3.00		

Income is $21; Lawns mowed _____6_____

Lawns mowed ____17____ ; Expenses ___$10.20___

Expenses ___$7.80___ ; Income ___$45.50___

Income $35; Expenses ___$6.00___ ; Lawns Mowed ____10____

3. Given the sequence 10, 17, 24, 31, __38__ , __45__ , __52__ , __59__ , ...

   a. Fill in the blanks.

   b. What is the 20th term?   143

   c. What rule can you use to find the 100th term?   703

   d. What is the 100th term?   7 x term number + 3

4. John has saved $48 to buy some 8-track tapes. The Record Rack is having a sale. He can buy $8.95 tapes for $6 and $6.95 tapes for $4. In how many different ways can he spend all his money?

$6 tapes	8	6	4	2	0
$4 tapes	0	3	6	9	12

   5 ways

5. At 6:30 A.M. the first two people arrived at the Super Bowl ticket office to purchase tickets for the game. Every 25 minutes after that, three more than the number of people already present arrived to get in line. How many people were in line at 9:00 A.M. when the office opened?

Time	6:30	6:55	7:20	7:45	8:10	8:35	9:00
People arrive	2	5	10	20	40	80	160
People in line	2	7	17	37	77	157	317

1. Six blocks are used in a staircase that has 3 steps. Can you make a staircase with 36 blocks? If so, show an example, and tell how many steps it has.

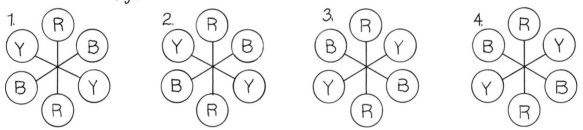

Yes, 8 steps

1 + 2 + 3 + 4 + 5 + 6 + 7 + 8 = 36

2. Six colored pin wheels are to be arranged in a circle. There are two red, two yellow, and two blue wheels. Wheels of the same color are placed opposite each other on the circle. One wheel of each color is spinning clockwise and one counterclockwise. Adjacent wheels always spin opposite directions. If the red wheels are vertical, how many possible ways can the colored spinning wheels be placed around the circle?   4 ways

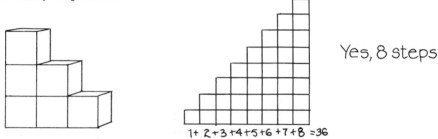

3. A person mows a lawn which is a square 10 meters on a side in 20 minutes. How long will it take that person working at the same rate to mow a lawn which is a square 5 m on a side?

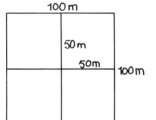

15 minutes since there is only one-fourth as much area to mow.

4. How many boxes 5 cm by 8 cm by 2 cm can you put in a box that is 20 cm by 32 cm by 16 cm?

128

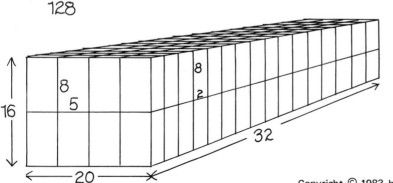

197

1. Mrs. Brussel wants to plant corn, carrots, cabbage, and cucumbers.

    a. Show how she can plant the vegetables so cabbage is next to corn and carrots, and corn is next to cabbage and cucumbers.

    b. Show how she can plant the vegetables so each type is next to each of the other three types.

    c. Mr. Sprout wants to plant peas, peppers, potatoes, parsnips and pumpkins. Can he plant the vegetables so each type is next to each of the other four types?

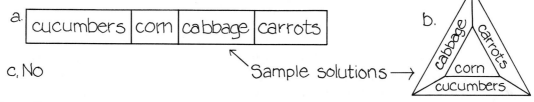

a. | cucumbers | corn | cabbage | carrots |

c. No   Sample solutions →   b. triangle: cabbage, carrots, corn, cucumbers

2. A family of four wants to cross a river. Their raft can hold at most 100 kilograms. The father weighs 85 kg, the mother weighs 54 kg, the son weighs 45 kg, and the daughter weighs 40 kg. How can they cross the river? Explain your answer.

    Son and daughter cross, and son returns with boat.
    Son and mother cross, and son returns with boat.
    Father crosses, daughter returns with boat.
    Son and daughter cross.

3. Five termites are eating through an old oak log.

    Enie is 20 millimeters ahead of Meanie.

    Meanie is twice as far as Miney.

    Miney is 60 millimeters behind Moe.

    Joe is a daring 15 millimeters behind Meanie.

    If Enie has munched 54 millimeters, how far has each of the others munched? Who's the fastest muncher in the oak? Explain your answer.

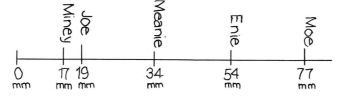

Moe is the fastest muncher in the Oak.

number line: 0 mm, Miney 17 mm, Joe 19 mm, Meanie 34 mm, Enie 54 mm, Moe 77 mm

4. The area of a rectangular room is 279 square meters. Its perimeter is 67 meters. What are the dimensions of the room?

    18m x 15.5m

1. A building has 6 stories, each the same height. It takes 10 seconds for the freight elevator to get from the first floor to the third floor. How long does it take for the elevator to go from the first to the sixth floor—20 seconds, 25 seconds, 30 seconds?

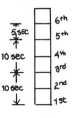

25 seconds

2. Two frogs have a race. One frog makes a jump of 80 cm once every 5 seconds. The other frog makes a jump of 15 cm every 1 second. The rules of the race state that the frogs must cross a line 5 m away and then come back to the starting point. Which frog wins the race?

Time	5	10	15	20	25	30	31	32	33	34	35	40	45	50	55	60	65	66	67	68
80 cm jumper	80	160	240	320	400	480	480	480	480	480	*560	480	400	320	240	160	80	80	80	80
15 cm jumper	75	150	225	300	375	450	465	480	495	*510	495	420	345	270	195	120	45	30	15	0

* note that they both must go past the 5m line before returning.

3. Two candles of equal length are lit at the same time. One candle takes 6 hours to burn out and the other 3 hours. After how much time will the slower burning candle be exactly twice as long as the faster burning one?

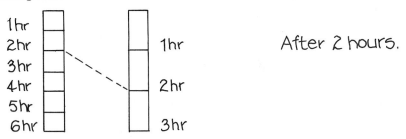

After 2 hours.

4. The Grundy Carpet Mart made a bid on carpeting the stairway in a split-level home. The upper level is four feet above the lower level. Each step is 5 feet long, 2 feet wide, and 6 inches above the one below.

Only the top of each step will be carpeted.

The roll of carpet chosen comes in a 12-foot width.

What is the smallest length of carpet which can be bought to cover the steps so that each step is covered by a solid piece of carpet. 6 feet

1.

	Cupboard 1	Cupboard 2	Cupboard 3
Row 1	B W W	B W W	B B W
Row 2	B W W	B B W	B W W
Row 3	B B W	B W W	B W W
Row 4	B B W	B B W	W W W
Row 5	B B W	W W W	B B W
Row 6	W W W	B B W	B B W

The table above shows six different ways that four blue plates and five white plates can be placed in three cupboards. Tell which row in the table meets all three of the following conditions.

a. Cupboard 1 has exactly 2 blue plates.   Rows 3,4,5 ⎫
                                                          ⎬ only possibilities
b. Cupboard 3 does not have 2 blue plates.   Rows 2,3,4 ⎭

c. Cupboard 1 does not have exactly 1 more blue plate than any other cupboard.

   Row 4

2. Find the number of marbles in a bag if:

   a. There are more than 50 and less than 100 marbles.

   b. If you divide the number of marbles by 8, you get a remainder of 5.

   c. If you divide the number of marbles by 9, you get a remainder of 4. 85 marbles

   Make a list that satisfies (a) and (c) [58,67,76,85,94] Eliminate using (b)

3. A man went to town one day with $12 in his pocket, but returned in the evening with $149. He bought a shirt at the clothing store and some cheese at the cheese market. Then he had his teeth checked at the dentist. Now, this man receives his paycheck every Thursday and always cashes his check at the bank which is open on Tuesday, Friday, and Saturday only. The dentist does not keep his office open on Saturday, and the cheese market is not open on Thursday and Friday. What day did the man go to town? He cashes his check at the bank on Tue., Fri., or Sat. The dentist is closed Sat. and the cheese market is closed Fri. Answer = Tuesday.

4. Ella has $1.15 made up of 6 American coins. With these coins, however, she cannot make change for a dollar, half dollar, quarter, dime or nickel. Which 6 coins does she have?

   She has 1 half dollar, 1 quarter, and 4 dimes.

1. Sue had a code where letters were used for digits. Each letter in the addition exercise stands for one of these digits: 0, 1, 4, 5. Match each letter with the correct digit.

   IS + SS = TEE   The sum of 2 two-digit numbers is < 200, so T=1
                      4+4=8, and S≠E, so S≠0 or 4, therefore S=5.
   45 + 55 = 100   Then E=0 and I=4.

2. Lester had a code too. In the addition exercise, each letter stands for one of these digits: 2, 6, 7, 8. What digit does each letter represent?

   PQ + PQ + PQ = RRS   If P=6,7,or 8, R≤2, therefore R=2
                         If Q=7, 3·Q=21, then S=1, therefore Q≠7
                         If Q=8, 3·Q=24, then S=4, therefore Q≠8
   76 + 76 + 76 = 228   So Q=6, 3·Q=18, then S=8, and P=7.

3. What am I?

   I am a three-digit number.   Since 7^3 > 200, the digits
   I am equal to the sum of the cubes of my digits. must be 1, 3, and 5
   I am between 100 and 200. $1^3 + 3^3 + 5^3$ ≠ 135
   My digits are odd numbers. $1^3 + 5^3 + 3^3 = 153$
                               The number is 153.

4. Dolores has some change in her purse. She has no silver dollars. She cannot make change for a nickel, dime, quarter, half dollar, or dollar. What is the greatest amount of money she can have?

   She has $1.19   1 half dollar, 1 quarter, 4 dimes, 4 pennies

5. A man has three hats, one red, one white, and one black. He has three coats, one red, one white, and one black.

   1. He never wears his black hat with his white coat.
   2. He never wears his white hat with his black coat.
   3. He never wears the same hat two days in a row.
   4. He never wears the same coat two days in a row.
   5. He always wears his white coat on Sunday.
   6. He always wears his white hat on Sunday.
   7. He always wears his black hat on Monday.
   8. His hat and coat match only on Sunday.

   What color hat and coat will he wear on Saturday?

   He wears a red hat and black coat.

1. In these problems, each letter represents one of the numbers 1 through 5. Determine the code word by filling in the blank above each number with the letter that represents it.

   U + N = H   H − C = L   C − U = U   H × L = H

   $\underline{\quad L \quad}$ $\underline{\quad U \quad}$ $\underline{\quad N \quad}$ $\underline{\quad C \quad}$ $\underline{\quad H \quad}$
   1   2   3   4   5

2. Four colored rings need to be arranged in order from smallest to largest.

   The yellow ring is smaller than the red ring.
   The orange ring is larger than the green ring.
   The green ring is smaller than the yellow ring.
   The red ring is three rings larger than the green ring.
   The green ring is two rings away from the orange ring.

   Find the arrangement of the rings.

   Large ⟶ Small

   Red – Orange – Yellow – Green

3. Ruth asked Alex to guess the middle initial of her name. She gave him this clue:

   You won't find the letter in the names for the numbers 1 through 999, but you will find it in the names for all the numbers 1000 through 999,999.

   What is Ruth's middle initial? The initial is A. It is in the word thousand

4.

First determine which is Tim who always tells the truth. Hikers 1 and 2 cannot be Tim, therefore he is Hiker 3. He tells the truth, so Hiker 1 is Herman and Don is in the middle.

The hiker in the middle is Tim.

I'm Don.

The hiker on the other end is Herman.

Herman   Don   Tim

Three hikers named Tim, Don, and Herman are walking along a trail. Tim always tells the truth. Don sometimes tells the truth, while Herman never does. Determine who is who and explain how you know.

1. Mary thought of a number. She multiplied the number by 4, then added 6. This result she divided by 2. Finally she subtracted 4. If her result was 59, what number was Mary thinking of?

30

2.

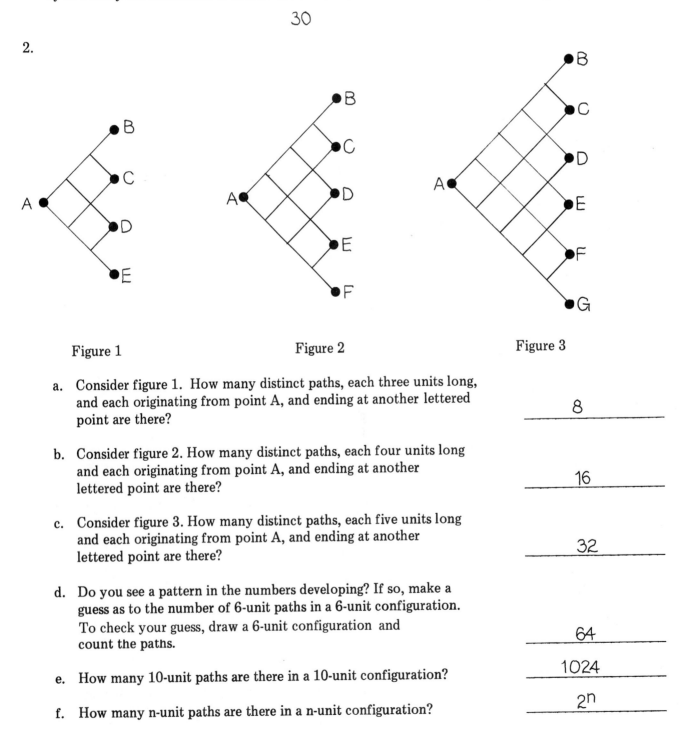

| Figure 1 | Figure 2 | Figure 3 |

a. Consider figure 1. How many distinct paths, each three units long, and each originating from point A, and ending at another lettered point are there?

8

b. Consider figure 2. How many distinct paths, each four units long and each originating from point A, and ending at another lettered point are there?

16

c. Consider figure 3. How many distinct paths, each five units long and each originating from point A, and ending at another lettered point are there?

32

d. Do you see a pattern in the numbers developing? If so, make a guess as to the number of 6-unit paths in a 6-unit configuration. To check your guess, draw a 6-unit configuration and count the paths.

64

e. How many 10-unit paths are there in a 10-unit configuration?

1024

f. How many n-unit paths are there in a n-unit configuration?

2^n

1. Two neighbors, Joe and Irma, are salespersons. They both work five days each week. Irma travels an average of 62 kilometers a day. Joe travels an average of 49 kilometers a day. After how many days will Irma have traveled 364 kilometers more than Joe?

Day	1	2	3	4	28
Irma	62	124			
Joe	49	98			
Difference	13	26	39	52	364

28 days

2. What is the sum of the numbers from 1 to 500 inclusive?

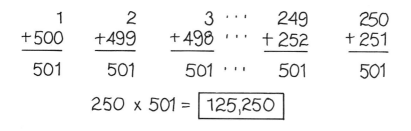

$$250 \times 501 = \boxed{125{,}250}$$

3. A mad scientist invented a machine that could duplicate any object or group of objects. The machine worked like this:

1. A special camera was used to photograph the object or objects to be duplicated.
2. The photograph was fed into the machine.
3. At the end of one hour, the machine ejected two duplicates of each object in the photograph.
4. Once an object had been photographed, the camera would not photograph it again.
5. Objects produced by the machine could be photographed and duplicated once.

After inventing the machine, the scientist decided to make a fortune by manufacturing golfballs. He bought some golfballs and began duplicating them. At the end of three hours, he had 105 golfballs. How many golfballs did he start with?

Time	Golf balls											
begin	1			2			3			7		
	Old	New	Total Time	Old	New	Total Time	Old	New	Total Time	Old	New	Total Time
1 hour	1	2	3	2	4	6	3	6	9	7	14	21
2 hours	3	4	7	6	8	14	9	12	21	21	28	49
3 hours	7	8	15	14	16	30	21	24	45	49	56	105

Total = 15 × Number at beginning

1. A lady and her daughter each bought a new outfit consisting of pants, blouse, and jacket. In each outfit, the blouse cost half as much as the pants, and the jacket cost three times as much as the blouse. If the price of each of the lady's items was twice that of her daughter's, and the daughter's pants cost $14.00:

   a. What did each of the lady's items cost?

   b. What was the total cost of each outfit?

	pants	blouse	jacket	Total
lady	$28.00	$14.00	$42.00	$84.00
daughter	$14.00	$7.00	$21.00	$42.00

2. A pirate stole a treasure chest containing gold coins. He buried ½ of them and threw ½ of the remaining coins into the sea. If he was left with 5000 gold coins, how many were in the treasure chest that he stole?

   20,000 coins

3. Ten men are fishing from a boat, five in the front, five in back, and there is one empty seat in the middle. The five in front are catching all the fish, so the five in back want to change seats. To avoid capsizing the boat, they agree to do so using the following rules:

   1. A man may move from his seat to an empty seat next to him.
   2. A man may step over only one man to an empty seat.
   3. No other moves are allowed.

   What is the MINIMUM number of moves necessary for the ten men to switch places?

   To solve this problem, experiment using chips of two different colors to represent the men and a Model like the one below to represent the seats in the boat.

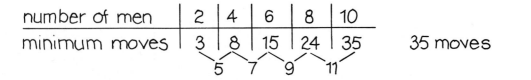

number of men	2	4	6	8	10
minimum moves	3	8	15	24	35

          5   7   9   11

35 moves

1. Three thieves, Mugs, Bugs, and Slug, robbed an armored car and stole 1321 gold bars valued at $50,000 each. They took the bars to their hideout and decided to divide them evenly the next day.

Mugs, not trusting the others, got up during the night and divided the gold bars into three equal piles. Having one left over, he buried it and took his one third. Later that night, Bugs, also not trusting the others, decided to take his one third. He also divided the remaining bars into three equal piles and had one remaining. He buried the extra bar, and took his one third. Slug, a heavy sleeper, waited until early morning and did the same thing with the remaining bars.

The next morning, the thieves divided the remaining bars and each received the same number of gold bars. How many bars did each thief get in the morning?

How many bars did each thief have altogether?

What was the total value of each man's gold?

	Bars taken at night	Bars left	Bars buried	Bars received in morning	Total	Value
Mugs	440	880	1	130	570	28,500,000
Bugs	293	586	1	130	423	21,150,000
Slug	195	390	1	130	325	16,250,000

2. This is a problem about Gauss High School and that favorite storage area, the high school locker.

At Gauss High there are 1000 students and 1000 lockers (numbered 1-1000). At the beginning of our story all the lockers are closed. The first student comes by and opens every locker. Following the first student, the second student goes along and closes every second locker. The third student changes the state (if the locker is open, he closes it; if the locker is closed, he opens it) of every third locker. The fourth student changes the state of every fourth locker, and so forth. Finally, the thousandth student changes the state of the thousandth locker.

When the last student changes the state of the last locker, which lockers are open?

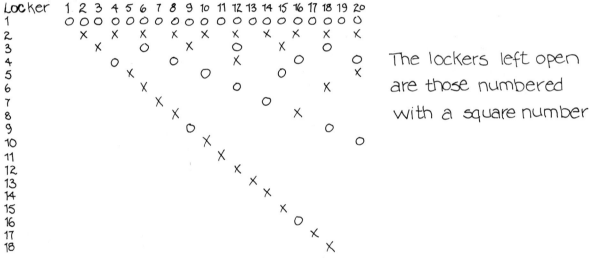

Gauss, for whom the school was named, said that this is a simple problem.

3. It takes 882 digits to number the pages of a book consecutively. How many pages are there?

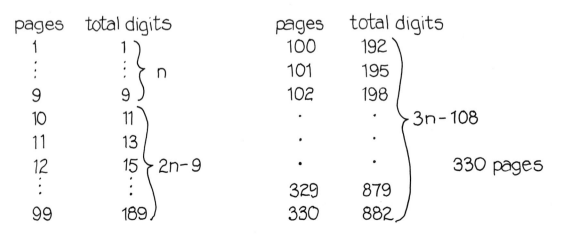

1. Travel on the commuter trains is very heavy. An empty train picked up three passengers at its first stop. At every stop thereafter, it picked up two more passengers than it had picked up at the previous stop. How many passengers got on at the fifteenth stop? If none of the passengers had gotten off, how many passengers would have been on the train after the fifteenth stop?

Stop	1	2	3	4	5	n	. . .	15
Passengers picked up	3	5	7	9	11	2n+1	. . .	31
Total	3	8	15	24	35	n(n+2)	. . .	255

2. The mathematician Augustus DeMorgan, who lived in the nineteenth century, stated that he was X years old in the year X^2. In what year was he born?

age	42	43	44
age²	1764	1849	1936
year of birth		1806	

3. Explain how single digits can be painted on the faces of two cubes so that the cubes can be placed so as to show each of the first 31 whole numbers.

   cube 1: 1, 2, 3, 4, 5, 6
   cube 2: 1, 2, 7, 8, 9, 0

4. During the softball season, the Angels won three times as many games as the Cardinals, and the Cardinals won one-fourth as many as the Beavers. If the Beavers won three more games than the Angels, which team won 12 games?

Angels	12		9	36
Beavers	16 ≠ 12 + 3		12	48 ≠ 36 + 3
Cardinals	4		3	12

The Beavers won 12 games

5. Certain types of examinations are scored by giving 2 points for every correct answer and subtracting one point for each incorrect answer. On an examination of 20 questions, Alice, Bob, Cloe, and David received scores of 31, 13, 25, and 37 respectively. How many questions did each of them answer correctly?

no. correct	19	18	17	15	11
points	38	36	34	30	22
no. wrong	1	2	3	5	9
points	1	2	3	5	9
total	37 DAVID	34	31 ALICE	25 CLOE	13 BOB

6. A rancher divided his herd of cows among his four sons. He gave one son half the herd; a second son one-fourth of the herd; a third son one-fifth of the herd; and the fourth son 48 cows. How many cows were in the herd originally?

$$1 - \left(\frac{1}{2} + \frac{1}{4} + \frac{1}{5} \right) = 1 - \frac{19}{20} = \frac{1}{20}$$

The fourth son received $\frac{1}{20}$ of the herd. Thus there were 960 cows originally.

SECTION IV

STUDENT PAGES

WORKSHEET 1—Guess the Answer

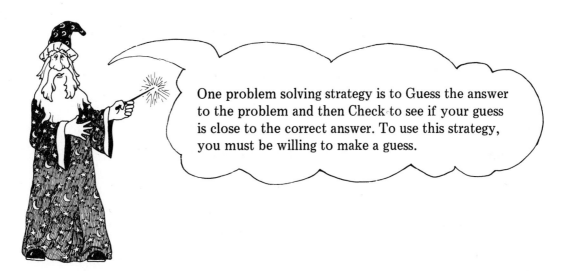

One problem solving strategy is to Guess the answer to the problem and then Check to see if your guess is close to the correct answer. To use this strategy, you must be willing to make a guess.

Write your guess for the answer to each question in the blank.

_____ 1. What is the weight of your math book?

_____ 2. How many people will visit Yellowstone National Park in an average year?

_____ 3. How long is the Golden Gate Bridge?

_____ 4. How far is it from New York to Paris?

_____ 5. How many shirts are in a gross?

_____ 6. What is the greatest speed ever recorded for a fastball thrown by a major league pitcher?

_____ 7. How much does a pickup truck weigh?

_____ 8. What is the greatest height ever recorded for a woman?

_____ 9. What is the heaviest weight ever recorded for a human being?

_____ 10. How fast can a man run 1500 meters?

_____ 11. How long is the longest river in the world?

WORKSHEET 2—*Likely or Unlikely*

Tell whether the following statements are likely or unlikely:

_____   1. The center on the high school basketball team is three meters tall.

_____   2. A ladybug is 5 millimeters long.

_____   3. A recipe for a casserole that serves four people calls for 500 grams of hamburger.

_____   4. Your math teacher weighs 150 kilograms.

_____   5. He drank 350 milliliters of lemonade in one swallow.

_____   6. It is 100° C outside.

_____   7. A tour group consisting of six young married couples is visiting the Washington Monument. The elevator to the top has a load limit of 1000 kg. It is safe for all six couples to ride the elevator at once.

> Did you have trouble with number 7? The following might help you make a good guess.

What is the weight of an adult female? _____

What is the weight of an adult male? _____

What is the weight of the 6 couples? _____

_____   8. A stack of notebook paper 50 centimeters tall contains 7000 sheets of paper.

_____   9. Bob and Steve are planning a 400-mile trip to Collegeville in Bob's car. $20.00 will pay for the gas for the trip.

_____ 10. The 16 members of the Drama Club are planning to go to the pizza parlor for pizza and soft drinks after the school play. Sixty-five dollars will be enough to pay the bill.

Having trouble? Think;

One large pizza will feed _____ people.

To feed everyone, they will need _____ large pizzas.

One large pizza costs _____ .

They will need _____ large soft drinks.

Each soft drink will cost _____ .

_____ 11. If you were to count continuously for eight hours a day, five days a week, it would take more than two weeks to count to one million.

_____ 12. A restaurant chain claims that it sells one billion hamburgers each year. If you could stack up all the hamburgers they sell in one year, the stack would reach from the earth to the moon.

WORSHEET 3—An Educated Guess

Use your knowledge of the real world and the methods you learned in Worksheet 2 to try to make a good guess.

Estimate the answer to each of the following questions.

————————————— 1. What is the length of this room?

————————————— 2. How high is the ceiling in this room?

————————————— 3. How many times does your heart beat in an hour?

————————————— 4. How many breaths do you take in a day?

————————————— 5. How heavy is a basketball?

————————————— 6. What is the length of a 10-speed bike?

————————————— 7. How long would it take an average junior high student to walk one kilometer?

————————————— 8. How many drops of water from a medicine dropper will it take to fill a one liter jar?

————————————— 9. How many egg cartons can you stack in your classroom?

————————————— 10. How far is it from your school to the state capitol building?

————————————— 11. What is the height of a stack containing 1,000,000 one-dollar bills?

WORKSHEET 4—Check Your Guess

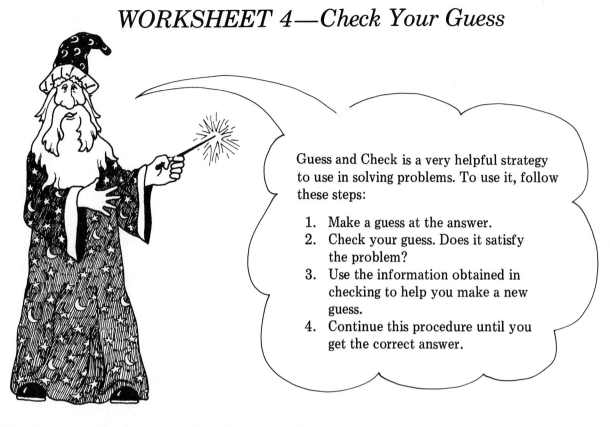

Guess and Check is a very helpful strategy to use in solving problems. To use it, follow these steps:

1. Make a guess at the answer.
2. Check your guess. Does it satisfy the problem?
3. Use the information obtained in checking to help you make a new guess.
4. Continue this procedure until you get the correct answer.

Use Guess and Check to solve the following problems.

1. "I am thinking of two whole numbers," Jose said. "When I add them the answer is 118, and when I subtract the smaller number from the larger one the result is 36. What are my numbers?"

   Guess 1: Choose any two numbers that add up to 118, like 100 and 18. Subtract the smaller from the larger.
   $100 - 18 = 82$.

   Think: 82 is too big. I must choose numbers that are closer together.

   Guess 2: Try 90 and 28

   $90 + 28 = 118$

   $90 - 28 = \underline{\qquad}$

   Think: The difference is closer to 36, but the numbers must be even closer together.

Guess 3: Try 82 and _____

82 − _____ = _____

Guess 4: _____ and _____

Think: Should the numbers be closer together or farther apart?

2. In a collection of quarters and nickels, there are two more nickels than quarters. How many quarters are there if the collection is worth $3.40?

Guess 1: Try 8 quarters, then there are 10 nickels.
8 quarters = $2.00 and 10 nickels = $.50.
Total value = $2.50.

Think: This is too small; we need more quarters.

Guess 2: Try 12 quarters, _____ nickels.

12 quarters = _____ and

_____ nickels = _____ .

Total value = _____ .

The total value should tell you whether to try more quarters or fewer quarters.

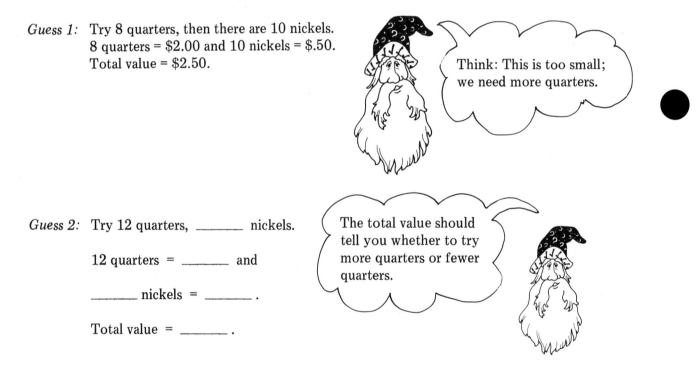

3. "I am also thinking of two whole numbers," said Matilda. "When I add them, the answer is 45, but when I multiply them the answer is 486. What are my numbers?"

4. Carmen bought some sweaters for $16 each and some blouses for $10 each. She spent $98. How many did she buy?

5. The sum of two numbers is 47, their difference is less than 10. What are *all* the possible pairs of numbers?

6. Dan's father makes furniture for a hobby. Last Christmas he made 4-legged tables and 3-legged stools as gifts for relatives. When he finished, he had used 37 legs. What are all of the possible combinations for the number of tables and stools that he made?

7. In order to encourage Sandy to do her science problems, Sandy's father promised to pay her $.25 for every problem she got right, but he would take away $.15 for every problem she missed. After working 20 problems, Sandy was paid $.20 by her father. How many of Sandy's answers were correct?

WORKSHEET 1—Complete the List

Solve the following problems by completing the list which is started for you.

To be a good problem solver, you must learn to organize your work.

1. How many three digit numbers can you make with the digits 4, 5, and 6.

    4   5   6   5   ___ ___   ___ ___ ___

    4   ___ ___   ___ ___ ___   ___ ___ ___

J & D MOTOR CO.

New Car Special

Any 3-Option Package FREE on Each New Car Purchased

Options Available
1. Factory Air
2. AM/FM Radio/Tape
3. Racing Stripes
4. Power Seats
5. Power Windows

Organize your list. Don't miss any possibilities.

2. How many different 3-Option Packages are available from J&D MOTORS?

    Air   Radio   _____   Air   _____ _____

    Air   Radio   _____   _____ _____ _____

    _____ _____ _____   _____ _____ _____

    _____ _____ _____   _____ _____ _____

WORKSHEET 2—Make the List

MEAT DISHES	VEGETABLES	SALADS	DESSERTS
Roast Beef	Corn	Fruit	Pie
Chicken	Peas	Fresh Green	Ice Cream
Lasagne			

1. The Busy Bee Cafe offers these choices on its dinner menu. If you choose one item from each category, how many days can you eat meals at the Busy Bee before you eat the same dinner a second time?*

2. After a football game, a group of students go to the Super Burger for a snack. Hamburgers cost 80¢, soft drinks are 40¢. They have $10 to spend.

   If they must buy at least 5 hamburgers and 5 drinks, how many of each can they buy? They must spend exactly $10.

   > Be sure to list all possibilities.

3. The five tags below are put in a box and drawn out three at a time. If a score is the *sum of the numbers* on the tags drawn, how many different scores are possible?

   What are they?

4. How many ways can you have coins that total exactly 37¢?

*You will need to put your answers on a separate sheet of paper.

WORKSHEET 3—Make the Table

For each situation below, make a table that shows at least six entries. Explain how you filled in the table by stating a rule for each situation:

1. A mechanic is paid $15.50 per hour.

Hours Worked	1	2				
Wages	15.50					

   Rule: Wages = $15.50 × hours worked.

2. Two ropes are tied together to form a rope 35m long.

Rope 1	15					
Rope 2	20					

   Rule: _____

3. The 80 chairs in the auditorium are arranged in rows with the same number of chairs in each row.

Rows						

   Rule: _____

4. Sam is seven years older than Maria.

Sam's Age						

   Rule: _____

5. The small wheel on a pulley goes around 3 times when the large wheel goes around 2 times.

   Rule: _____

WORKSHEET 4—Table the Situation

Complete the table and state a rule for each situation.

1. Margo's mother is 27 years older than Margo.

Margo's Age	2	7	14			30	
Margo's Mother's Age	29			39	45		58

Rule: _____

2. Each year of a dog's life is approximately equal to seven years of a human's life.

Human's Age	7				21	35	63
Dog's Age	1	4	10	15			

Rule: _____

3. The seventh and eighth grade classes sold a total of 127 tickets to the school play.

Tickets sold by 8th	70		96		80		33
Tickets sold by 7th	57	42		65		21	

Rule: _____

4. The directions on Sun Pak Orange Drink mix are: "Mix 16 g of Sun Pak Orange mix with one liter of cold water, stir, and chill."

Orange Drink Mix	16 g	8 g		48 g			160 g
Water	1 L		4 L		250 mL	100 mL	

Rule: _____

5. Amy saves 30¢ from each $1.00 she earns babysitting.

Amount earned	1.00	3.00		5.00		8.50	
Amount saved	.30		.15		2.40		3.60

Rule: _____

WORSHEET 5—Using Tables

Use the information given in the following tables to solve the problems:

1.

Bags	1	2	3	4	5	6	7	8
Cost	$.59	$1.18	$1.77	$2.36	$2.95	$3.54	$4.13	$4.72

10 bags	13 bags	cost = $17.70	24 bags
cost = _____	cost = _____	_____ bags	cost = _____

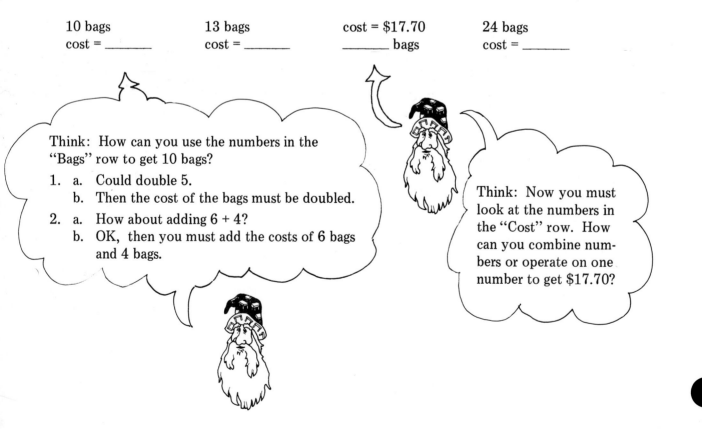

Think: How can you use the numbers in the "Bags" row to get 10 bags?

1. a. Could double 5.
    b. Then the cost of the bags must be doubled.
2. a. How about adding 6 + 4?
    b. OK, then you must add the costs of 6 bags and 4 bags.

Think: Now you must look at the numbers in the "Cost" row. How can you combine numbers or operate on one number to get $17.70?

2. Beginning salary $4.50 per hour.

Hours worked	1	2	3	4	5	6	7
Salary	4.50	9.00	13.50	18.00	22.50	27.00	31.50

TIME CARD

Name: Joan

Hours: _____
Salary:
$ 45.00

TIME CARD

Name: Eric

Hours: 20
Salary:
$ _____

TIME CARD

Name: Kevin

Hours: _____
Salary:
$ 36.00

TIME CARD

Name: Linda

Hours: _____
Salary:
$ 81.00

TIME CARD

Name: Tanya

Hours: 42
Salary:
$ _____

3. During last year's softball season Andrea got a hit 3 out of every 5 times at bat.

Hits	3	6	9		15		
Times at Bat	5	10	15	20			

Times at Bat 20; Hits _____ .

Hits 36; Times at Bat _____ .

Times at Bat 45; Hits _____ .

Hits 75; Times at Bat _____ .

4. Peppermint Sticks cost 15¢ apiece, 2 for 25¢.

P. Sticks	1		3	4	5	
Cost	15	25	40		65	

13 sticks

$ _____

20 sticks

$ _____

_____ sticks

$ 1.15

$ _____

Be sure you found the *least* cost.

5. A stamping machine in a toy factory can produce 35 toy cars each minute at a cost of 77¢. What does it cost to produce 385 toy cars? How long does it take?

Cars	35	70	140	280		
Minutes	1	2				
Cost	.77	1.54				

Combine some of the numbers in your table to obtain the 385 cars you need to solve the problem.

6. Ms. Smith's third period math class has 32 students.

Boys	5	9				
Girls			12	13		

1. If there are the same number of boys and girls, how many girls are there? _____

2. If there are six more girls than boys, how many girls are there? _____

3. If there are three times as many girls as boys, how many boys are there? _____

4. If the ratio of boys to girls is 5 to 3, how many boys are there? _____

WORKSHEET 6—Table Problems

Make a Table to solve the following. Use the Guess and Check strategy. The table should help you to organize the guessing procedure.

1. Tracy said, "When I add two whole numbers, the result is 46. If I multiply them the answer is 493. What are the two numbers?"

First Number	40	35				
Second Number	6	11	14			
Sum	46	46	46	46		
Product	240	385				

Think: Need two numbers whose sum is 46. Product is TOO SMALL. Second number should be larger.

Think: Getting closer, second number still needs to be larger. Try 14 and _____.

2. The sum of two whole numbers is 41. If you subtract the smaller from the larger, the result is 5. What are the two numbers?

Larger Number	40					
Smaller Number	1					
Sum	41	41	41	41		
Difference						

3. Gwen said, "If I multiply two numbers the result is 360. When I divide the larger by the smaller the result is 40." What are the two numbers?

4. The product of two whole numbers is 36. When the first number is added to three times the second, the answer is 31. What are the numbers?

5. On a TV game show called "The Big 24", a contestant is paid $7 for each correct answer, but must pay back $5 for each wrong answer. After answering 24 questions on the show, Sam broke even (he did not win or loose money). How many questions did he answer correctly?

6. When asked about the ages of her brothers, Carmen said, "Al is twice as old as Doug; Lance is 3 years older than Doug, and their ages add up to 35." How old is each brother?

WORKSHEET 1—What's Missing?

Look at the sequences below and fill in the blanks so that your answers complete the Pattern.

1. 1, 4, 7, 10, _____ , _____ , _____ , _____ , 25

2. 0, 5, 10, 15, _____ , _____ , _____ , _____ , 40

3. 61, 57, 53, _____ , _____ , _____ , _____ , 33

4. 1×2, 2×3, 3×4, _____ , _____ , _____ , 8×9

5. 3, 6, 12, _____ , _____ , _____ , _____ , 384

6. 1, 3, 6, 10, _____ , _____ , _____ , _____ , 45

7. 101, 99, 96, _____ , _____ , _____ , _____ , 66

8. 2, 4, 8, _____ , _____ , _____ , 256

9. 720, 360, 120, _____ , _____ , _____ , 1/7

10. 1, 4, 3, 6, 5, _____ , _____ , _____ , 9, 12

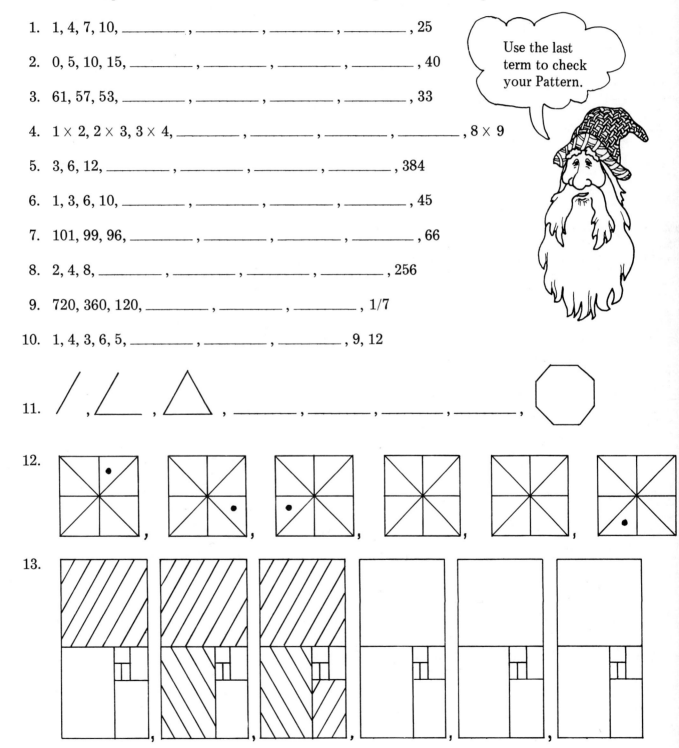

> Use the last term to check your Pattern.

WORKSHEET 2—What Comes Next?

Given the sequence 15, 21, 27, 33, · · ·

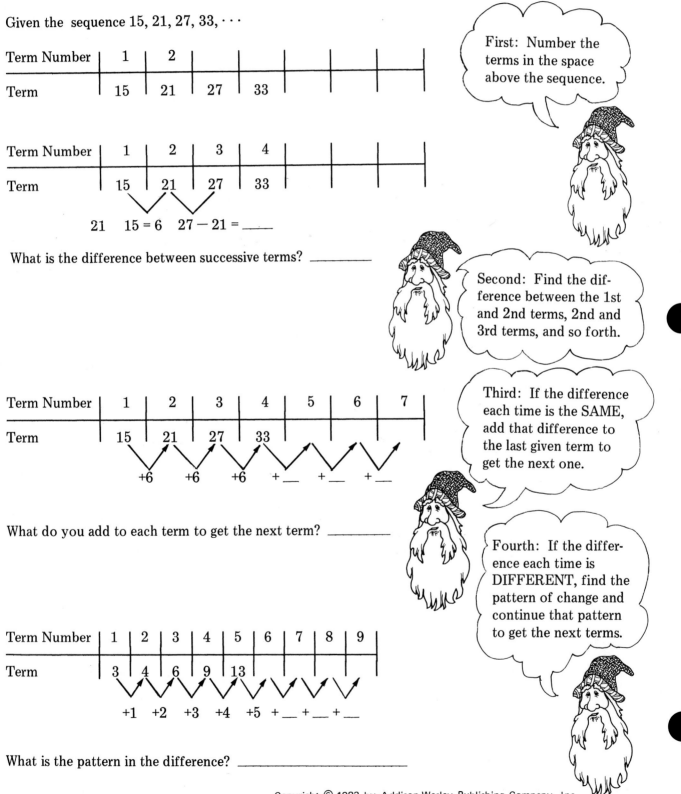

First: Number the terms in the space above the sequence.

Term Number | 1 | 2
Term | 15 | 21 | 27 | 33

Term Number | 1 | 2 | 3 | 4
Term | 15 | 21 | 27 | 33

21   15 = 6   27 – 21 = ____

What is the difference between successive terms? _____

Second: Find the difference between the 1st and 2nd terms, 2nd and 3rd terms, and so forth.

Third: If the difference each time is the SAME, add that difference to the last given term to get the next one.

Term Number | 1 | 2 | 3 | 4 | 5 | 6 | 7
Term | 15 | 21 | 27 | 33

+6   +6   +6   + __   + __   + __

What do you add to each term to get the next term? _____

Fourth: If the difference each time is DIFFERENT, find the pattern of change and continue that pattern to get the next terms.

Term Number | 1 | 2 | 3 | 4 | 5 | 6 | 7 | 8 | 9
Term | 3 | 4 | 6 | 9 | 13

+1   +2   +3   +4   +5   + __   + __   + __

What is the pattern in the difference? _____

USE these Four Steps and find WHAT COMES NEXT.

1. Term Number

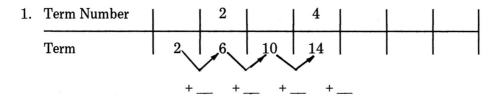

    + __ + __ + __ + __

2. Term Number

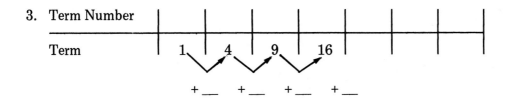

    +__ +__ +__ +__

3. Term Number

    + __ + __ + __ + __

WORKSHEET 3—Make a Sequence

Compute the first seven terms in each sequence.

EXAMPLE: Use the term number, multiply it by 5.

1st Term	2nd Term	3rd Term	4th Term	5th Term
1×5	2×5	3×5	4×5	__ × __
5	10	15		

1.   Term number times 2.

Term Number	1st	2nd	3rd	4th	5th	6th	7th
Term	2	4	___	___	___	___	___

2.   Term number times 3, minus 1.

Term number	1st	2nd	3rd	4th	5th	6th	7th
Term	2	___	___	___	___	___	___

3.   Term number times (-5), plus 55.

Term number	1st	2nd	3rd	4th	5th	6th	7th
Term	___	___	___	___	___	___	___

4.   Term number times 7, plus 2.

Term Number	1st	2nd	3rd	4th	5th	6th	7th
Term	___	___	___	___	___	___	___

5.   Term number times (-4), plus 91.

Term Number	1st	2nd	3rd	4th	5th	6th	7th
Term	___	___	___	___	___	___	___

6. Square the term number.

Term Number	1st	2nd	3rd	4th	5th	6th	7th
Term	——,	——,	——,	——,	——,	——,	——

7. Term number times the next term number.

Term Number	1st	2nd	3rd	4th	5th	6th	7th
Term	——,	——,	——,	——,	——,	——,	——

WORKSHEET 4—The Constant Difference

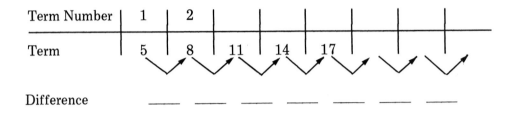

Term Number | 1 | 2

Term | 5 | 8 | 11 | 14 | 17

Difference _____ _____ _____ _____ _____ _____ _____

What is the Constant Difference? _____

Term Number		Constant Difference						What To Do?					
1	×	3	=	3	→	3	+	_____	=	5	1st Term
2	×	3	=	6	→	6	+	_____	=	8	2nd Term
3	×	_____	=	_____	→	_____	+	_____	=	11	3rd Term
4	×	_____	=	_____	→	_____	+	_____	=	_____	4th Term
.											
.											
.											
10	×	_____	=	_____	→	_____	+	_____	=	_____	10th Term
.											
.											
.											
50	×	_____	=	_____	→	_____	+	_____	=	_____	50th Term

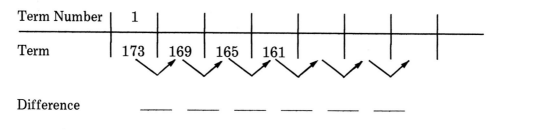

Term Number	1								
Term	173	169	165	161					

Difference _____ _____ _____ _____ _____ _____

What is the Constant Difference? _____

Term Number		Constant Difference				What To Do?					
1	×	−4	=	−4	⟶	−4	+	177	=	173	1st Term
2	×	−4	=	−8	⟶	−8	+	177	=	169	2nd Term
3	×	___	=	___	⟶	___	+	___	=	165	3rd Term
4	×	___	=	___	⟶	___	+	___	=	___	4th Term
.											
.											
10	×	___	=	___	⟶	___	+	___	=	___	10th Term
.											
.											
30	×	___	=	___	⟶	___	+	___	=	___	30th Term

WORKSHEET 5—Guess My Rule

Build a table for each sequence as shown on the previous worksheet. Answer each question for each sequence.

    a.   What are the missing numbers?
    b.   What is the 20th term?
    c.   What is the 50th term?
    d.   What is the rule you used to determine the 50th term?

1. 8, 13, 18, 23, _____ , _____ , _____ , · · ·

2. 4, 5, 6, 7, _____ , _____ , _____ , · · ·

3. 4, 9, 14, 19, _____ . _____ . _____ . · · ·

4. 5, 8, 11, 14, _____ , _____ , _____ , · · ·

5. 23, 30, 37, 44, _____ , _____ , _____ , · · ·

6. 200, 197, 194, _____ , _____ , _____ , · · ·

7. 8, 22, 36, 50, _____ , _____ , _____ , · · ·

8. 6, 10, 14, 18, _____ , _____ , _____ , · · ·

9. 383, 379, 375, 371, _____ , _____ , _____ , · · ·

10. 1, 4, 7, 10, _____ , _____ , _____ , · · ·

WORKSHEET 6—Solve with Patterns

Use your knowledge of Patterns to solve the following:

1. An empty commuter train is picking up passengers at the
    following rate. One passenger jumped on at the first stop,
    three jumped on at the second stop, five at the third stop,
    seven at the fourth, and so on. How many passengers got
    on the train at the 15th stop?

Stops	1	2	3	4		
Number of Passengers that get on the Train						

Do you see a pattern in
the problem? Let's set up
a table to help solve it.

What is the constant difference in the number of passengers? _____
Rather than carry the table to 15 stops, use the method you learned in the last lesson to find the
correct answer.

2. Now that you know how many
    passengers got on at each stop, what
    was the total number of passengers
    on the train after 10 stops? After
    15 stops?

Be sure you understand
the question—Now you
want total passengers.
How about using a table
again—but now add a
third row—Total Passengers.

Stops	1	2	3	4			
Number of Passengers that get on the Train	1	3					
Total Passengers on the Train	1	4					

3. Suppose you were offered a job and the employer said she would pay your salary as follows: one penny the first day, 2 pennies the second day, 4 pennies the third day, 8 pennies the fourth day and so on to the end of the month.

    How much would you be paid for working on the thirteenth day?

    How much money would you have earned altogether for 13 days?

4.

    a. Describe the pattern in the twentieth picture. _____

    b. How many dots are there in the twentieth picture? _____

5. The Talk-A-Lot Phone Company installs party lines with various numbers of customers. It charges $7 a month per phone. After much research on costs, it discovered that it costs $2 a month to install and service one phone on a line, $4 a month for two phones, $7 a month for three phones, and so forth. If this pattern continues, how many phones can be put on a party line before the company would lose money?

6. Harry Heartburn had the largest garden in the neighborhood. Instead of growing beets, carrots, corn, and beans (vegetables that everyone enjoys), he had a garden of exotic foods.

   Ten days after he planted, the first shoots began to appear. The kohlrabi came up first at the rate of one plant a day. The collards started a day after the first kohlrabi at a rate of two a day. The first rutabagas came up two days after the first collards at a rate of three plants a day.

   Thirty days after the first kohlrabi came up, how many total plants could be seen growing in Harry's garden?

WORKSHEET 1—Selecting a Model

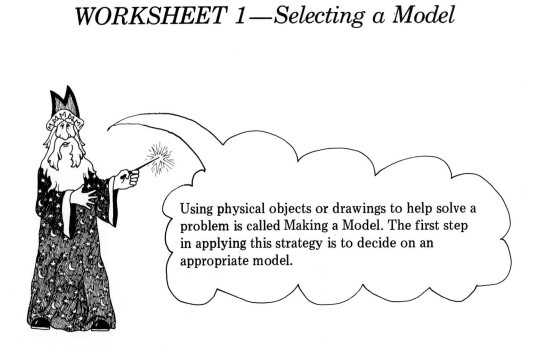

Using physical objects or drawings to help solve a problem is called Making a Model. The first step in applying this strategy is to decide on an appropriate model.

For each of the following problems:

   a. Decide whether or not a model would help you solve the problem.

   b. If you WOULD NOT use a model, give the answer to the problem and explain your solution.

   c. If you think a model would help, describe the model you would use, but DO NOT solve the problem.

1. How many different ways can three postage stamps be torn from a sheet so that all three stamps are still attached to one another?

2. A fruit punch dispenser mixes 4 mL of orange juice with 6 mL of pineapple juice. How many milliliters of orange juice does it mix with 240 mL of pineapple juice?

3. If it takes 12 minutes to cut a log into 3 pieces, how long would it take to cut the log into 4 pieces?

4. The length of a tennis court is six feet more than twice its width. If the court is 36 feet wide, what is its perimeter?

5. Cannon balls for an antique cannon are stacked next to it in four layers forming a square pyramid. How many cannon balls are there in the pyramid?

6. Find the maximum number of 3 cm × 5 cm rectangles that can be placed inside a 10 cm × 20 cm rectangle, if none of the small rectangles overlap.

7. In the spring, a bear left its cave in search of food. It walked 10 km due south, 10 km due west, and 10 km due north and arrived back at its cave. What color was the bear?

8. a. Is it possible to plant roses, mums, and asters in a single plot so that the roses are next to the asters, but the asters are not next to the mums?

   b. Is it possible to plant the flowers so that each type of flower is next to each of the other two types?

WORSHEET 2—Using a Model

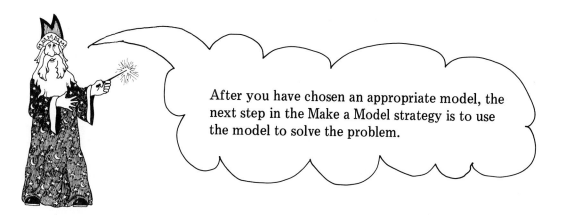

After you have chosen an appropriate model, the next step in the Make a Model strategy is to use the model to solve the problem.

Use the hints provided to solve the following problems.

1. How many different ways can three postage stamps be torn from a sheet so that all three stamps are still attached to one another?

Placing the rectangles side by side like this gives one solution.

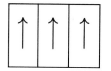

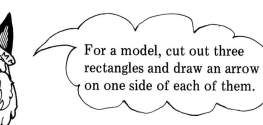

For a model, cut out three rectangles and draw an arrow on one side of each of them.

Here is one new arrangement:

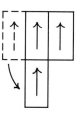

But there are others. To find them, change the model by moving one rectangle around the other two.

Continue moving this rectangle around the other two to find three other arrangements and draw them below.

Now see if you can find any new arrangements by moving two of the rectangles in the original arrangement.

2. How many different ways can four squares be arranged in a single shape so that if two squares touch they border along a full side?

What model would you use? _____

Use the procedure in problem 1 to find all the possible arrangements. Be sure to keep a record of each one!

3. Cannon balls for an antique cannon are stacked next to it in four layers to form a square pyramid. How many cannon balls are in the pyramid?

A good model for this problem would be to stack marbles (or cubes) in a square pyramid and count the number of marbles in the top four layers. If you don't have marbles, you can accomplish the same thing by making a drawing of each layer.

Layer	Drawing	Number of Cannon Balls in the Layer	Total Number of Cannon Balls
1	◯	1	1
2	(four circles)	4	5
3	_____	_____	_____
4	_____	_____	_____

Suppose that the original problem asked for the number of cannon balls in 10 layers.

Sometimes a model suggests another strategy that could be used to solve a problem more quickly.

Use *patterns* to extend the last two columns in the table and answer the question.

4. The length of a tennis court is six feet more than twice its width. If the court is 36 feet wide, what is its perimeter?

The model here is very simple. Its main purpose is to help us organize the information in the problem.

Draw a rectangle to represent the tennis court, and label the length and width using the information in the problem.

What is the perimeter?

5. Find the maximum number of 3 cm × 5 cm rectangles that can be placed inside a 10 cm × 20 cm rectangle, if none of the small rectangles overlap.

6. a. Is it possible to plant roses, mums, and asters in a single plot so that the roses are next to the asters, but the asters are not next to the mums?

    b. Is it possible to plant the flowers so that each type of flower is next to each of the other two types?

WORKSHEET 3—Solve Using Models

Use a model to solve each of the following problems.

1. How many different ways can five squares be arranged in a single shape so that if two squares touch, they border along a full side?

2. How many of the arrangements in problem 1 can be folded to form an open topped box?

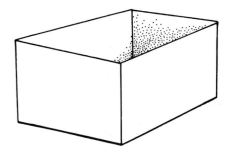

3. If it costs a nickel each time you cut and weld a link, what is the minimum cost to make a length of chain out of five separate links?

4. A little squirrel went up a tree,
   Which was forty feet and three.
   Every day she climbed up eleven;
   Every night she slid down seven.
   Tell me, if she did not drop,
   When did her paws touch the top?

5. Each of the following is a different view of the same cube. What are the two missing numbers?

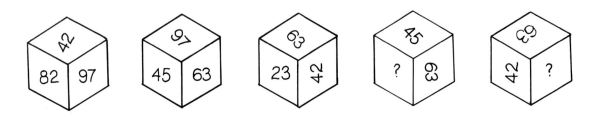

6. Have you ever heard a story about people who are lost in a forest? They often walk for hours thinking they are traveling in a straight line, and suddenly find themselves back where they started. The reason for this is simple. No one's legs are exactly the same length, so the length of a step taken with one leg is longer than the length of a step taken with the other. This difference in the lengths of the steps causes people to walk in circles.

Wierd Willie had a similar problem. While hiking in a forest one day, he became lost. He came upon a marker which indicated he was at the exact center of the forest. Now Willie knew that the forest area was a square 60 km on a side, so he decided to walk out in a straight line. But, the route he actually traveled went like this: 5 km south, then 10 km west, then 15 km north, 20 km east, 25 km south, and so on.

How far did Willie walk before he got out of the forest, and on which side of the forest did he exit?

WORKSHEET 1—*Solve by Elimination*

1. Ace Detective Shamrock Bones of the City Homicide Squad is investigating a murder at the Old Grand Hotel. Five men are being held as suspects.

    - "Giant Gene" Green. He is 250 cm tall, weighs 140 kg, and loves his dear mother so much that he has never spent a night away from home.
    - "Yoko Red." He is a 200 kg Sumo wrestler.
    - "Hi" Willie Brown. He is a small man only 130 cm tall; he hates high places because of a fear of falling.
    - "Curly" Black. His nickname is a result of his totally bald head.
    - Harvey "The Hook" White. He lost both of his hands in an accident.

    Use the following clues to help Detective Bones solve this crime.

    a. The killer was registered at the hotel.
    b. Before he died, the victim said the killer had served time in prison with him.
    c. Brown hair from the killer was found in the victim's hand.
    d. The killer escaped by diving from the third floor balcony into the river running by the hotel and then swimming away.
    e. Smudges were found on the glass table top indicating that the killer wore gloves.

2. Find the number described by the clues below. Circle the correct number.

    a. It is divisible by 4.
    b. It is larger than 8641.
    c. It is an even number.
    d. The sum of the digits is 21.
    e. It is less than 9756.

    What does this eliminate? _____

    Which clue(s) should you use first? _____

	9078			5483		
6552		8948	9984		9341	9714
	9096				3242	
	9462	8643	8832			
10341				2359		
	1874		8706	8814		

WORKSHEET 2—Bigger or Smaller Revisited

1. The object of the Bigger or Smaller game is to determine an unknown number by a series of guesses. The strategy is to eliminate certain guesses based on each response of the teacher.

    In each game below, put the guesses and the responses of the teacher in the correct order. Use the hints to help you solve the problems. *WATCH the order.*

    In these games, each guess is a *good* one. That is, if the guess is 54 and the response is SMALLER, all guesses after that will be LESS THAN 54.

Game A

Guesses   12,   19,   9,   14,   13

Guess	Teacher Response
_____	Bigger _____
_____	_____
_____	_____
_____	Bigger _____
13	Right _____

1. All guesses are good. This FIRST response tells you what guess was made.

3. There are two numbers left. Could 14 be a correct guess here? Explain.

2. You know the number is 13. This response should tell you what guess was made here.

Game B

Guesses 63, 74, 11, 72, 85, 24, 75, 47

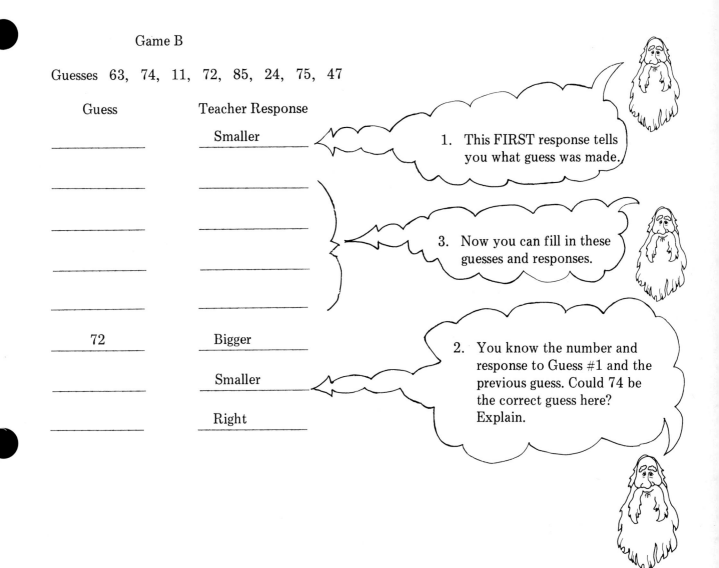

Guess	Teacher Response
_____	Smaller
_____	_____
_____	_____
_____	_____
_____	_____
72	Bigger
_____	Smaller
_____	Right

1. This FIRST response tells you what guess was made.

3. Now you can fill in these guesses and responses.

2. You know the number and response to Guess #1 and the previous guess. Could 74 be the correct guess here? Explain.

2. For the Bigger or Smaller games below, put the guesses and the teacher responses in the correct order. All guesses are *GOOD* guesses.

Game A

Guesses 35, 30, 25, 33, 50, 31

Guess	Teacher Response
_____	Smaller
_____	Bigger
_____	Smaller
_____	Bigger
_____	Smaller
_____	Right

Game B

Guesses 65, 49, 55, 35, 47, 45

Guess	Teacher Response
_____	Smaller
_____	_____
_____	Smaller
_____	_____
49	Smaller
47	Right

3. Study the clues that are given below and explain how you can tell exactly which marbles are in each box.

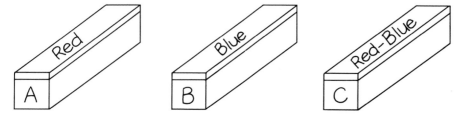

a. One box contains 2 red marbles.

b. One box contains 2 blue marbles.

c. One box contains 1 red and 1 blue marble.

d. None of the lids are on their correct box.

e. Jason reached into the box with the Red–Blue lid and pulled out a blue marble.

(1.) Since a blue marble was picked, can the other marble be red? _____

Explain. _____

_____

What is the correct lid for Box C?

(2.) Can Box B contain the Red and Blue marbles? _____

Explain. _____

_____

What are the correct lids for boxes A, B, and C?

Box	Correct Lid
A	
B	
C	

4. Three teams in the Ice-Cold Hockey League played each other at home and away. Find the win-loss record for the six games shown in the schedule below if:

   a. The Ants never defeated the Bats.

   b. The Cats never lost a home game.

   c. The Cats lost 2 games.

Game	1	2	3	4	5	6
Home Team	Ants	Cats	Bats	Ants	Bats	Cats
Visitors	Cats	Ants	Ants	Bats	Cats	Bats

Team	Ants	Bats	Cats
Won			
Lost			

5. Study the clues. Eliminate all but the correct number.

9135	5731	8361	7591	
5241	3715	5263	3175	
2537	1693	5313	3174	7621
1935	9731	9371	1469	

   a. The sum of the first and last digit is equal to the sum of the two middle digits.

   b. The four digits in the number are all different.

   c. The hundreds digit is smaller than the thousands digit and the tens digit.

   d. All of the digits are odd.

   e. The units digit is the smallest natural number.

WORKSHEET 3—Elimination Illustrated

1. Clues:

    (a) I am not even.

    (b) I am greater than 200.

    (c) I am not a square number.

    (d) I am divisible by 5.

    (e) I am less than 400.

    (f) I am divisible by 9.

    Who am I?

Which clue(s) might best be used FIRST? _____

Would it help to make a list based on these clues? Try it.

2. Linda received four stamps from England, Spain, France, and Italy for her collection. The stamps are not marked so she does not know which stamp came from each country. A fellow stamp collector gave her the following clues:

    The French stamp is red.

    The English stamp has a picture of a castle.

    The white stamp has a picture of a fountain.

    The flower is on the blue stamp.

    The Spanish stamp is not white.

    The tower is not on the green stamp.

    Use the clues and complete the table below.

Color	_____	_____	_____	_____
Picture	_____	_____	_____	_____
Country	_____	_____	_____	_____

3. Old MacDonald was on his way to market when a case of eggs fell off the back of the truck. Looking at the huge omelet on the road, a man asked how many eggs were in the case.

"When I counted by 2s, there was one left over; when I counted by 3s or 4s, there was one left over; but when I counted by 5s, there were no eggs left over," said MacDonald.

If MacDonald had less than 100 eggs in the case, what are the possible numbers of eggs he could have had?

4. Juanita, Ester, and Grace left school together. In their rush to leave, they mixed up their caps and gloves. Each one wore someone else's cap and the gloves that belonged to yet another. If Grace wore Ester's cap, determine whose cap and whose gloves each girl wore.

Name	Cap	Gloves
Grace	Ester	
Juanita		
Ester		

Can Juanita be wearing Grace's gloves?

_____ . Explain.

_____

_____

_____

WORKSHEET 4—*Constructing Solutions*

1. An archeologist digging in a ruin found a set of measuring containers used by an ancient tribe of people. There were five different jars with the names MUG, LUG, PUG, BUG, and HUG printed on them. Study of some writings which were also found indicated that the names were not on the correct jars.

   Use the following clues and place the correct name on each jar shown below.

   a. A LUG is more than a BUG.

   b. A MUG is never the least.

   c. A LUG is not the greatest.

   d. Only one thing is less than a HUG.

   e. A PUG is more than a MUG.

   f. More than one thing is greater than a MUG.

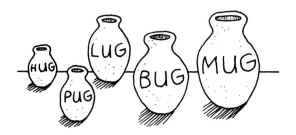

2. Lee has a collection of records. When he puts them in piles of two, he has one left over. He also has one left over when he puts them in piles of 3 or piles of 4. He has none left over when he puts them in piles of 7. What is the least number of records he can have?

3. The Lopez family, the Stein family, and the Brewster family live in 3 houses on the same side of 54th Street.

   a. The Lopez's live next to the Steins.

   b. There are no children in the middle house.

   c. The family on the right does not have the Shepherd.

   d. Kathy thinks her Poodle is the best dog a person can have.

   e. Ramona Lopez and Kathy Brewster are best friends and go to the same junior high.

   f. The Shepherd and the Poodle are not neighbors.

From the clues, determine which family lives in each house and who has which dog.

4. There was a dog show in which four places were awarded. A poodle, beagle, setter, and terrier all entered. All had collars of different colors. There were no ties. Find which dog won each place and the color of his collar.

   a. The poodle wore the red collar, not the green collar.

   b. The beagle received the place next to the dog with the purple collar.

   c. The dog with the yellow collar received first.

   d. The dog with the purple collar was second.

   e. The colors of the poodle's collar and the terrier's collar mix to form orange.

WORSHEET 1—Divide and Conquer

Sometimes a problem is too complex to solve in one step. When this happens, it is often useful to Simplify the problem by dividing it into cases and solving each one separately.

Use the hints provided to solve each of the following problems.

1. How many palindromes are there between 0 and 1000? (A *palindrome* is a number like 525 that reads the same backward or forward.)

    a.   How many of the numbers 1 through 9 are palindromes?

    Simplify the problem. Find the number of one, two, and three digit palindromes separately.

    b.   How many of the numbers 10 through 99 are palindromes?

    Make a list.

    c.   Find the number of palindromes from 100 through 999.

    | 1 | 0 | 1 | | 2 | 0 | 2 | ... |
    | 1 | 1 | 1 | | 2 | 1 | 2 | ... |
    | 1 | 2 | — | | — | — | — | |
    | 1 | — | — | | | . | | |
    | | . | | | | . | | |
    | | . | | | | . | | |
    | | . | | | | | | |

    Use the list I've started, and look for a pattern!

    d.   What is the answer to this original question?

2. If you add the digits in a number, how many numbers between 0 and 1000 have a sum of 10? (One of the numbers is 334 because 3 + 3 + 4 = 10.)

3. During a recent sale, the Sound Palace sold $2070 worth of records and tapes. They received twice as much income from the tapes as from the records. They sold 150 records—classical lps selling for $5 each and country-western lps selling for $4 each. They sold 210 tapes—disco tapes selling for $8 each and rock tapes selling for $6 each. How many classical lps did they sell? Country-western lps? Each variety of tape?

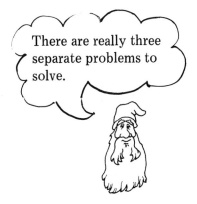

There are really three separate problems to solve.

a. First, determine how much of the $2070 was from records, and how much was from tapes.

Record Sales	500		
Tape Sales = 2 × Record Sales	1000		
Total Sales	1500		

The tape sales must be two times the record sales. Build a Table and use Guess and Check. Total sales must be $2070.

b. How many classical lps and how many country-western lps did they sell?

Number of classical	100		
Number of country-western	50		
Total	150		
Value of classical lps	500		
Value of country-western lps	200		
Total Value	700		

The number of classical lps plus the number of country-western lps is 150. Classical lps sell for $5 each, country-western lps sell for $4 each. Try a Table and use Guess and Check.

c. How many disco tapes and how many rock tapes did they sell?

Build a Table and use Guess and Check.

4. A man's age at death was 1/29th of the year of his birth. He was alive in 1900. How old was he in 1900?

There are really two problems to be solved. What do you need to know to find his age in 1900?

5. Harry is twice Becky's age now. Four years ago Becky was twice as old as Jill. However, Jill is now 1/3 Harry's age. Which one will be 13 on their next birthday?

One of the people is 12 years old now, but we don't know which one. Try three separate cases and use Elimination.

    a. Suppose Harry is 12?

        How old is Becky? _____

        How old is Jill? _____

        How old was Becky 4 years ago? _____

        How old was Jill 4 years ago? _____

        Was Becky twice as old as Jill? _____

        What does this tell you?

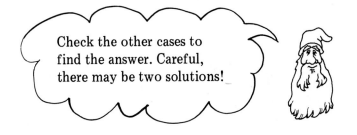

Check the other cases to find the answer. Careful, there may be two solutions!

    b.   c.

TO MARRY OR NOT TO MARRY?

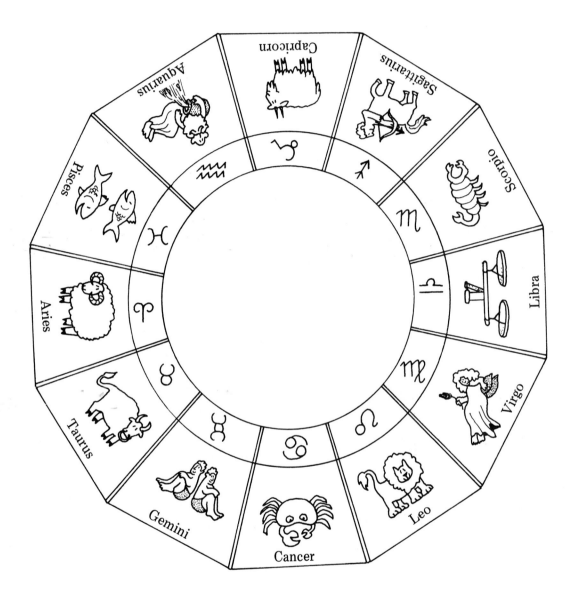

In the world of astrology, Madam Zodia considers it unwise for people born under the same sign to marry. One should also avoid marriage to persons born under a sign adjacent to one's own. Marriage between other pairs of signs are considered good.

How many pairs of signs will result in good marriages?

WORKSHEET 2—*Simplify to Solve*

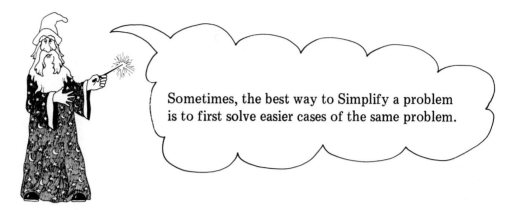

Sometimes, the best way to Simplify a problem is to first solve easier cases of the same problem.

1. Use the hints provided to solve this problem.

The nine directors of the Whacky Widget Corporation always open their annual board meetings with a special ceremony in which each director shakes hands with each of the other directors. How many hand shakes take place?

2 directors
1 handshake

2 directors,
1 handshake
The new director must shake hands with each of them. This adds 2 more handshakes. Three handshakes altogether.

4 directors
3 more handshakes

_____ total handshakes

Simplify the problem by solving it for 2 directors instead of nine.

How many handshakes are there for three directors?

Now, try solving the problem with 4 directors. Don't forget to Organize your results.

Number of Directors	Added Handshakes	Total Handshakes
2	1	1
3	1 + 2	3
4	1 + 2 + 3	_____
5	1 + 2 + 3 + 4	_____
6	_____	_____
7	_____	_____
8	_____	_____
9	_____	_____

5 directors

_____ more handshakes

_____ total handshakes

Look at the Pattern and complete the table for nine directors.

2. The Round Tuit Corporation has 15 directors. They also open their annual board meeting with the handshaking ceremony. How many handshakes take place?

Use the method explained in the preceding problems to solve the following:

3. It is traditional in many families at Christmas time for each family member to give a gift to each of the other members. If a family of ten followed this tradition, how many total gifts would be given?

4. A pie can be cut into seven pieces with three straight cuts. What is the largest number of pieces that can be made with eight straight cuts?

THE MEATY MYSTERY

Shamrock Bones and Winston were investigating a robbery at Paoli's Pastrami Factory. In one room, Winston found a strange balance scale used to weigh the meat for the pastrami. Mr. Paoli had only four masses, 1 kg, 3 kg, 9 kg and 27 kg. He stated that he could find the mass of any whole kilogram of meat between 1 and 40 kg.

Winston said it was impossible. Shamrock said it was an elementary problem, and explained it to Winston.

How did he do it?

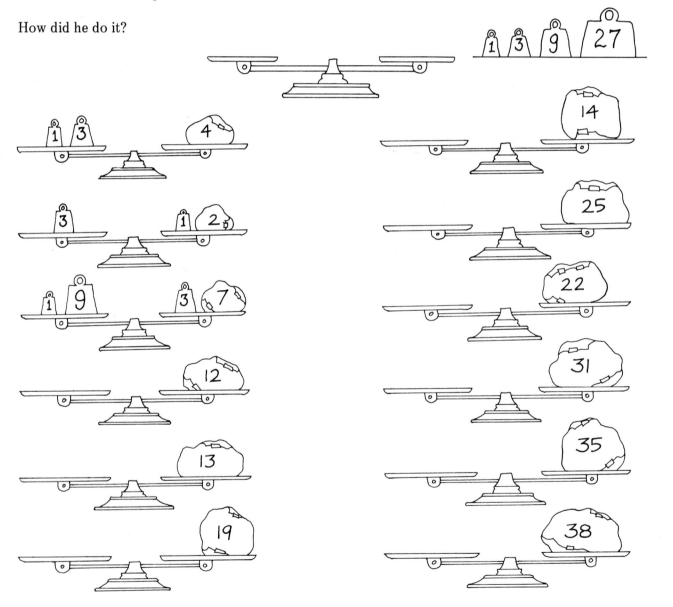

Challenge: Can you also explain to Winston how Mr. Paoli weighed the missing masses between 1 and 40?

A RIGID TASK

1. Use the materials provided to make a triangle, a quadrilateral, a pentagon, and a hexagon.

2. Which one of these do you think is the most fun to play with? _____
Why?

3. Which of the polygons cannot be changed in shape? _____

4. The triangle is called a rigid polygon because its shape cannot be changed.

   a. Can you make the quadrilateral rigid by adding supports? _____

   b. If so, what is the minimum number of supports that you need? _____

   c. Answer questions a and b for the pentagon and hexagon.

5. Complete the table below. Build more polygons if necessary.

Number of Sides in the Polygon	Minimum Number of Supports Required to Make it Rigid	Number of Triangles Formed by the Supports
3		1
4		
5		
6		
7		
8		
9		
10		
⋮		
n		

6. The fact that triangles are the only rigid polygons makes them very important. List some situations in which triangles are used because they are rigid.

TRIANGLE PROPERTIES I
THE SIDES

1. a. Use a ruler to construct three different triangles in which one side is 3 cm and another side is 4 cm.

   b. Compare your triangles with a fellow student's. What do you notice?

   c. How many different triangles could you construct given the lengths of two sides?

   _____

2. In each of the following, use a ruler and compass to construct a triangle in which the sides have the lengths indicated.

   a. 4 cm, 4 cm, 3 cm   e. 8 cm, 5 cm, 3 cm

   b. 3 cm, 5 cm, 6 cm   f. 4 cm, 4 cm, 4 cm

   c. 7 cm, 3 cm, 2 cm   g. 1 cm, 2 cm, 8 cm

   d. 3 cm, 8 cm, 7 cm   h. 6 cm, 8 cm, 6 cm

3. a. Which parts of exercise 2 did not result in a triangle? _____

   b. In these cases, what is true about the sum of the lengths of the two shorter sides?

   c. What is true about the sum of the lengths of the two shorter sides in the parts of exercise 2 that did result in a triangle?

   d. List four more sets of three lengths that CAN BE used to construct a triangle. Do not use more than one set in which all three lengths are equal.

   _____   _____   _____   _____

   e. List four sets that CANNOT be used to construct triangles.

   _____   _____   _____   _____

4. One way to classify triangles is by the number of congruent sides in the triangle.

   a. How many congruent sides do each of the following triangles have? Measure each side if necessary.

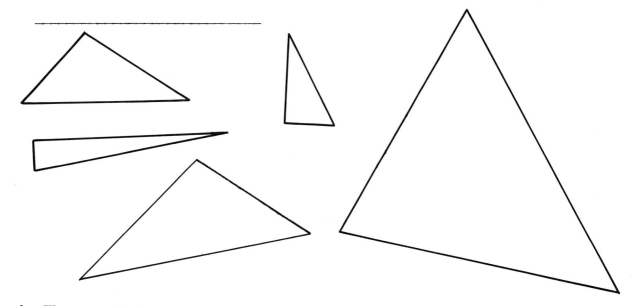

   b. These are called *scalene triangles.* How many congruent sides does a scalene triangle have?

   _____

5. An *isosceles triangle* has at least two congruent sides.

   a. Construct two isosceles triangles.

   b. Which of the triangles in exercise 2 were isosceles? _____

6. a. A third type of triangle is called an *equilateral triangle.* How many congruent sides do you think it has? _____

   b. Construct an equilateral triangle.

   c. Which of the triangles in exercise 2 were equilateral? _____

7. Are all equilateral triangles isosceles? _____

   Explain. _____

   _____

TRIANGLE PROPERTIES II
THE ANGLES

1. In each of the following, use a ruler and protractor to construct a triangle which contains a pair of angles with the indicated measures. Record your results in the table.

   a. 30°, 40°

   b. 80°, 80°

   c. 60°, 60°

   d. 55°, 35°

   e. 130°, 80°

   f. 120°, 50°

   g. 128°, 70°

   h. 95°, 90°

Problem	Sum of the Given Angles	Is a Triangle Possible?	If Yes, What is the Measure of the Third Angle?
a.			
b.			
c.			
d.			
e.			
f.			
g.			
h.			

2. a. List four more pairs of angles that CAN BE used to construct a triangle.

   _____ _____ _____ _____

   b. List four pairs of angles that CANNOT be used to construct a triangle.

   _____ _____ _____ _____

   c. What can you conclude about the sum of the measures of the angles of a triangle?

3. a. Use a ruler and a protractor to construct two more triangles in which one angle is 30° and another is 40° as in exercise 1a.

   b. Compare your triangles with a fellow student's. What do you notice?

4. Triangles can be classified by the types of angles they contain.

   a. An *obtuse triangle* is a triangle that contains one angle that is greater than 90° but less than 180°. Construct an obtuse triangle.

   b. Would it be possible to have a triangle with two obtuse angles? If yes, construct one. If no, explain why.

   c. Which of the triangles that you constructed in exercise 1 were obtuse triangles? _____

5. a. All of these triangles have the same special property. What is it? _____

   _____

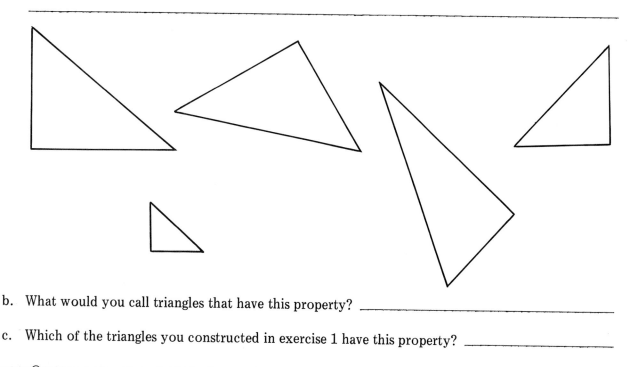

   b. What would you call triangles that have this property? _____

   c. Which of the triangles you constructed in exercise 1 have this property? _____

6. a. What do each of the following triangles have in common? If necessary, measure each angle in each triangle.

b. Why would triangles with this property be called *acute triangles*?

c. Which of the triangles you constructed in exercise 1 are acute triangles? _____

KINDS OF TRIANGLES

1. In the preceding activities, you learned that triangles can be classified in two ways:

    a. By the number of congruent sides:
        (1) A *scalene triangle* has no congruent sides.
        (2) An *isosceles triangle* has at least two congruent sides.
        (3) An *equilateral triangle* has three congruent sides.

    b. By the type of angles:
        (1) An *obtuse triangle* has one obtuse angle.
        (2) A *right triangle* has one right angle.
        (3) An *acute triangle* has three acute angles.

It is also possible for a triangle to be classified by the number of congruent sides and the types of angles at the same time. For example, this is a right-scalene triangle. Why?

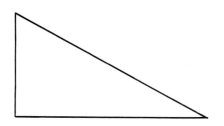

2. Each of the following combinations is possible. Construct one example of each type.

    a. Right-scalene   b. Right-isosceles

c.   Obtuse-scalene

d. Obtuse-isosceles

e. Acute-scalene

f. Acute-isosceles

g. Acute-equilateral

3. There are two combinations such as those above, that are impossible. Can you name them?

_____   _____

4. Why are these two types impossible? _____

_____

A SQUARE EXPERIMENT

Use square chips and form all of the rectangular arrays possible with each different number of chips. Record your results in the table below.

Example: Number of Chips   Arrays

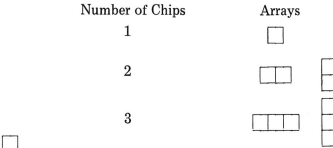

Note: is not a rectangular array.

TABLE 1

Number of Chips	Dimensions of Rectangular Arrays	Total Number of Arrays
1	1 × 1	1
2	1 × 2, 2 × 1	2
3	1 × 3, _____	
4		
5		
6		
7		
8		
9		
10		
11		
12		

1. Use the results from Table 1 to complete Table 2.

TABLE 2
Number of Squares that Produced

A	B	C	D
Only One Array	Only Two Arrays	More Than Two Arrays	An Odd Number of Arrays
—			

2. Suppose that you had 15 chips:

   a. How many rectangular arrays could be made? _____

   b. In which column in Table 2 would you place 15? _____

   c. What are the factors of 15? _____

3. a. What are the factors of 16? _____

   b. How many rectangular arrays can you make with 16 chips? _____

   c. In which column of Table 2 would you place 16? _____

4. Look at the data in Table 1 and Table 2. How is the number of rectangular arrays related to the number of factors of any given number? _____

   _____

5. a. Why is it that the numbers in column D have an odd number of arrays? _____

   _____

   b. What are the next two numbers that you would place in column D? _____

6. What is the mathematical name for the list of numbers in

    a. Column B? _____

    b. Column C? _____

    c. Column D? _____

7. Which numbers can be placed in two lists? _____

_____

8. Can any numbers be placed in three lists? _____

    If so, which ones? _____

THE POOL FACTOR

While investigating a jewelery robbery at the Parrington mansion, Detective Shamrock Bones became distracted from the case while looking for clues in the Billiard Room. He found several tables of various sizes, each having four pockets and a square grid on it as shown below.

On the wall he found this sign.

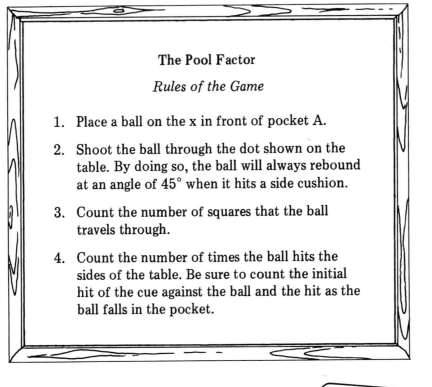

The Pool Factor

Rules of the Game

1. Place a ball on the x in front of pocket A.

2. Shoot the ball through the dot shown on the table. By doing so, the ball will always rebound at an angle of 45° when it hits a side cushion.

3. Count the number of squares that the ball travels through.

4. Count the number of times the ball hits the sides of the table. Be sure to count the initial hit of the cue against the ball and the hit as the ball falls in the pocket.

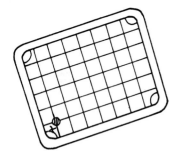
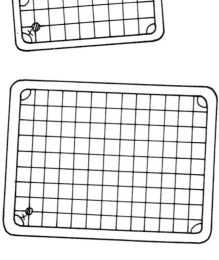
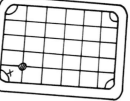

Bones became so interested in the pool table game that he forgot about the robbery case. See if you can help him solve The POOL FACTOR. Use graph paper to construct models of pool tables with the measurements given in the table. If necessary, extend the table by drawing additional pool tables with other measurements until you discover a pattern that you can use to determine the Number of Hits and Number of Squares when given any measurements for the base and altitude.

Example:

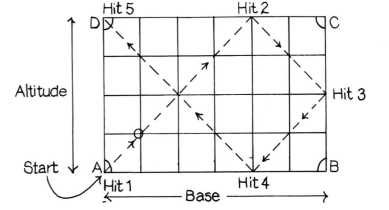

Base	Altitude	Number of Hits	Number of Squares
6	4	5	12
3	5		
5	4		
3	2		
8	4		

SQUARE FRACTIONS

Follow the folding and cutting directions carefully. If scissors are not used, make a sharp crease in the paper, and tear along the crease. Answer each question as you proceed through the activity.

1. Fold the square on the diagonal and cut along the fold:

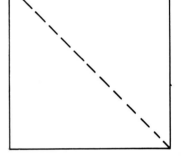

   a. What are the resulting polygons?

   _____   _____

   b. How are the two polygons realted?

   _____

   c. Each polygon is what fraction of the original square? _____

2. Select one of the triangles and fold it so that two congruent polygons result. Cut along the fold and label the polygons 1 and 2 as shown.

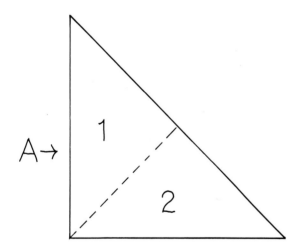

   Note: The large triangle will be referred to later as triangle A.

   a. What are the resulting polygons?

   _____   _____

   b. How are the two polygons related? _____

   c. Triangle 1 is what fraction of triangle A? _____

   d. Triangle 1 is what fraction of the original square? _____

Copyright © 1983 by Addison-Wesley Publishing Company, Inc.

3. Locate the midpoint of the longest side of the remaining large triangle. Fold the vertex of the right angle to the midpoint of the longest side and cut along the fold. Mark the triangle 3.

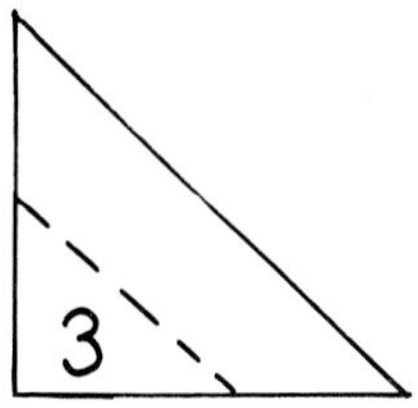

a. What are the resulting polygons?

_____   _____

b. How is triangle 3 related to:

   1. triangle 1? _____   2. triangle A? _____

c. Triangle 3 is what fractional part of:

   1. triangle 1? _____   2. triangle A? _____

   3. the original square? _____   4. the isosceles trapezoid? _____

4. Using the isosceles trapezoid, fold one of the vertices of the long side to the midpoint and cut along the fold. Mark the triangle 4.

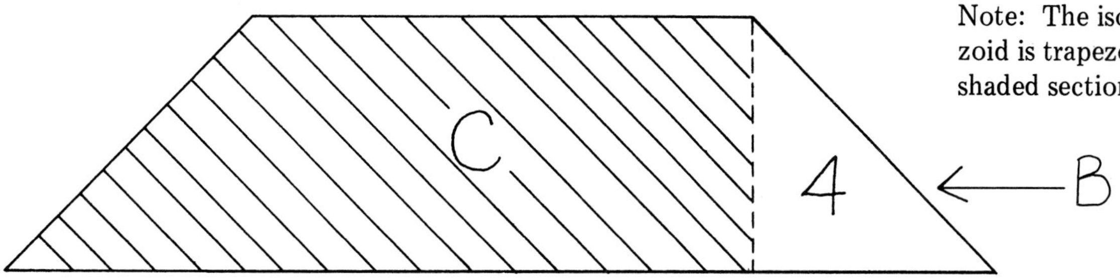

Note: The isosceles trapezoid is trapezoid B. The shaded section is C.

a. What are the resulting polygons?

_____   _____

b. How is triangle 4 related to:

   1. triangle 3? _____   2. triangle 1? _____

   3. triangle A? _____

c. Triangle 4 is what fraction of:

1. triangle 3? _____   2. triangle 1? _____

3. triangle A? _____   4. trapezoid C? _____

5. trapezoid B? _____   6. the original square? _____

5. Using trapezoid C match the endpoints of the shortest of the parallel sides and fold. Cut along the fold and mark 5 as shown.

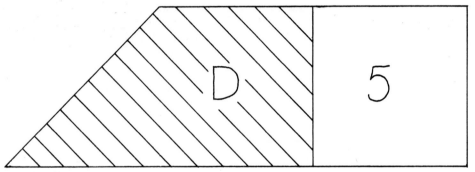

Note: The large trapezoid is trapezoid C. The shaded section is D.

a. What are the resulting polygons?

_____   _____

b. Square 5 is what fractional part of:

1. trapezoid C? _____   2. trapezoid D? _____

3. triangle 3? _____   4. trapezoid B? _____

5. triangle 4? _____   6. triangle 1? _____

7. triangle A? _____   8. the original square? _____

c. C is what fraction of:

1. trapezoid D? _____   2. square 5? _____

3. the original square? _____

6. Using the trapezoid that is left, fold as shown, matching opposite corners. Cut along the fold and mark 6 and 7 as shown.

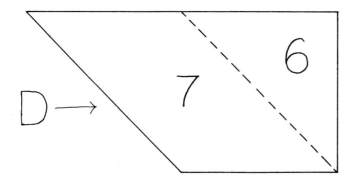

Note: The trapezoid shown here is trapezoid D.

a. What are the resulting polygons?

_____   _____

b. How is triangle 6 related to:

   1. triangle 4? _____   2. triangle 3? _____

   3. triangle A? _____

c. Triangle 6 is what fraction of:

   1. trapezoid D? _____   2. trapezoid C? _____

   3. parallelogram 7? _____   4. triangle 3? _____

   5. triangle 1? _____   6. square 5? _____

   7. trapezoid B? _____   8. traingle A? _____

   9. the original square? _____

7. Parallelogram 7 is what fraction of:

   a. trapezoid D? _____

   b. triangle 3? _____

   c. trapezoid C? _____

   d. trapezoid B? _____

   e. triangle 4? _____

   f. square 5? _____

   g. triangle 1? _____

   h. triangle A? _____

   i. the original square? _____

PATTERNS OF REPEATING DECIMALS

In order to change a fraction to a decimal, divide the numerator by the denominator. To correctly write a repeating decimal:

1. Put a bar over those digits that repeat.
2. Write only those digits necessary to show the repeating pattern.

Example:
.428428428 · · · should be written .$\overline{428}$.
.1676767 · · · should be written .1$\overline{67}$.

Use your calculator to change the following fractions to decimals. Look for patterns in the digits of the decimals, you may find a way to write the answer without doing the division.

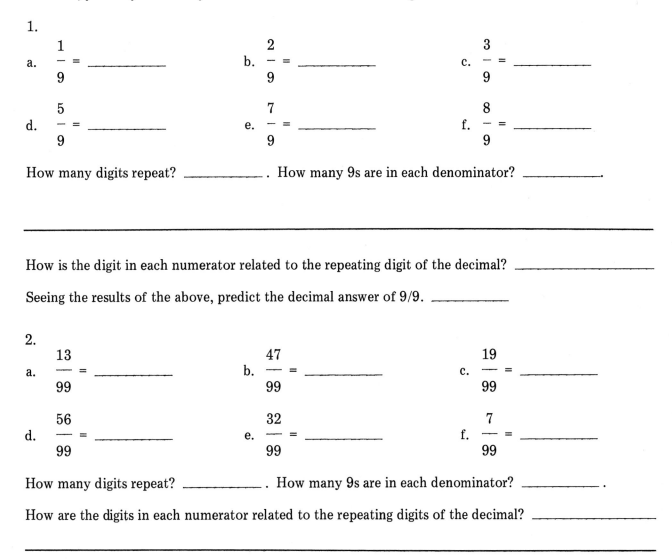

1.

a. $\dfrac{1}{9}$ = _____   b. $\dfrac{2}{9}$ = _____   c. $\dfrac{3}{9}$ = _____

d. $\dfrac{5}{9}$ = _____   e. $\dfrac{7}{9}$ = _____   f. $\dfrac{8}{9}$ = _____

How many digits repeat? _____ . How many 9s are in each denominator? _____ .

How is the digit in each numerator related to the repeating digit of the decimal? _____

Seeing the results of the above, predict the decimal answer of 9/9. _____

2.

a. $\dfrac{13}{99}$ = _____   b. $\dfrac{47}{99}$ = _____   c. $\dfrac{19}{99}$ = _____

d. $\dfrac{56}{99}$ = _____   e. $\dfrac{32}{99}$ = _____   f. $\dfrac{7}{99}$ = _____

How many digits repeat? _____ . How many 9s are in each denominator? _____ .

How are the digits in each numerator related to the repeating digits of the decimal? _____

3.

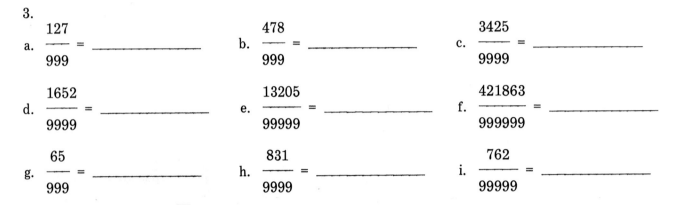

a. $\dfrac{127}{999}$ = _____

b. $\dfrac{478}{999}$ = _____

c. $\dfrac{3425}{9999}$ = _____

d. $\dfrac{1652}{9999}$ = _____

e. $\dfrac{13205}{99999}$ = _____

f. $\dfrac{421863}{999999}$ = _____

g. $\dfrac{65}{999}$ = _____

h. $\dfrac{831}{9999}$ = _____

i. $\dfrac{762}{99999}$ = _____

How does the number of 9s in each denominator relate to the number of repeating digits in the decimal?

How do the digits in each numerator relate to the repeating digits in the decimal?

Having observed the pattern of repeating digits in each of the decimals, state a general rule which describes the decimal equivalent of a fraction whose denominator contains only 9s.

EQUIVALENT RATIOS

1. Circle the pairs in which the two given ratios are equal.

a. $\frac{1}{2}$ and $\frac{3}{6}$ b. $\frac{2}{4}$ and $\frac{1}{3}$ c. $\frac{2}{3}$ and $\frac{4}{5}$ d. $\frac{2}{3}$ and $\frac{5}{6}$

e. $\frac{3}{4}$ and $\frac{30}{40}$ f. $\frac{2}{5}$ and $\frac{3}{4}$ g. $\frac{4}{5}$ and $\frac{8}{10}$ h. $\frac{1}{3}$ and $\frac{9}{10}$

i. $\frac{3}{4}$ and $\frac{6}{8}$ j. $\frac{5}{6}$ and $\frac{10}{12}$ k. $\frac{1}{2}$ and $\frac{5}{10}$ l. $\frac{4}{6}$ and $\frac{2}{5}$

2. For each pair of ratios in exercise 1, find the pairs of products as shown in this example:

$$\frac{2}{3} \quad \text{and} \quad \frac{6}{9}$$

$$2 \times 9 = 18 \qquad 3 \times 6 = 18$$

a. $\frac{1}{2}$ and $\frac{3}{6}$

$1 \times 6 =$ _____ $2 \times 3 =$ _____

b. $\frac{2}{4}$ and $\frac{1}{3}$

$2 \times 3 =$ _____ $4 \times 1 =$ _____

c. $\frac{2}{3}$ and $\frac{4}{5}$

$2 \times 5 =$ _____ $3 \times 4 =$ _____

d. $\frac{2}{3}$ and $\frac{5}{6}$

___ $\times 6 =$ _____ $3 \times$ ___ $=$ _____

e. $\frac{3}{4}$ and $\frac{30}{40}$

___ $\times$ ___ $=$ ___

f. $\frac{2}{5}$ and $\frac{3}{4}$

___ $\times$ ___ $=$ ___

g. $\dfrac{4}{5}$ and $\dfrac{8}{10}$ h. $\dfrac{1}{3}$ and $\dfrac{9}{10}$

i. $\dfrac{3}{4}$ and $\dfrac{6}{8}$ j. $\dfrac{5}{6}$ and $\dfrac{10}{12}$

k. $\dfrac{1}{2}$ and $\dfrac{5}{10}$ l. $\dfrac{4}{6}$ and $\dfrac{2}{5}$

3. What did you notice about the products in the problems which have equal ratios?

In the problems which do not have equal ratios?

4. Use this method to find which of the following pairs of ratios are equal.

a. $\dfrac{6}{3}$ and $\dfrac{16}{9}$ b. $\dfrac{5}{7}$ and $\dfrac{7}{9}$ c. $\dfrac{9}{6}$ and $\dfrac{6}{4}$

5. How would you use this method to help find the missing number in each of the following equations?

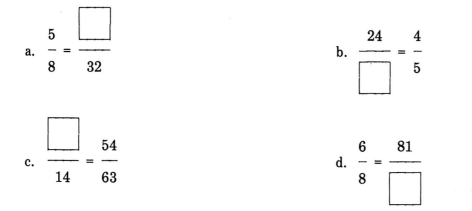

a. $\dfrac{5}{8} = \dfrac{\square}{32}$

b. $\dfrac{24}{\square} = \dfrac{4}{5}$

c. $\dfrac{\square}{14} = \dfrac{54}{63}$

d. $\dfrac{6}{8} = \dfrac{81}{\square}$

REGULAR POLYGONS IN A ROW

Fill in each blank with the correct answer. Draw a Model for the figures not given and construct a Table so that you will be able to determine a Pattern.

1. 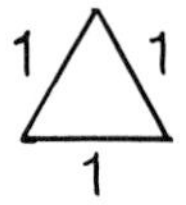
1
1
1
Perimeter = 3

2. 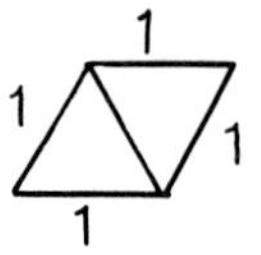
1
1
1
1
Perimeter = ________

3. 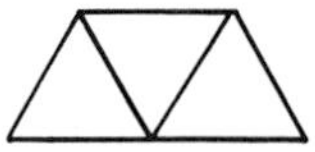
Perimeter = ________

4. 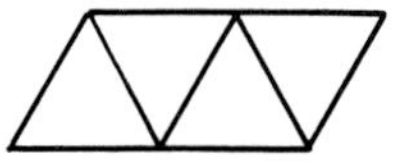
Perimeter = ________

5. What is the perimeter of 5 Δs placed end to end as shown above? ________ 12 Δs? ________

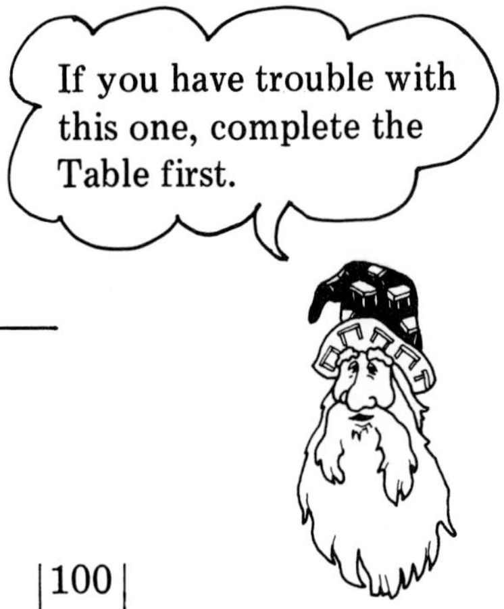
If you have trouble with this one, complete the Table first.

6. How many triangles would have a perimeter of 19? ________________

Perimeter of 37? ________

7. Complete the following table

Number of Δs	1	2	3	4	5	9	13			28		100
Perimeter								19	23		35	

8. How would you find the perimeter given any number (k) of triangles?

9. 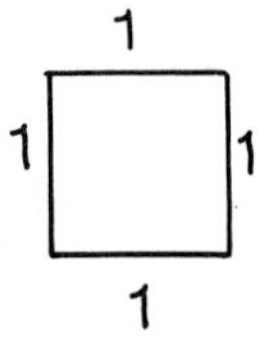
1
1
1
1
Perimeter = 4

10. 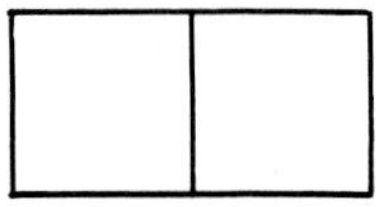
Perimeter = ________

11. 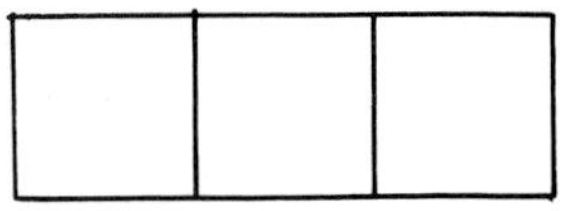
Perimeter = ________

12. What is the perimeter of 4 □s? ________ 5 □s? ________

13. Complete the following table to help you answer the questions below.

Number of □s	1	2	3						100
Perimeter									

14. What is the perimeter of 11 □s? _____ 19 □s? _____

15. How many squares would have a perimeter of 26? _____ Perimeter of 40? _____

16. How would you find the perimeter given any number (k) of squares?

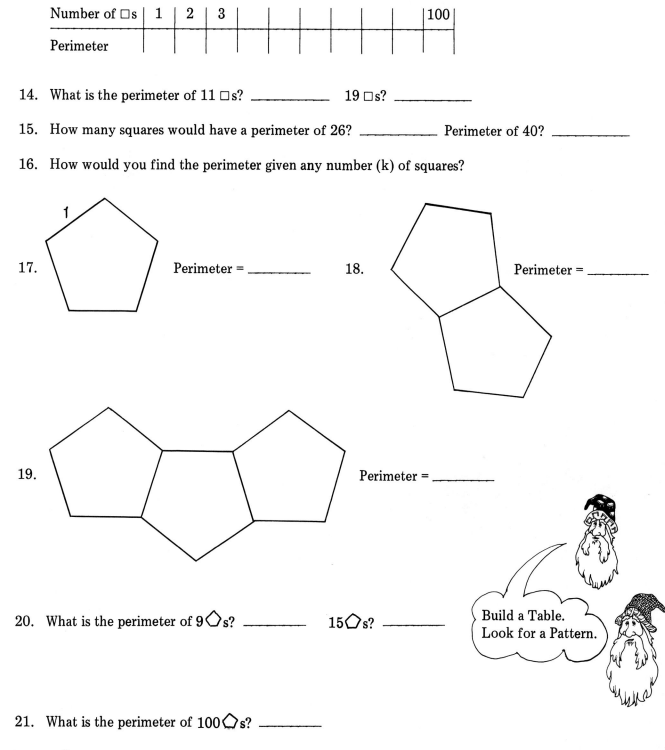

17. Perimeter = _____   18. Perimeter = _____

19. Perimeter = _____

20. What is the perimeter of 9 ⬠s? _____ 15 ⬠s? _____

Build a Table.
Look for a Pattern.

21. What is the perimeter of 100 ⬠s? _____

290 (161)

22. How would you find the perimeter given any number (k) of pentagons?

23. Now that you have developed a method for determining the perimeter of some regular polygons placed end to end, use the above procedure to find the following:

a. The perimeter given any number (k) of hexagons? (6 sides)

b. The perimeter given any number (k) of heptagons? (7 sides)

c. The perimeter given any number (k) of octagons? (8 sides)

24. Complete the table below with the rule you developed to determine the perimeters given any number (k) of polygons placed end to end.

Regular Polygons	Number of Sides in Each Polygon	Rule
Triangles	3	k + 2
Squares	4	
Pentagons		
Hexagons		
Heptagons		
Octagons		
⋮		
n(gon)	n	

FROM TRIANGLES TO POLYGONS

Study the example and complete the table.

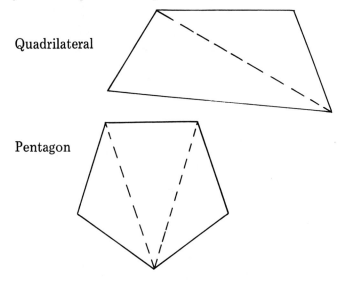

Quadrilateral

4 sides
1 diagonal from a vertex
2 triangles

Pentagon

5 sides
2 diagonals from a vertex

_____ triangles

Polygon	Number of Sides	Number of Diagonals from One Vertex	Number of Triangles Formed by the Diagonals From One Vertex	Sum of the Interior Angles of the Polygon
Triangle	3	0	1	180
Quadrilateral	4	1	2	360
Pentagon	5	2		
Heptagon				
Nonagon				
Dodecagon				
N gon	n			

PENTOMINOES

Cut out each of the figures.

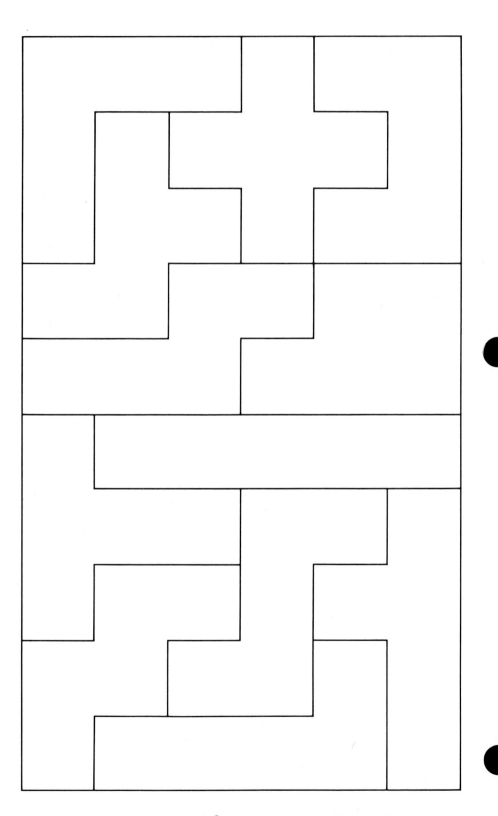

PENTOMINOES AND RECTANGLES

Study the example and complete the table. Look for rectangles with different dimensions in each case. Sketch your solutions on graph paper.

Number of Pentominoes

Record of Solution

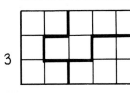

3

5

Dimensions 3 × 5

Area   15

Perimeter 16

_____

Number of Pentominoes	Can You Make a Rectangle?	Dimensions	Area	Perimeter
1	Yes			
2				
3	Yes	3 × 5	15	16
4	Yes	2 × 10, 4 × 5		
5				
6				
7				
8				
9				
10				
11				
12				

PENTOMINO TRIPLICATION

1. a. Fill in figure A with one pentomino piece.
   b. Fill in figure B with nine of the remaining pieces.

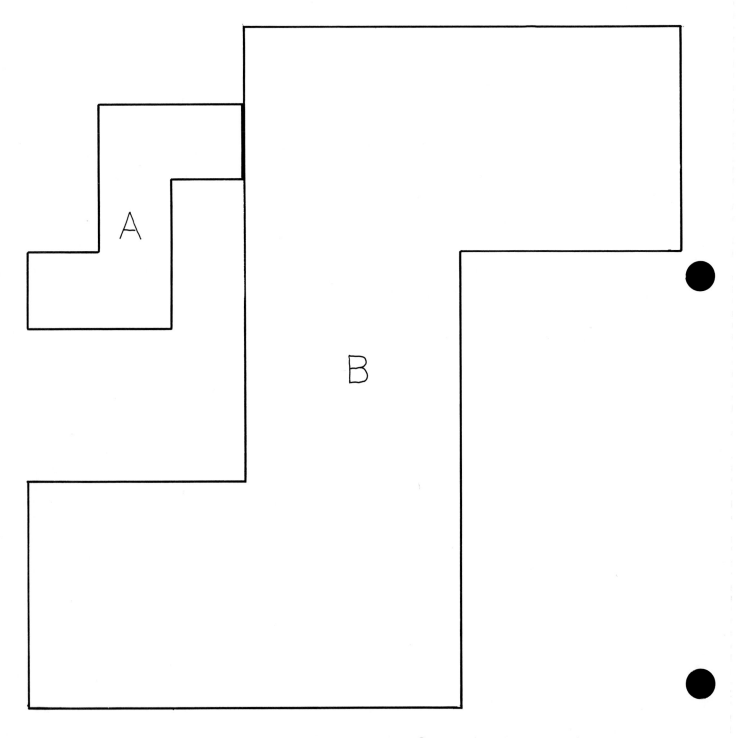

2. a. Select any pentomino.
    b. As in exercise 1, use nine of the remaining pentominoes to make an enlargement of the pentomino you selected. Record your solution on graph paper.

3. a. How does the area of the enlargement compare with the area of the single pentomino?

    b. How do the dimensions of the enlargement compare with the dimensions of the single pentomino?

4. Which pentominoes can you enlarge in this fashion?

PENTOMINO COVER UP
GAME BOARD I

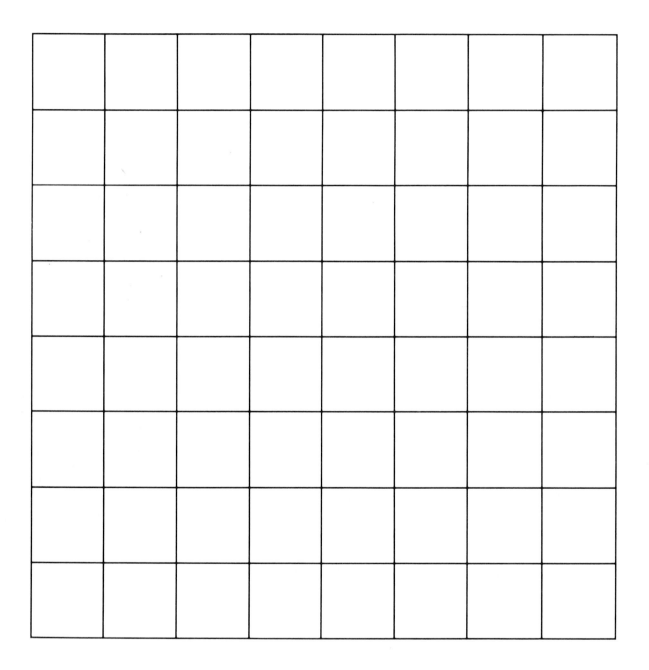

PENTOMINO COVER UP
GAME BOARD II

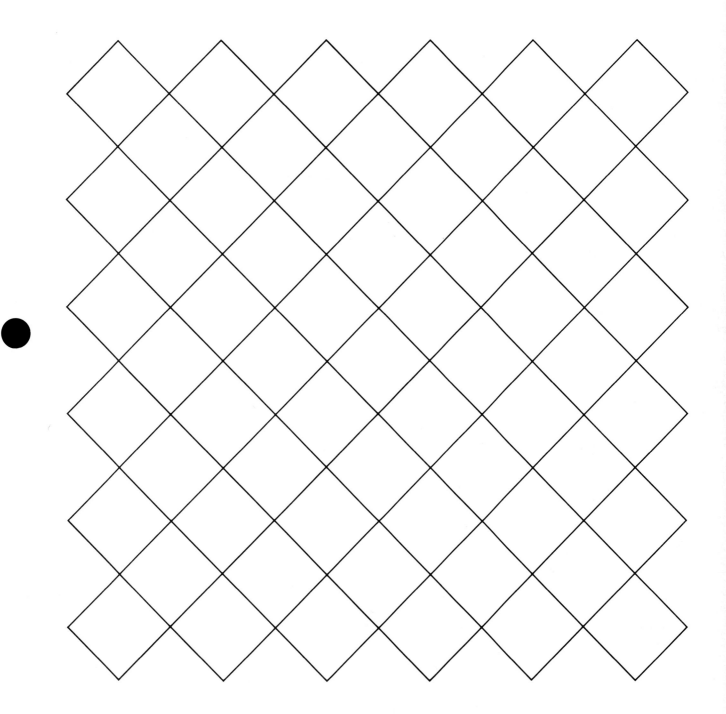

INTEGER PATTERNS

1. Complete the list of problems by looking for patterns.

2. Use the completed list to help answer the following questions.

   When is the sum of a positive number and a negative number

   a. positive?

   b. zero?

   c. negative?

   d. Write a rule for adding a positive and a negative number.

$$5 + 5 = 10$$

$$5 + 4 = 9$$

$$5 + 3 = 8$$

$$5 + 2 = 7$$

$$5 + 1 = \underline{\hspace{1cm}}$$

$$5 + 0 = \underline{\hspace{1cm}}$$

$$5 + \underline{\hspace{1cm}} = \underline{\hspace{1cm}}$$

$$5 + \underline{\hspace{1cm}} = \underline{\hspace{1cm}}$$

$$5 + \underline{\hspace{1cm}} = \underline{\hspace{1cm}}$$

$$5 + \underline{\hspace{1cm}} = \underline{\hspace{1cm}}$$

$$\underline{\hspace{1cm}} + \underline{\hspace{1cm}} = \underline{\hspace{1cm}}$$

$$\underline{\hspace{1cm}} + \underline{\hspace{1cm}} = \underline{\hspace{1cm}}$$

$$\underline{\hspace{1cm}} + \underline{\hspace{1cm}} = \underline{\hspace{1cm}}$$

$$\underline{\hspace{1cm}} + \underline{\hspace{1cm}} = \underline{\hspace{1cm}}$$

$$\underline{\hspace{1cm}} + \underline{\hspace{1cm}} = \underline{\hspace{1cm}}$$

$$\underline{\hspace{1cm}} + \underline{\hspace{1cm}} = \underline{\hspace{1cm}}$$

3. Use your results from exercise 2 to find these sums.

   a. $10 + {}^-5 = \underline{\hspace{1cm}}$ b. $6 + {}^-5 = \underline{\hspace{1cm}}$ c. $4 + {}^-5 = \underline{\hspace{1cm}}$ d. $1 + {}^-5 = \underline{\hspace{1cm}}$

4. Addition is a commutative operation. That is, a + b = b + a for all numbers a and b. Use the commutative property of addition and your answers in exercise 3 to find the following sums.

   a. $^-5 + 10 = 10 + {}^-5 = \underline{\hspace{1cm}}$ b. $^-5 + 6 = \underline{\hspace{1cm}} = \underline{\hspace{1cm}}$

   c. $^-5 + 4 = \underline{\hspace{1cm}} = \underline{\hspace{1cm}}$ d. $^-5 + 1 = \underline{\hspace{1cm}} = \underline{\hspace{1cm}}$

5. Use the results of exercise 2 and the commutative property to complete the problems in this list.

$$-5 + 10 = \underline{\hspace{1cm}}$$
$$-5 + 9 = \underline{\hspace{1cm}}$$
$$-5 + 8 = \underline{\hspace{1cm}}$$
$$-5 + 7 = \underline{\hspace{1cm}}$$
$$-5 + 6 = \underline{\hspace{1cm}}$$
$$-5 + 5 = \underline{\hspace{1cm}}$$
$$-5 + 4 = \underline{\hspace{1cm}}$$
$$-5 + 3 = \underline{\hspace{1cm}}$$
$$-5 + 2 = \underline{\hspace{1cm}}$$
$$-5 + 1 = \underline{\hspace{1cm}}$$

6. Write the next five problems in the list by looking for patterns in the numbers.

$$\underline{\hspace{1cm}} + \underline{\hspace{1cm}} = \underline{\hspace{1cm}}$$
$$\underline{\hspace{1cm}} + \underline{\hspace{1cm}} = \underline{\hspace{1cm}}$$
$$\underline{\hspace{1cm}} + \underline{\hspace{1cm}} = \underline{\hspace{1cm}}$$
$$\underline{\hspace{1cm}} + \underline{\hspace{1cm}} = \underline{\hspace{1cm}}$$
$$\underline{\hspace{1cm}} + \underline{\hspace{1cm}} = \underline{\hspace{1cm}}$$

Is the sum of the two negative numbers positive or negative? _____

Write a rule for adding two negative numbers.

7. Use your results from exercises 2 and 6 to find these sums:

a. $18 + -6 = \underline{\hspace{1cm}}$ b. $-6 + -8 = \underline{\hspace{1cm}}$

c. $-11 + 7 = \underline{\hspace{1cm}}$ d. $-6 + 18 = \underline{\hspace{1cm}}$

e. $12 + -15 = \underline{\hspace{1cm}}$ f. $-11 + -13 = \underline{\hspace{1cm}}$

1. Place the numbers 1, 2, 3, 4, 5, 6 in the circles in such a way that each side of the triangle adds up to 10, 11, 12.

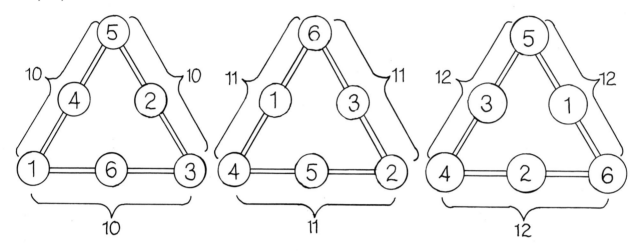

2. A math book is lying open on a desk. To what pages is it opened if the product of the facing pages is 8556?

3. The difference between two numbers is 75. If the larger number is divided by the smaller number, the quotient is 6 and the remainder is 5. What are the two numbers?

4. Gina and Tom raise cats and birds. They counted all the heads and got 10. They counted all the feet and got 34. How many birds and cats do they have?

5. Adult tickets to the Boya 1 Theater cost $2.00 more than student tickets. The total receipts from 100 students and 200 adults were $850.00. What was the cost of the student ticket?

1. The mile relay team of Central High consists of four runners; Speedy, Flash, Dasher, and Stumbles. Each runner runs one-quarter of a mile in the order listed. As they race, each member runs his quarter mile two seconds faster than the previous runner. If they run the mile in 3 minutes and 40 seconds, what is the time for each runner's lap?

2. The difference between two numbers is 37, their sum is 215. What are the numbers?

3. A farmer went to market and sold 62 chickens. He sold the hens for $1.50 each and the roosters for $0.75 each; his total receipts were $61.50. How many hens and roosters did he sell?

4. Three girls received a quarter each to spend for candy. The candy store contained lollipops at 3 for a nickel, licorice sticks at 4 for a nickel, and cinnamon bears at one cent each. Each girl ended up with a different selection of candy, but each spent her entire quarter. Each girl received exactly 20 pieces of candy. What were their selections?

1. Roofing nails sell for $0.60 per pound.

Pounds of Nails	1	2	5					
Cost	0.60	1.20		3.60	0.30			

   a. What is the cost of 11 pounds? _____ .

   b. If you have only $0.30, how many pounds of nails can you buy? _____ .

   c. How many pounds can you buy for $12.00? _____ .

   d. If you have $0.75, how many pounds can you buy? _____ .

2. With five minutes left to play in the championship game between the Cougars and the Huskies, the Cougars were leading by 16 points. In the last five minutes, the Cougars scored 6 points per minute and the Huskies scored 9 points per minute. Who won the game and by how much?

3. A drippy water faucet will fill a 100 ml cup in 10 minutes. Make a table and answer the following:

Time	10 min	20 min	5 min		1 hr		
Water Wasted	100 ml	200 ml					

   a. How much water is wasted in 1 day? _____ .

   b. How long does it take to waste 10 liters of water? _____ .

   c. How much water is wasted in one week? _____ .

   d. How long does it take to waste 1 kiloliter of water? _____ .

4. George has $3.71 in pennies, nickels, dimes, and quarters in his pocket. He has twice as many dimes as nickels, two more nickels than quarters, and three fewer pennies than three times the number of nickels. How many of each kind of coin does he have?

1. The stockholders receive an 8% dividend.

Stock Value	$100	$200	$50	$300		$700		
Dividend	$8	$16			$40			

   a. If you own $500 in stock, what is your dividend? _____ .

   b. If you own $750 in stock, what is your dividend? _____ .

   c. You receive a $72 dividend, what is the value of your stock? _____ .

2. Terry has five objects, all having a different weight from 1 through 5 kg. If she weighs them three at a time, what is the largest possible number of different weights she can have?

3. A cashier found that he was often asked to give change for a dollar to people who had made no purchases but wanted 20 cents for a telephone call. He started thinking one day about the number of ways he could make change. If he gave no more than four of any coin, in how many different ways could he give change for a dollar to people who wanted to make a telephone call?

4. While attending "The Great Mandini" magic show, Brett was asked to come on stage to be part of the program. When asked how much change he had, Brett said he had 55¢ in dimes and nickels. Mandini said he would change all the nickels to dimes and the dimes to nickels. After the change was made, Brett counted his money and had 65¢. How many nickels and dimes did Brett have before he went on stage?

1. Two clocks show the correct time to be one o'clock. One clock is running properly; the other is also running at the correct rate, but backwards. When is the next time that both clocks will show the same time?

2. Colleen is going to buy a new car. The local dealer has cars with exterior colors of black, white, and turquoise.

   The same colors are available for the interiors, however, the interior color is always the same as, or lighter than the exterior color.

   Pin stripes are found only on cars with a black exterior.

   How many styles are available?

3.

SPECIAL!!!

Assorted Greeting Cards

15¢ each

$1.50 — Box of 12 Cards

Cards	1	5	10	12			
Boxes	0	0	0	1	2		
Cost	$0.15	$0.75		$1.50			

   a. What is the cost of 3 boxes? _____

   b. What is the least cost for 30 cards? _____

   c. Which costs more — 12 cards or 11 cards? _____

   d. Eileen spent $7.20 for cards. What is the greatest number of cards she could buy? _____

4. Joan buys 3 skirts, 4 blouses, and 3 sweaters. She intends to wear them in various combinations. The blue skirt doesn't go with the green sweater, but otherwise any combination of the three garments is attractive. How many different combinations can Joan make that include a skirt, a blouse, and a sweater?

1. Two planes leave Denver at the same time from adjoining runways; one flies west to San Francisco, the other east to Baltimore. The westbound plane travels at 400 km/hr, and the other at 450 km/hr. When will the planes be 3825 km apart?

2. Number 1 apples sell for $5.00 a bushel and number 2 apples sell for $4.00 a bushel. If the value of a crop of 100 bushels is $460.00, how many bushels are number 1 apples and how many bushels are number 2 apples?

3. If 3 people can complete 1/2 of a job in 20 days, how long would it take 12 people to do the complete job?

4. Three boxes labeled A, B, and C all contain a number of beans. The sum of the number of beans in A and B is 385. The difference between the numbers of beans in B and C is 65. The sum of the numbers of beans in A and C is 320. The difference between the numbers of beans in A and C is 70. Use this information to determine how many beans are in each box.

1. Joe Gardener is a greenhouse operator. Each spring, he plants cucumbers, peppers, and tomatoes. He plants 50 rows, each row containing 100 plants according to the following scheme:

1st Row — 100 cucumber plants

2nd Row — 98 cucumber plants, 2 pepper plants

3rd Row — 96 cucumber plants, 3 pepper plants, 1 tomato plant

4th Row — 94 cucumber plants, 4 pepper plants, 2 tomato plants

5th Row — 92 cucumber plants, 5 pepper plants, 3 tomato plants

6th Row — _____ cucumber plants, _____ pepper plants, _____ tomato plants

7th Row — _____ cucumber plants, _____ pepper plants, _____ tomato plants

8th Row — _____ cucumber plants, _____ pepper plants, _____ tomato plants

How many of each type of plant are in the:

a. 10th Row? _____

b. 15th Row? _____

c. 28th Row? _____

d. 50th Row? _____

2. At 3:20 p.m., a jeweler set three antique clocks to the correct time. The next afternoon at 3:20, she found that one clock was correct, one was 2 minutes slow and one was 2 minutes fast. At those rates, how long will it take before all three clocks show 3:20 again?

PERIMETER PATTERNS 1

Stack rectangles end to end only.

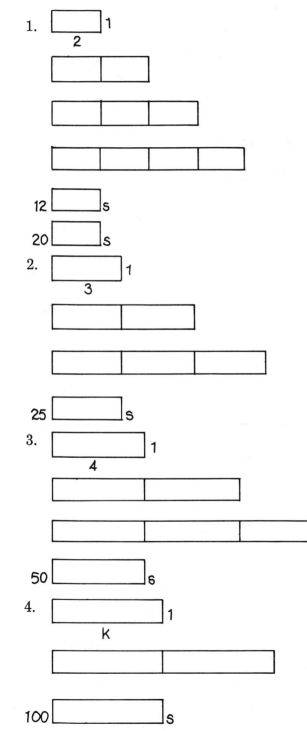

1.

perimeter = _____

perimeter = _____

perimeter = _____

perimeter = _____

perimeter = _____

perimeter = _____

2.

perimeter = _____

perimeter = _____

perimeter = _____

perimeter = _____

3.

perimeter = _____

perimeter = _____

perimeter = _____

perimeter = _____

4.

perimeter = _____

perimeter = _____

perimeter = _____

PERIMETER PATTERNS 2

Stack rectangles end to end only.

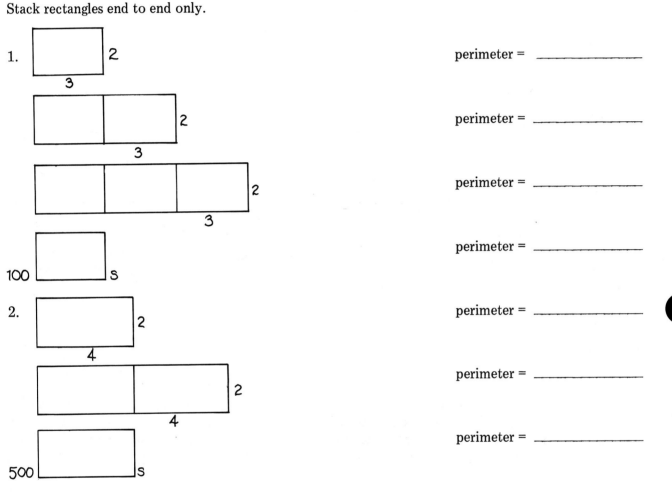

1.

perimeter = _____

perimeter = _____

perimeter = _____

perimeter = _____

2.

perimeter = _____

perimeter = _____

perimeter = _____

3. Can you write a rule that could be used to find the perimeter of each of the following for any number (n) of rectangles?

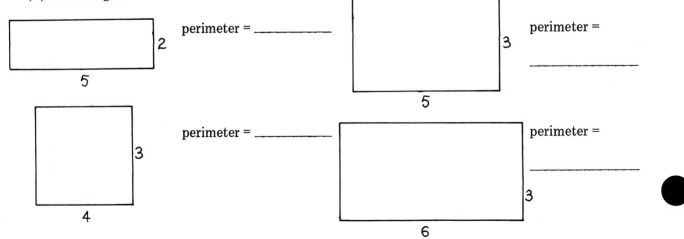

perimeter = _____

perimeter = _____

perimeter = _____

perimeter = _____

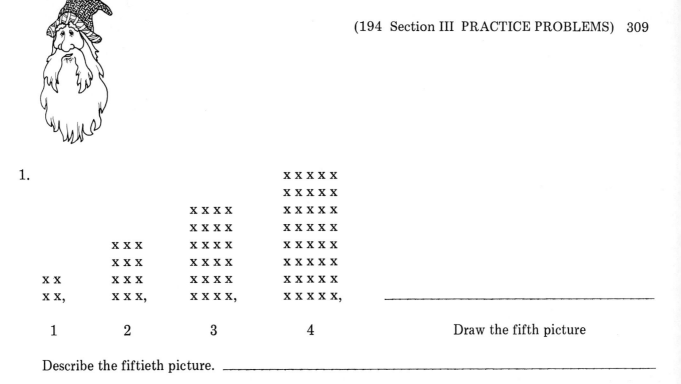

1.

			x x x x x
			x x x x x
		x x x x	x x x x x
		x x x x	x x x x x
	x x x	x x x x	x x x x x
	x x x	x x x x	x x x x x
x x	x x x	x x x x	x x x x x
x x,	x x x,	x x x x,	x x x x x,

1	2	3	4	_____

Draw the fifth picture

Describe the fiftieth picture. _____

2. A raft on the Yellowstone Boat Float can hold 270 liters of water before sinking. During the float last year, Randy hit a rock and the raft began to leak. It gained 10 liters of water the first kilometer, 15 liters the second kilometer, 20 liters the third, and so on. How far could it travel before sinking?

3. Good news travels fast. For instance, Jan Smith received a new car from her parents. Being excited, she immediately told two friends who, ten minutes later, each repeated the news to two other friends. Ten minutes later, these four friends each told two others. If the news continues to spread in this fashion, how many friends know about Jan's new car after 80 minutes?

4. One afternoon, the Royal Duck Squadron was resting on the Palace lawn. The Head Quack dismissed them to the Royal Pond in the following manner. At 1:00 p.m. one duck was dismissed. Every 10 minutes after, two times the number that had already left were dismissed. If there were 243 ducks, and it took ten minutes to get to the Pond, at what time were all the ducks in the Pond?

1. Which number between 1 and 150 when multiplied times itself results in a product which is closest to 300?

2. Joe charges $3.50 to mow a lawn. His expenses for gas and repairs average $0.60 per lawn.

Lawns Mowed	1	2	3	4	5		
Income	3.50	7.00	10.50	14.00	17.50		
Expenses	.60	1.20	1.80	2.40	3.00		

Income is $21; Lawns mowed _____

Lawns mowed _____17_____ ; Expenses _____

Expenses _____$7.80_____ ; Income _____

Income $35; Expenses _____ ; Lawns Mowed _____

3. Given the sequence 10, 17, 24, 31, _____ , _____ , _____ , _____ , · · ·

   a. Fill in the blanks.
   b. What is the 20th term?
   c. What rule can you use to find the 100th term?
   d. What is the 100th term?

4. John has saved $48 to buy some 8-track tapes. The Record Rack is having a sale. He can buy $8.95 tapes for $6 and $6.95 tapes for $4. In how many different ways can he spend all his money?

5. At 6:30 A.M. the first two people arrived at the Super Bowl ticket office to purchase tickets for the game. Every 25 minutes after that, three more than the number of people already present arrived to get in line. How many people were in line at 9:00 A.M. when the office opened?

1. Six blocks are used in a staircase that has 3 steps. Can you make a staircase with 36 blocks? If so, show an example, and tell how many steps it has.

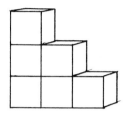

2. Six colored pin wheels are to be arranged in a circle. There are two red, two yellow, and two blue wheels. Wheels of the same color are placed opposite each other on the circle. One wheel of each color is spinning clockwise and one counterclockwise. Adjacent wheels always spin opposite directions. If the red wheels are vertical, how many possible ways can the colored spinning wheels be placed around the circle?

3. A person mows a lawn which is a square 10 meters on a side in 20 minutes. How long will it take that person working at the same rate to mow a lawn which is a square 5 m on a side?

4. How many boxes 5 cm by 8 cm by 2 cm can you put in a box that is 20 cm by 32 cm by 16 cm?

1. Mrs. Brussel wants to plant corn, carrots, cabbage, and cucumbers.

   a. Show how she can plant the vegetables so cabbage is next to corn and carrots, and corn is next to cabbage and cucumbers.

   b. Show how she can plant the vegetables so each type is next to each of the other three types.

   c. Mr. Sprout wants to plant peas, peppers, potatoes, parsnips and pumpkins. Can he plant the vegetables so each type is next to each of the other four types?

2. A family of four wants to cross a river. Their raft can hold at most 100 kilograms. The father weighs 85 kg, the mother weighs 54 kg, the son weighs 45 kg, and the daughter weighs 40 kg. How can they cross the river? Explain your answer.

3. Five termites are eating through an old oak log.

   Enie is 20 millimeters ahead of Meanie.

   Meanie is twice as far as Miney.

   Miney is 60 millimeters behind Moe.

   Joe is a daring 15 millimeters behind Meanie.

   If Enie has munched 54 millimeters, how far has each of the others munched? Who's the fastest muncher in the oak? Explain your answer.

4. The area of a rectangular room is 279 square meters. Its perimeter is 67 meters. What are the dimensions of the room?

1. A building has 6 stories, each the same height. It takes 10 seconds for the freight elevator to get from the first floor to the third floor. How long does it take for the elevator to go from the first to the sixth floor—20 seconds, 25 seconds, 30 seconds?

2. Two frogs have a race. One frog makes a jump of 80 cm once every 5 seconds. The other frog makes a jump of 15 cm every 1 second. The rules of the race state that the frogs must cross a line 5 m away and then come back to the starting point. Which frog wins the race?

3. Two candles of equal length are lit at the same time. One candle takes 6 hours to burn out and the other 3 hours. After how much time will the slower burning candle be exactly twice as long as the faster burning one?

4. The Grundy Carpet Mart made a bid on carpeting the stairway in a split-level home. The upper level is four feet above the lower level. Each step is 5 feet long, 2 feet wide, and 6 inches above the one below.

   Only the top of each step will be carpeted.

   The roll of carpet chosen comes in a 12-foot width.

   What is the smallest length of carpet which can be bought to cover the steps so that each step is covered by a solid piece of carpet.

1.

	Cupboard 1	Cupboard 2	Cupboard 3
Row 1	B W W	B W W	B B W
Row 2	B W W	B B W	B W W
Row 3	B B W	B W W	B W W
Row 4	B B W	B B W	W W W
Row 5	B B W	W W W	B B W
Row 6	W W W	B B W	B B W

The table above shows six different ways that four blue plates and five white plates can be placed in three cupboards. Tell which row in the table meets all three of the following conditions.

a. Cupboard 1 has exactly 2 blue plates.

b. Cupboard 3 does not have 2 blue plates.

c. Cupboard 1 does not have exactly 1 more blue plate than any other cupboard.

2. Find the number of marbles in a bag if:

a. There are more than 50 and less than 100 marbles.

b. If you divide the number of marbles by 8, you get a remainder of 5.

c. If you divide the number of marbles by 9, you get a remainder of 4.

3. A man went to town one day with $12 in his pocket, but returned in the evening with $149. He bought a shirt at the clothing store and some cheese at the cheese market. Then he had his teeth checked at the dentist. Now, this man receives his paycheck every Thursday and always cashes his check at the bank which is open on Tuesday, Friday, and Saturday only. The dentist does not keep his office open on Saturday, and the cheese market is not open on Thursday and Friday. What day did the man go to town?

4. Ella has $1.15 made up of 6 American coins. With these coins, however, she cannot make change for a dollar, half dollar, quarter, dime or nickel. Which 6 coins does she have?

1. Sue had a code where letters were used for digits. Each letter in the addition exercise stands for one of these digits: 0, 1, 4, 5. Match each letter with the correct digit.

   IS + SS = TEE

2. Lester had a code too. In the addition exercise, each letter stands for one of these digits: 2, 6, 7, 8. What digit does each letter represent?

   PQ + PQ + PQ = RRS

3. What am I?

   I am a three-digit number.
   I am equal to the sum of the cubes of my digits.
   I am between 100 and 200.
   My digits are odd numbers.

4. Dolores has some change in her purse. She has no silver dollars. She cannot make change for a nickel, dime, quarter, half dollar, or dollar. What is the greatest amount of money she can have?

5. A man has three hats, one red, one white, and one black. He has three coats, one red, one white, and one black.

   1. He never wears his black hat with his white coat.
   2. He never wears his white hat with his black coat.
   3. He never wears the same hat two days in a row.
   4. He never wears the same coat two days in a row.
   5. He always wears his white coat on Sunday.
   6. He always wears his white hat on Sunday.
   7. He always wears his black hat on Monday.
   8. His hat and coat match only on Sunday.

   What color hat and coat will he wear on Saturday?

1. In these problems, each letter represents one of the numbers 1 through 5. Determine the code word by filling in the blank above each number with the letter that represents it.

   U + N = H   H − C = L   C − U = U   H × L = H

   _____   _____   _____   _____   _____
       1   2   3   4   5

2. Four colored rings need to be arranged in order from smallest to largest.

   The yellow ring is smaller than the red ring.
   The orange ring is larger than the green ring.
   The green ring is smaller than the yellow ring.
   The red ring is three rings larger than the green ring.
   The green ring is two rings away from the orange ring.

   Find the arrangement of the rings.

3. Ruth asked Alex to guess the middle initial of her name. She gave him this clue:

   You won't find the letter in the names for the numbers 1 through 999, but you will find it in the names for all the numbers 1000 through 999,999.

   What is Ruth's middle initial?

4.

   Three hikers named Tim, Don, and Herman are walking along a trail. Tim always tells the truth. Don sometimes tells the truth, while Herman never does. Determine who is who and explain how you know.

1. Mary thought of a number. She multiplied the number by 4, then added 6. This result she divided by 2. Finally she subtracted 4. If her result was 59, what number was Mary thinking of?

2.

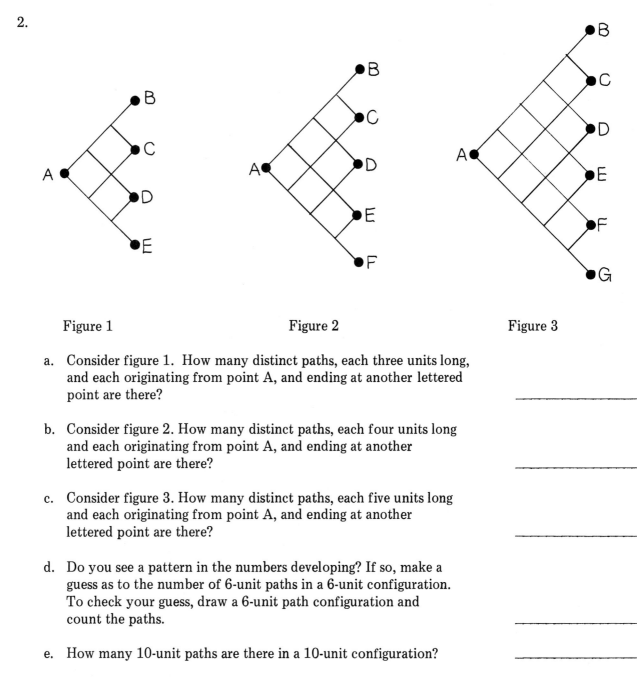

Figure 1   Figure 2   Figure 3

a. Consider figure 1. How many distinct paths, each three units long, and each originating from point A, and ending at another lettered point are there? _____

b. Consider figure 2. How many distinct paths, each four units long and each originating from point A, and ending at another lettered point are there? _____

c. Consider figure 3. How many distinct paths, each five units long and each originating from point A, and ending at another lettered point are there? _____

d. Do you see a pattern in the numbers developing? If so, make a guess as to the number of 6-unit paths in a 6-unit configuration. To check your guess, draw a 6-unit path configuration and count the paths. _____

e. How many 10-unit paths are there in a 10-unit configuration? _____

f. How many n-unit paths are there in a n-unit configuration? _____

318   (203)

1. Two neighbors, Joe and Irma, are salespersons. They both work five days each week. Irma travels an average of 62 kilometers a day. Joe travels an average of 49 kilometers a day. After how many days will Irma have traveled 364 kilometers more than Joe?

2. What is the sum of the numbers from 1 to 500 inclusive?

3. A mad scientist invented a machine that could duplicate any object or group of objects. The machine worked like this:

    1. A special camera was used to photograph the object or objects to be duplicated.
    2. The photograph was fed into the machine.
    3. At the end of one hour, the machine ejected two duplicates of each object in the photograph.
    4. Once an object had been photographed, the camera would not photograph it again.
    5. Objects produced by the machine could be photographed and duplicated once.

    After inventing the machine, the scientist decided to make a fortune by manufacturing golfballs. He bought some golfballs and began duplicating them. At the end of three hours, he had 105 golfballs. How many golfballs did he start with?

1. A lady and her daughter each bought a new outfit consisting of pants, blouse, and jacket. In each outfit, the blouse cost half as much as the pants, and the jacket cost three times as much as the blouse. If the price of each of the lady's items was twice that of her daughter's, and the daughter's pants cost $14.00:

   a. What did each of the lady's items cost?

   b. What was the total cost of each outfit?

2. A pirate stole a treasure chest containing gold coins. He buried ½ of them and threw ½ of the remaining coins into the sea. If he was left with 5000 gold coins, how many were in the treasure chest that he stole?

3. Ten men are fishing from a boat, five in the front, five in back, and there is one empty seat in the middle. The five in front are catching all the fish, so the five in back want to change seats. To avoid capsizing the boat, they agree to do so using the following rules:

   1. A man may move from his seat to an empty seat next to him.
   2. A man may step over only one man to an empty seat.
   3. No other moves are allowed.

   What is the MINIMUM number of moves necessary for the ten men to switch places?

   To solve this problem, experiment using chips of two different colors to represent the men and a Model like the one below to represent the seats in the boat.

1. Three thieves, Mugs, Bugs, and Slug, robbed an armored car and stole 1321 gold bars valued at $50,000 each. They took the bars to their hideout and decided to divide them evenly the next day.

   Mugs, not trusting the others, got up during the night and divided the gold bars into three equal piles. Having one left over, he buried it and took his one third. Later that night, Bugs, also not trusting the others, decided to take his one third. He also divided the remaining bars into three equal piles and had one remaining. He buried the extra bar, and took his one third. Slug, a heavy sleeper, waited until early morning and did the same thing with the remaining bars.

   The next morning, the thieves divided the remaining bars and each received the same number of gold bars. How many bars did each thief get in the morning?

   How many bars did each thief have altogether?

   What was the total value of each man's gold?

2. This is a problem about Gauss High School and that favorite storage area, the high school locker.

   At Gauss High there are 1000 students and 1000 lockers (numbered 1–1000). At the beginning of our story all the lockers are closed. The first student comes by and opens every locker. Following the first student, the second student goes along and closes every second locker. The third student changes the state (if the locker is open, he closes it; if the locker is closed, he opens it) of every third locker. The fourth student changes the state of every fourth locker, and so forth. Finally, the thousandth student changes the state of the thousandth locker.

   When the last student changes the state of the last locker, which lockers are open?

   Gauss, for whom the school was named, said that this is a simple problem.

3. It takes 882 digits to number the pages of a book consecutively. How many pages are there?

1. Travel on the commuter trains is very heavy. An empty train picked up three passengers at its first stop. At every stop thereafter, it picked up two more passengers than it had picked up at the previous stop. How many passengers got on at the fifteenth stop? If none of the passengers had gotten off, how many passengers would have been on the train after the fifteenth stop?

2. The mathematician Augustus DeMorgan, who lived in the nineteenth century, stated that he was X years old in the year X^2. In what year was he born?

3. Explain how single digits can be painted on the faces of two cubes so that the cubes can be placed so as to show each of the first 31 whole numbers.

4. During the softball season, the Angels won three times as many games as the Cardinals, and the Cardinals won one-fourth as many as the Beavers. If the Beavers won three more games than the Angels, which team won 12 games?

5. Certain types of examinations are scored by giving 2 points for every correct answer and subtracting one point for each incorrect answer. On an examination of 20 questions, Alice, Bob, Cloe, and David received scores of 31, 13, 25, and 37 respectively. How many questions did each of them answer correctly?

6. A rancher divided his herd of cows among his four sons. He gave one son half the herd; a second son one-fourth of the herd; a third son one-fifth of the herd; and the fourth son 48 cows. How many cows were in the herd originally?